BEGGARS IN RED

PEN & SWORD MILITARY CLASSICS

We hope you enjoy your Pen and Sword Military Classic. The series is designed to give readers quality military history at affordable prices. Below is a list of the titles that are planned for 2003. Pen and Sword Classics are available from all good bookshops. If you would like to keep in touch with further developments in the series, including information on the Classics club, then please contact Pen and Sword at the address below.

2003 List

PEN AND SWORD BOOKS LTD

47 Church Street • Barnsley • South Yorkshire • S70 2AS

Tel: 01226 734555 • 734222

E-mail: enquiries@pen-and-sword.co.uk • **Website:** www.pen-and-sword.co.uk

BEGGARS IN RED

The British Army
1789–1889

JOHN STRAWSON

PEN & SWORD MILITARY CLASSICS

First published in 1991 by Hutchinson
Published in 2003, in this format, by
PEN & SWORD MILITARY CLASSICS
an imprint of
Pen & Sword Books Limited
47 Church Street
Barnsley
S. Yorkshire
S70 2AS

ISBN 0 85052 951 4

A CIP record for this book is available from the British Library

Printed in England by
CPI UK

'Ave you 'eard o' the Widow at Windsor
With a hairy gold crown on 'er 'ead?
She 'as ships on the foam — she 'as millions at 'ome,
An' she pays us poor beggars in red.

RUDYARD KIPLING

Contents

Illustrations

Acknowledgements

I would like to thank Alex McIntosh for his assistance in editing the text; Anne-Marie Ehrlich for organizing the pictures and the painting on the jacket; Barbara Hird for providing an index; Rodney Paull for dealing with the maps; and Patrick McCreeth for arranging the dust cover.

I wish to record a very special debt to *The Pax Britannica Trilogy* by James/Jan Morris, in particular its first volume, *Heaven's Command*, as much of my story is concerned with Imperial progress, the sub-title of this first volume, and I have quoted freely from it. No recent historian has written more vividly or readably about the British Army's part in the Napoleonic Wars than Sir Arthur Bryant, and I have found his trilogy, *The Years of Endurance*, *Years of Victory* and *The Age of Elegance* indispensable for reference. Three volumes of *The Oxford History of England* – J. Steven Watson's *The Reign of George III*, Sir Llewellyn Woodward's *The Age of Reform* and Sir Robert Ensor's *England 1870–1914* were constantly at hand and, as always, wholly rewarding. The Marquess of Anglesey's *History of the British Cavalry*, Volumes 1, 2, and 3, was once again full of valuable and lively material. Rudyard Kipling's *Barrack Room Ballads* reflect, as nothing else, the life and language of Thomas Atkins, and are often made use of. Jock Haswell's *The British Army: A Concise History* was as usual invaluable. For the Indian Army the works of Philip Mason are, of course, both essential and a superb tribute to the soldiers he writes about. Books for particular campaigns are listed in the Bibliography, *The Army Quarterly and Defence Journal* was a rich source of information and narrative. For stories by numerous soldiers on active service I am again greatly indebted to *Rank and File* compiled by T.H. McGuffie. I wish to thank The Queen's Royal Irish Hussars for permission to use a passage which I wrote for their Regimental History.

The author and publishers wish to thank the following for their kind permission to quote from the works named: the *Army Quarterly and Defence Journal*, 'The Hicks Pasha Expedition' (Clark); Barrie & Jenkins, *Flashman* (Fraser); *Blackwood's Magazine*; Jonathan Cape,

A Matter of Honour and *The Men Who Ruled India* (Mason);
Constable, *Lord Palmerston* (Ridley) and *The Reason Why* (Wood-
ham-Smith); Leo Cooper Ltd, *A History of the British Cavalry*
(Marquess of Anglesey); Curtis Brown Inc, *In Defense of the Public
Liberty* (Griffith); Faber & Faber, *Heaven's Command* (Morris);
HarperCollins, *The Age of Elegance, The Years of Endurance* and
Years of Victory (Bryant); Hutchinson, *In Relief of Gordon: Lord
Wolseley's Campaign Journal* (Preston, Ed.) and *Rank and File*
(McGuffie); Longman Group, *The Dragon Wakes* (Hibbert); Mac-
millan, *Napoleon and his Marshals* (Macdonnell) and *Rudyard
Kipling* (Carrington); Society for Army Historical Research and Dr
Julia Trevelyn, *The British Army and Royal Jubilees* (Sir Charles
Oman).

The author and publishers are also very grateful to the following for
their permission to reproduce the pictures in this book: City of Bristol
Museum & Art Gallery (12); Essex Regiment Museum (11); E. T.
Archive (3,7,13); H. M. The Queen (14); The Mansell Collection (17);
National Army Museum (1,4,6,10,15,16); National Portrait Gallery
(2); Royal Greenjackets Museum (5); Royal Military College, Sandhurst (8); Victoria and Albert Museum (9).

My thanks also go to Mr J.C. Andrews FLA, Chief Librarian,
Ministry of Defence library, and his staff for their splendid help in
producing books and periodicals for me to study.

As always I would like to thank my wife for her unfailing support
during the writing and production of this book.

JOHN STRAWSON
Boyton, Warminster
December 1990

Preface

I am the model soldier of the future.
I don't want to get married.
I have no feelings.
I am equal to any amount of unnecessary night duty.
And I want no food or pay.

Caption of a cartoon entitled
THE ARMY OF THE FUTURE from
Fun magazine 1876

This book is not a comprehensive account of all that the British Army did during the years 1789–1889. In so relatively short a work that would not be possible, and we already have Sir John Fortescue's definitive and incomparable History. Rather, what I have done is to take a look here and there at circumstances leading to war, at those in power shaping and responding to these circumstances, at military leaders, at battles fought by the Army, at some of the officers and men who took part in them. Such a version of events is necessarily selective. It strives also to be representative. It will be seen that one of the consistent themes of this story is that of government's economy in and neglect of Army affairs as soon as the soldiers had saved government's skin by winning its wars. It will also be clear that in winning these wars one of the British Army's most valuable and enduring strengths – which generally enabled it to triumph over great difficulties of terrain and climate, numerically superior enemies, and all too often inept management by its generals – was its priceless regimental spirit. Some battles have been described briefly, others more fully, as interest and inclination dictated. I have avoided too much discussion of matters like strengths and recruiting, pay and conditions, weapons and drill, rules, regulations and administrative matters, preferring to dwell more on the active service of 'us poor beggars in red'.

There is always a danger that the soldiers of today, and not only soldiers, will forget their history. In this volume I try to give them an opportunity to relive some of it, and at this particular time when debate about the British Army's future composition and role has given rise to many different opinions – some from those least qualified to give them – it may be that a look at the past will help to shape the future, so that what has proved of enduring worth throughout our infinitely varied history is not lightly discarded.

That there must be change is not in dispute. It is what change is to be made that merits discussion. In 1868 Disraeli declared that 'in a progressive country change is constant; and the great question is not whether you should resist change which is inevitable, but whether that change should be carried out in deference to the manners, the customs, the laws, and the traditions of a people, or whether it should be carried out in deference to abstract principles, and arbitrary and general doctrines'. Disraeli, of course, was in no doubt that the former recipe was the proper one for managing the country, and we similarly should be in no doubt that in effecting inevitable change in the British Army's size, structure and capability, we should do it in deference to the manners, customs, laws and traditions of the Army itself. In being guided by this rule, there is still much to learn from the past and much to be gained by preserving what has for so long shown its worth in either keeping the peace or, if that peace were broken, restoring it by resort to force of arms – always provided, mind you, that such preservation is compatible with the two overriding requirements of economy and efficiency.

In June 1979 *Blackwood's Magazine* published an article of mine called *The Future of the British Army*. It was based on a prediction that between then and the year 2000 – in other words roughly about now – new circumstances would come about which would demand a new look at the Army's size, structure and role. Among the circumstances which I suggested might prevail were these:

(1)   the decline and partial disintegration of the Soviet Union and the dissolution of the Warsaw Pact;

(2)   the loosening of America's ties with Europe and the emergence of a European defence force;

(3)   continued terrorism in Great Britain;

(4)   more European involvement in the affairs of Africa and the Middle East;

(5)   uncertainties about roles for the Armed Forces;

(6)   continued need for simply means of moving soldiers about the world – ie air and sea transport;

(7)   a defence budget unable to sustain today's level of forces.

After discussing how these and some other, now less relevant, considerations might affect things, I came to the conclusion that, given these circumstances most of which have recently come about, the future British Army would not change fundamentally, that there would not be (most certainly *should* not be) any revolutionary restructuring, no stark division into a combat arm and a logistic arm, no doing away with those traditional features of the Army which are most valued by those in it. I therefore suggested that the future British Army would be like this:

(1)   it will still be built round horse, foot, guns and sappers;

(2)   the regimental system will continue because it is the best system of raising, grouping, training and leading men in action that any Army has yet devised;

(3)   there will be fewer units of this sort, perhaps only seventy or so – fifteen armoured,* fifteen artillery, forty infantry† and some sappers;

(4)   the Army's strength might be little more than 100,000;

(5)   the Army will be deployed in Germany as part of a European Defence Force, in the UK, and in Hong Kong, Cyprus, Belize, Gibraltar (and Falkland Islands) as long as these places require garrisons;

(6)   there will be frequent changes of station consistent with military efficiency and domestic stability;

(7)   above all the soldiers will belong to a well-found, well-trained, well-equipped, well-paid, well-led Army.

It will be interesting to observe whether these predictions and suggestions are realized in the government's choice among its current options for change. Much more recently than the *Blackwood's Magazine* article, I suggested in two letters to *The Times* (7 February and 26 May 1990) that when the regular part of the British Army is reduced, it will be important to arrange that the Reserve Army is greatly enhanced; that regular regiments become infinitely versatile so that they can undertake roles of peacekeeping, UN duties, disaster relief, internal security; that training be exciting and demanding; that every use be made of overseas territories to vary tasks and deployment. Furthermore in order that as many infantry battalions as possible are retained, the Army should be *de-specialized*, regiments and corps being given back duties they used to perform for themselves (cooking, repair, accounting, education) so that some specialist corps with their costly staffs and overheads can be done away with. In short, if we are to have fewer soldiers, they must all be more versatile, so that with the indispensable help of the Royal Navy and Royal Air Force, we can say, as Arnold White said a hundred years ago: 'The British Army, though small, can do anything and go anywhere.'

One last thing – no more amalgamations! If a cavalry or infantry regiment has to go, let it become part of the Reserve Army, with a strong regular cadre, and keep its name and traditions in being. For the

---

* Four regiments fewer than now.
† A loss of ten battalions.

infantry, as my old friend and regimental comrade, Brigadier John Paley, CBE MC, has suggested, go once and for all to a solution, which allows further expansion or reduction without pain, and at the same time preserves the names, history, pride and honours which so frequently feature in this book. Forget about The Queen's Division, for example – historically it is meaningless. Choose instead a title such as The Queen's Own Royal Regiment of Foot, with the necessary number of battalions in it, regular and reserve, and let each of them glory in preserving for ever the record of service, gallantry and devotion to duty that names such as The Buffs or The Diehards – in parenthesis after the Regiment's title and battalion's number – will ensure. Then, those officers and men of the future serving in such Regiments will understand what is meant in the second paragraph of this Foreword by the importance of looking at the past to help shape the future and by not discarding from the British Army what has throughout its history proved of such enduring worth.

Rudyard Kipling – to whom I owe the title of this book and much else in it – understood as few others in his time did the worth of the British soldier. He had seen and heard much of him in India. With his ballads and tales he made many of his contemporaries aware of this worth too. Yet today not many of those who, a score of times, have praised the strength of the Sergeants' Mess in this regiment or that know that it was Kipling who wrote: 'But the backbone of the Army is the non-commissioned man!' In his majestic biography of Kipling, Charles Carrington observed that the Victorian English did not on the whole think much of or greatly respect their soldiers, whether officers or rankers.

> Yet, underlying the surface flow of anti-militarism there remained a hidden current of admiration, not rational and not articulate, for the redcoats with their strange insignia and pomp, whose life seemed far removed from the workaday world of England in the nineteenth century. Who were they then, these smart neat young officers, this rough and hearty rank and file who led a double life: appearing sometimes in the police-court news as drunken, diseased reprobates; sometimes as the heroes of quite fabulous adventures in far distant lands, the thin red line at Balaclava, the storming columns of Delhi, the defenders of Rorke's Drift, the men who advanced across the desert by night to Tel-el-Kebir, who marched through the mountain passes in tropical heat from Kabul to Kandahar?

In the following pages I try to answer the question and show the reader both what these men did to establish so remarkable a tradition of service, courage, devotion to duty and comradeship, and what it is that the soldier of today is required to live up to and preserve.

CHAPTER ONE

Triumph and Disaster

No one can guarantee success in war, but only deserve it.
SIR WINSTON CHURCHILL

If we wanted to select a century in which the British Army did more than in any other to astonish the world, to indulge in spectacular triumphs as well as humiliating defeats, moving on from the final despatch of history's greatest soldier to the subjugation of innumerable Asian and African potentates, a century which saw the British tighten their hold on India, extend their Imperial possessions to unimagined frontiers, and at length – despite blunders in the Crimea and mutiny by Indian sepoys – establish a kind of peace-keeping cordon around the globe, then the century we would choose is the one which began with the French Revolution and ended just after Queen Victoria had celebrated her first Jubilee with incomparable Imperial splendour.

Even before this period the British public had been treated to striking extremes of fortune and misfortune in the conduct of the nation's military affairs, illustrating as so often before and since that whereas the calibre of the ordinary British soldier remained broadly unchanged, his success or failure was usually attributable to the calibre of those directing his activities. Sometimes the *age* of those directing operations played its part. It cannot be said that many of Britain's great captains distinguished themselves when they were young. Unlike Alexander, who conquered the world before he was thirty, or Napoleon, who at twenty-seven shocked Europe with his Italian campaign, Marlborough was fifty-four at Blenheim, Wellington* forty-six at Waterloo, and Montgomery fifty-five at Alamein. Yet there were notable exceptions. Robert Clive was only twenty-five at Arcot; a mere six years later he utterly routed the Nawab of Bengal's army at Plassey. James Wolfe was but thirty-two

* Wellington in fact thought of himself as young in command, and when compared with others – he was only thirty at Seringapatam in 1799; Abercromby was sixty-seven at Alexandria in 1801 – we may agree with him.

when he triumphed at Quebec. These two men showed what a handful of redcoats commanded by soldiers of genius could do, overcoming daunting odds with almost insolent ease and audacity and winning for the Crown great tracts of Empire. Let us briefly accompany Clive to his splendid victories and Wolfe to his rendezvous with the last enemy before looking at the other side of the coin.

It may seem ironical that a Frenchman's vision of founding a great European empire on the crumbling remains of an Indian monarchy should have led in the end to this same empire's falling into the hands of the British. There was nothing unusual about the British and the French being at war, nor with initial French successes being gradually reversed by the British. So it was in the Carnatic in the middle of the eighteenth century. Had it not been for Dupleix, Governor of Pondicherry, Clive might never have been heard of, for it was Dupleix's imperial ambitions which made him seize Madras, threaten Trichinopoly and, in alliance with Indian pretenders to the throne, set himself in the way of becoming master of the Carnatic. And it was Clive, at this time a captain and commissary to the troops, who saw that unless some bold, dramatic blow was struck, the French would become absolute masters of the southern part of India. He therefore proposed an attack on Arcot, capital of the Carnatic.

When we consider what Clive did, it must even today, with countless tales before us of what daring can do to overcome greatly superior number, strike us as remarkable. Having persuaded his masters in the East India Company that what he proposed was necessary and that he himself was the man to execute it, he set off with a mere 500 soldiers less than half of whom were British, 300 being sepoys trained by the Company. Only two of the officers accompanying Clive had, like himself, seen action before. After a march from Trichinopoly in appalling weather he arrived with his puny force at the gates of Arcot, whose garrison, panic-stricken, instantly rushed out of the fort allowing Clive and his men to occupy it without a fight. It is not given to every young soldier in his first major campaign to practise almost every phase of war – advance, attack and defence – yet such was Clive's fortune. Nor do most soldiers of twenty-five have the foresight, the thoroughness, the political sagacity, the determination and the inspiring leadership which he was now to show. As we follow events, we see how Clive set about putting the seal of decisive victory on what up to this time had been no more than an enterprising raid. First, knowing that an effort to regain the fort could not be long delayed, he took two steps, one precautionary, the other bold. He made preparations for a siege, and made a night sortie to disperse the very enemy reinforcements that were planning to attack him. But before long the siege began in earnest, and Rajah Sahib, who conducted it, was able to muster some 10,000 troops against Clive's small band, which had by now dwindled to about 300, only one-third of them European. At length a threat of interference with his designs by Mahrattas induced Rajah Sahib to attempt an assault.

There is no more colourful account of the siege of Arcot than Macaulay's. He tells us how well the day chosen for the assault, being the Mohammedan festival of Husein, augured for the Moslem cause. All those who fell in battle against the infidel during this festival instantly atoned for whatever sins they might have committed during their lives and found themselves translated to that paradise represented by the garden of the Houris. Nor did Rajah Sahib depend only on this alluring prospect. Drugs reinforced the fanaticism of religion so that the besiegers 'drunk with enthusiasm, drunk with bhang, rushed furiously to the attack'. In spite of their being led by armoured elephants, whose weight and momentum were expected, like battering-rams, to drive in the gates and demolish the defences, a warm reception awaited the attacking hordes. Indeed it was the elephants who were the first to experience both the accuracy and discomfort of musket-balls delivered by disciplined redcoats. So dismayed were these huge animals that they turned about, rushing away from the fusillade that had greeted them and causing their followers either to scatter or be trampled beneath their thundering feet. This initial repulse, however, did not dampen the ardour of Rajah Sahib's men. Having launched a raft on the water filling one section of the defensive moat, they again attacked. But when Clive saw that his artillerymen were not managing their gun properly, he himself directed its fire and succeeded in sweeping the raft clear of the enemy in a few moments. Elsewhere the fanatical hordes attacked across dry parts of the ditch with great courage and dash, but the discipline, volume and accuracy of the British infantry's fire – the rear rank constantly loading spare muskets for those in front – took such heavy toll of the besiegers that after three attempts, they withdrew beyond the defensive ditch. The battle had lasted for an hour, had cost the assailants some 400 killed, while Clive's garrison lost but a handful. Next morning Rajah Sahib's army had gone.

It was Clive who had done it, alone in command, tireless, thinking of everything, supervising everybody, now giving the order to fire the first volley, now training the artillery piece on its target, burning with enthusiasm and a sense of duty, completely in control of himself and the situation, indomitable, victorious. The British soldiers and native sepoys had responded magnificently, steady in line, taking careful aim at their attackers, as confident in their weapons as they were in their leader. And the whole business at Arcot, which began as a venture, 'to strike a daring blow', became the beginning of the end for the French in India. Clive had shown not only a remarkable capacity for the essentials of leadership – imagination, determination and example – but a sure appreciation of what war's principles are. The value of surprise, the need for offensive action, the harmony with which clear purpose may be allied to economy of effort – how conclusively he had illustrated these fundamentals at Arcot in 1751!

Before we leave Clive, however, let us glance at him six years later at the battle of Plassey, which determined India's future and ranks with Assaye in the annals of tiny, British-led expeditions overwhelming huge numbers of Indian-led troops. By 1757 Great Britain and France are again at war and Clive is in Bengal. In the previous year the vicious, grasping and treacherous Nawab, Surajah Dowlah, had marched on Calcutta, taken it and then had been unwise enough to imprison nearly 150 Europeans in a tiny cell, which became known as the Black Hole. This savage cruelty simply hastened Surajah Dowlah's own downfall. His own court was resolved to turn him off the throne and place Mir Jafar on it instead. Clive was to help and by June 1757 had assembled an army of some three thousand,* of whom less than one-third were British, although the whole force had British officers in command and the benefit of having been trained by them. Surajah Dowlah's host was somewhat larger – nearly 60,000 in all, with more than 40,000 infantry, 15,000 cavalry, and fifty huge guns which required great teams of oxen to pull them and elephants to push. It was these two armies which met at Plassey. One was incomparably superior in numbers; the other was astonishingly superior in discipline and valour.

The contest when it began was hardly a contest at all. There was an exchange of artillery fire, but while that of Surajah Dowlah's guns had hardly any effect at all, Clive's new and well-handled artillery pieces caused many casualties; among those killed were some of the Nawab's subordinate commanders. Whatever other qualities the ruler may have had – and certainly he was evil, degenerate and vicious – courage and resolution were not among them. Confusion among the ranks brought about by Clive's artillery, suspicion of treachery by his own people, together with his own ready and extreme fear were more than enough for him to accept the insinuations of those who were conspiring against him. A general withdrawal was ordered and once this order had been given, all was over for him. A detachment of Clive's army had already begun to advance, and Clive, seeing his opportunity, ordered his whole force forward. 'The confused and dispirited multitude,' wrote Macaulay, 'gave way before the onset of disciplined valour. No mob attacked by regular soldiers was ever more completely routed.' The victory was complete. Surajah Dowlah's forces were scattered, his guns, baggage train, supplies captured and he himself was murdered a few days later. Clive had lost some twenty men killed and fifty wounded. It could not be said of either Arcot or Plassey, with such puny numbers pitted against such multitudes, that Clive could have guaranteed victory. But he had certainly deserved it.

---

* Including the 39th Foot, later the Dorset Regiment.

At Arcot he had made himself master of the Carnatic, at Plassey master of Bengal. And what Clive had done on one side of the world, Wolfe was to do on the other.

If James Wolfe had bitten some of his fellow generals, as George II had suggested, the Seven Years War might not have lasted so long. As it was, in a single encounter on 13 September 1759 outside the walls of Quebec, Wolfe conquered an entire province of Canada, which together with Amherst's subsequent occupation of Montreal established British supremacy in Canada. Wolfe has sometimes been likened to Nelson, and indeed the two had much in common – frail in constitution, fearless in action, indomitable in spirit. But there is more to it than that. Wolfe was Nelson's hero, and often when confronted with the problem of an amphibious operation to seize some stronghold ashore he would ask himself what Wolfe would have done. It was in 1759, 'The Year of Victories', that Nelson was born, and Wolfe's deeds and daring were soon brought to his notice, in particular by the election campaign of George Townshend, a brigadier and Wolfe's second-in-command at Quebec, now in 1768 a marquess and a Whig candidate in Norfolk. The electors were reminded of Townshend's conduct in command of his brigade, always at its head, brave, humane, accessible, high-spirited (the words exactly fit Nelson) and how worthy he had been to succeed to the command after Wolfe's death at the very moment of victory. Nelson's admiration for Wolfe was constantly reinforced by those who had been with him at Quebec – in Jamaica by General Dalling, the Governor; in Quebec itself by Colonel Simpson, the Provost-Marshal; and later by Admiral Sir John Jervis, who had served with Wolfe and actually accompanied him in reconnoitring the beaches below the Heights of Abraham.

It was in the preliminaries to the battle that Wolfe displayed such daring – with, as so often, the skilful and dauntless support of the Royal Navy – in floating his army across the St Lawrence river, scaling the cliffs by means of a narrow and precipitous path, confronting Montcalm's 16,000 men and strong artillery with little more than half that number, and then by the discipline, accuracy and sheer volume of his infantry's fire-power deciding the issue in a mere fifteen minutes, sustaining during the exchange of volleys his mortal wound. His immortality was assured. The historian J. Steven Watson thinks it probable that 'no event has ever been more celebrated on canvas than Wolfe's capture of Quebec. Wolfe died in every style from the classical to the naturalistic to suit all tastes and rouse one general emotion.' Certainly it was an emotion that Nelson was never to lose, as he explained to the painter, Benjamin West, when he told West that he would always stop to look at the *Death of Wolfe** if it was in the window of a print-shop.

* West was President of the Royal Academy. His *Death of Nelson* was painted in 1806.

That Wolfe was revered by his men is made plain by a light infantryman of Fraser's Regiment.* On 12 September 1759 they were told that the Light Infantry would lead and land first in order to engage the enemy while the army disembarked and scaled the Heights. When it was further explained that volunteers were needed to precede even the main body of Light Infantry, this NCO of Fraser's together with his comrades replied how conscious they were of the honour that General Wolfe did them and assured their commanding officer that the General's 'agreeable order would be put in execution with the greatest activity, care, and vigour in our power'. This plan was carried out by twenty-four men under Captain Fraser (who succeeded in persuading French sentries that they were a party from the Montreal provision boats) who went on up the Heights with the main body of Light Infantry behind them. On reaching the top they encountered a party of enemy, but quickly dispersed them and then went on to silence an artillery battery which was firing on British ships in the river. Doughty goes on to describe the battle:

> About 6 o'clock observed the enemy coming from town, and forming under cover of their cannon; we saw they were numerous, therefore the General made the proper disposition for battle; they marched up in one extended line. When we came within a reconnoitring view they halted, advancing a few of their Irregulars, who kept bicquering with one or two platoons, who were advanced for that purpose, at the same time playing with three field pieces on our line. On which the General ordered the line to lay down till the enemy came close, when they were to rise up and give their fire. The enemy, thinking by our disappearing, that their cannon disconcerted us, they thought proper to embrace the opportunity; wheeling back from the centre, and formed three powerful columns, advanced very regular with their cannon playing on us. By this time we had one field piece on the right, and two howats on the left who began to give fire; the enemy huzza'd, advancing with a short trott (which was effectually shortened to a number of them) they began their fire on the left, the whole of them reclining that way, but received and sustained such a check that the smell of gunpowder became nauseous; they broke their line, to all parts of the compass.

The writer goes on to say how grievous was their concern and loss when it became known that General Wolfe had been mortally wounded. All the brigadiers, except one, were also wounded, but they still gave orders, as soon as they saw the enemy breaking, for 'the Grenadiers to charge in among them with their bayonets, as also the Highlanders with their swords, which did some execution, particu-

* *The Siege of Quebec and the Battle of the Plains of Abraham*, A. Doughty, Quebec, 1901.

larly in the pursuit'. There was no doubt in battles like this that generals and brigadiers led from the front. There was no doubt either that the French did not like 'English medicines'. The whole affair, concluded our Light Infantry NCO, gave great spirit to the army, notwithstanding the loss of General Wolfe, the 'Life of the Army'. Moreover 'the men kept sober, which was a great maxim of their bravery'.

Wolfe, like many another soldier, had a deep love of literature, and after completing his reconnaissance on the evening before the battle, diverted his fellow commanders by reciting for them from memory almost the whole of Gray's *Elegy*. He would rather, he concluded, be the author of those lines than enjoy the glory of defeating the French on the morrow. How prophetic was his repetition of one line of the *Elegy*, for in his case the path of glory did lead to the grave.

In 1759 victory was not confined to Canada. In West Africa, in the Caribbean, in India, in Europe, British arms were triumphant. Pitt's strategy of destroying French sea-power and relieving France of her possessions overseas had succeeded. At the battle of Minden the British infantry* had won golden opinions even from their enemies. Yet even though the Peace of Paris in 1763 confirmed British conquests in Canada, North America, India and the West Indies, Pitt, now out of power, foresaw that it would not be long before France took up arms again to seek retribution and restoration of her losses. When this time came, it was because Britain found itself at odds with its own people, the Colonists of North America. The British Army's generals in the American War of Independence were faced with very different problems from those in the Seven Years War. In the latter men like Clive, Wolfe and Amherst deserved victory and gained it, often against daunting odds and with little guarantee of success. In the former, it might have been possible almost to guarantee success by an adequate supply of resources, concentrated sea-power and a bold, clear policy of employing them. But the campaigns conducted by Burgoyne and Cornwallis neither deserved success nor were rewarded with it. This was not the fault of the soldiers, nor even their commanders. Strategy was flawed, purpose unclear, direction unco-ordinated.

As was customary with the British, as soon as the Seven Years War was over, the Army's establishment was drastically reduced. In 1764 with George Grenville in control of the Treasury and the extra-ordinary expenditure caused by war no longer needed, the number of infantry regiments was reduced from about a hundred to seventy, and

* Six Regiments fought at Minden – 12th, 20th, 23rd, 25th, 37th and 51st Foot, ie Suffolks, Lancashire Fusiliers, Royal Welch Fusiliers, KOSB, Hampshires, KOYLI. The French Commander, Duc de Contades, wrote that to see a line of infantry break through three lines of cavalry and tumble them to ruin was to witness something he had thought to be impossible.

the strengths of these ruthlessly cut, giving rise to Pitt's condemnation that the bravest men in the world were now being dispatched to their villages to starve and forget all their skill at arms. The Army's strength fell from about 120,000 to little more than 30,000, mainly horse, foot and guns, for there was still no supply organization and no permanent system of transport, both of which had to be improvised by requisition and 'impressment' in time of war. Some 10,000 soldiers were deployed in the Empire overseas, plus 4,000 in Minorca and Gibraltar. The rest were at home.

It is not given to every sovereign to preside over the acquisition of one empire, the loss of another and the gradual but sure consolidation of a third, yet such was the destiny of George III. On his accession in 1760 it may be said that one of the principal disadvantages under which he laboured was the fact that his principal minister was William Pitt, one of the greatest men of action that this country has ever seen, and of whom Carlyle wrote that Pitt had in effect himself been King of England for four years (1756–60). The resounding success of the Royal Navy and the British Army under Pitt was not only because of his command of large resources and the strategic skill with which he deployed them. It was also because, like Churchill almost 200 years later, he inspired the nation. 'The ardour of his soul,' wrote Macaulay, 'had set the whole kingdom on fire. It inflamed every soldier who dragged the cannon up the heights of Quebec, and every sailor who boarded the French ships among the rocks of Brittany. The Minister, before he had been long in office, had imparted to the commanders whom he employed his own impetuous, adventurous, and defying character.' No wonder Pitt's audacity and vigour were crowned with the Year of Victories, for by this time whenever there was an encounter between the French and British, it was almost a foregone conclusion that the British would win. So that by the time George III succeeded his grandfather in 1760, Pitt occupied a uniquely renowned position in the country, in the House of Commons and in Europe. He was, according to Macaulay, the first Englishman of his time, having made England the first country in the world. What chance had George III, with his tendency to melancholy, knowledge of his own limitations and devotion to second-rate, insinuating favourites, of exercising his will over such a man?

There were other reasons why George got rid of Pitt. In the first place George had regarded his grandfather, the late King, as unworthy to be a British monarch, and therefore Pitt, who had served such shuffling unworthiness, was to be condemned as 'a snake in the grass' with the 'blackest of hearts'. Moreover Pitt had nothing but justified contempt for Bute, friend and adviser of the young George and, to the young King, disregard of Bute was the same as disregard for himself. George II's son and heir, Prince Frederic (who, of course, pre-deceased him) had looked on Bute as the sort of man to be envoy at a small

dignified German court where there was little or nothing to do. None
the less George III made Bute his first minister, in which position it did
not take Bute long to show that a cultivated mind and an elegant leg
were insufficient qualifications for the direction of a great empire.
Bute, however, did relatively little harm as he was in office for but a
short time. Lord North, on the other hand, was the King's first
minister for twelve years and did irreparable damage. Although an
oversimplification, it would not be inaccurate to say that the loss of the
American colonies was brought about by the inflexibility and
stubbornness of the one man who most ardently desired their
retention – George III. In this achievement he was ably assisted by
Lord North. Neither of them could see what Edmund Burke so clearly
saw and so eloquently tried to impress upon others that magnanimity
was very often the wisest policy and that 'a great empire and little
minds go ill together'. Alas, both North and his sovereign did have
little minds and set about trying to coerce the uncoercible. They paid
no heed to Burke's further warning that if the colonies were denied
their share of freedom, the only bond which could preserve the
empire's unity would be broken. Force might do much – temporarily.
'It may subdue for a moment; but it does not remove the necessity of
subduing again: and a nation is not governed, which is perpetually to
be conquered.' Even when Pitt pointed out that America could not be
conquered, even when General Howe (who succeeded General Gage
in command in October 1775) advised that America could not be held,
still the King persisted. He had already been obliged to stomach
Burgoyne's surrender at Saratoga; he had yet to savour the humiliation of Cornwallis at Yorktown. Let us accompany these two
generals while they proceed to lose two armies.

The strategy, if it may be called that, by which the war was to be
ended in 1777 had been devised by Lord George Sackville – at this time
he was calling himself Germain. The likelihood of its success may
perhaps be gauged by remembering that at the battle of Minden,
Sackville had been disgraced for disobedience and cowardice. This
disgrace, however, inflicted as it was by George II and his ministers,
did not discourage George III from making Sackville Secretary of State
for American affairs in 1775. Indeed the very antipathy felt for
Sackville by Pitt and others was a recommendation in George's eyes.
The plan itself was to detach New England from the rest of the
colonies by two internal thrusts. Burgoyne, with his army of rather
more than 7,000 men, was to move from Canada through the Hudson
gap towards Albany, while Howe would link up with Burgoyne by
driving northwards from New York. The difficulty was one of timing,
and Howe, appreciating that he would have to remain inactive for too
long – thus allowing Washington to act against him – decided instead
to draw Washington to battle by seizing Philadelphia. Although he
succeeded in doing both, it meant that he could not now return to join

Burgoyne in the Hudson area. Thus Burgoyne found himself with the
option of either retiring to Ticonderoga or attempting to force his way
through to Albany in accordance with the original plan. Not only was
he short of food, there was no means of getting more, and his attempts
to break through the enemy forces surrounding him failed. Gentleman
Johnny's own conduct during various encounters was admirable and,
as Sergeant Lamb recorded, he 'behaved with great personal bravery,
he shunned no danger; his presence and conduct animated the troops
(for they greatly loved the general); he delivered his orders with
precision and coolness; and in the heat, fury and danger of the fight
maintained the true characteristics of the soldier – serenity, fortitude,
and undaunted intrepidity'. As Burgoyne and his army fell back on
Saratoga, depleted in numbers, short of provisions, harassed by
incessant rain, mud so thick that the exhausted, starved horses and
oxen could not drag guns and ammunition-wagons out of bogs,
leaving them there, the soldiers, exhausted, wet-through and hungry,
the American forces commanded by General Gates hemmed them in.
On 14 October Burgoyne asked for terms, and three days later the
formal instrument of surrender was signed. Gates was triumphant,
writing to his wife that 'if Old England is not by this lesson taught
humility, then she is an obstinate old Slut, bent upon her ruin'.
Burgoyne, on the other hand, showed no humility, admitted no errors
and even maintained that if his entire command had been British
(some of it was German) he would have succeeded in fighting his way
through. At this time Burgoyne was fifty-five.*

What was not instantly realized, however, was that Burgoyne's
surrender at Saratoga changed the whole nature of the war, for from
this time forward the French decided to give their open and whole-
hearted support to the Americans. Thus the balance of power was
significantly changed, and Britain was no longer able to rely on the key
to success in the American War – command of the sea. And it was want
of this supremacy at sea which brought about the further disaster of
Yorktown. Warlike activities in 1778 and 1779 began to dispose
George III's ministers to the idea of peace. The French fleet was
threatening the American coast, Spain entered the conflict and laid
siege to Gibraltar, there was even talk of England itself being invaded.
Yet if ministers were wavering, the King was firm, arguing that
America's aim was independence, and that if it were granted, the West
Indies with their close economic ties to America would then want
theirs. Even Ireland might go. Britain would face financial ruin.
Therefore they must fight on. The year 1780 produced more hope.
Rodney, the new naval commander in the West Indies, prevented the
French fleet from re-supplying the American army at Charleston,

---

* Now the age at which most generals in the British Army are retired.

which surrendered to Clinton. 'Bloody' Tarleton* with his mounted legion, including 17th Dragoons, pursued and annihilated an American force on the North Carolina border, and Cornwallis attacked and defeated Gates in South Carolina. Yet in the following year the joint price of dispersed British forces, no very clear aim as to what they were to do and indecision at sea proved to be a heavy one, when Cornwallis at Yorktown with some 7,000 men was hemmed in by almost double that number of French and American troops, and with the French navy preventing relief from the sea, resisted, but resisted in vain. On 17 October 1781 after a series of ineffectual attempts to delay the advancing enemy forces 'a Redcoat drummer, accompanied by an officer with a white flag, appeared on the British parapet. All firing ceased. The drummer beat a parley. Cornwallis proposed a cessation of hostilities for twenty-four hours.'† Washington agreed, asked Cornwallis to make his proposals in writing, and on the following day amended these proposals which Cornwallis in his turn accepted. It was agreed that on 19 October the British and German troops would march out of Yorktown, the bands to be playing a slow march, colours to be cased and arms shouldered. That afternoon Washington, his senior commanders, including Lafayette, and their staff officers, were sitting on their horses, when they heard melancholy music following drums which had beaten a solemn slow march:

At the head of the column rode not the noble earl for whom the thousands were anxiously waiting, but his deputy, Brigadier General Charles O'Hara, the handsome fighting Irish general who had commanded the Guards Brigade in the Carolinas and was representing his 'indisposed' commander in chief.‡ He approached Rochambeau and reined in. The French generals nodded towards Washington. Washington, always courteous, indicated that Major General Benjamin Lincoln, who had surrendered to Clinton at Charleston, should receive the sword. O'Hara bared his head and tendered the earl's sword. Lincoln accepted it and returned it. O'Hara wheeled his horse and rode with his staff slowly back to Yorktown. The British and German troops laid down their arms.

Six and a half years earlier, several hundred Redcoats had marched confidently from Boston to disperse rebels at Lexington.

---

* Later Lieutenant-General Sir Banastre Tarleton, Colonel 8th King's Royal Irish Hussars. The nickname 'Bloody' was given to him by the Americans for allegedly sabring a young American officer who was surrendering, and also because of his troops' supposed ruthless behaviour.
† *In Defense of the Public Liberty*, Samuel B. Griffith II, Cape, 1977.
‡ Cornwallis was forty-three at Yorktown and, as we shall see, went on to do great things in India, Ireland and as Master General of the Ordnance.

From the field at Yorktown 7,000 would march to prisoner-of-war camps.*

A second British army had been forfeited in the struggle against America, largely because of a temporary loss of command of the sea. This last deficiency was soon corrected by Rodney and Hood when, in the battle of 'The Saints' in April 1782 he surrendered the reins French fleet under de Grasse was decisively defeated. Control of the Atlantic was back in British hands. The British Army also retained control of New York and Charleston, and although the war dragged on until 1783, it was at length ended by the Treaty of Versailles.

Cornwallis's surrender of the army at Yorktown spelt the end of Lord North's administration. In March 1782 he surrendered the reins of office, and Rockingham took over. When the latter died a few months later, Shelburne succeeded him and it was he who conducted negotiations for a peace settlement. The great issue for which the Americans had fought – their independence – was granted. A frontier with Canada was agreed. Newfoundland remained British. France, which was almost bankrupt, also made peace with Britain, keeping her Indian possessions and those in the West Indies. Her object of assisting the Thirteen Colonies had been achieved. Britain had been weakened. Some retribution for the losses and humiliations of the Seven Years War had been realized. Spain fared less well. Although she obtained Minorca, the principal prize for which she had fought, Gibraltar, remained in British hands, greatly to the advantage of the British in the wars with France and Spain shortly to break out once more. Holland, without allies, had no choice but to make peace. Shelburne's treaties were far-seeing in one particular respect, for Britain retained most of those strategic areas essential to her manipulation of sea-power with all that this meant for reviving British economic strength through overseas trade. The coming wars with France were to show how sound this policy was, and it was Shelburne's chancellor of the exchequer, the young William Pitt, who was to reap the rewards of Shelburne's farsightedness.

As for the British Army, Jock Haswell[†] has reminded us that it had learned much from its American experiences – how to adapt to new forms of war in great tracts of country, using more open formations, exploiting the mobility of cavalry and mounted infantry, abandoning rigidity, using cover and developing fieldcraft. 'British troops' writes Haswell, 'won notable victories, indeed they won practically all their battles. The two surrenders at Saratoga and Yorktown were the results of flaws in overall strategy combined with a complete lack of communications; they were not battlefield defeats.' Haswell summed it all up by echoing the warnings of Burke and Pitt that no matter how

* Griffith, *op. cit.*
† *The British Army: A Concise History*, Jock Haswell, Thames & Hudson, 1975.

brave the soldiers and competent their commanders, relatively small numbers could not conquer an entire continent. In the forthcoming contest in which once more France, Spain and, very briefly, the United States, were to be enemies of Britain, the use of British sea-power and modestly sized British armies were to be decisive. France as usual was to be the principal foe. In the American war the French had savoured retribution and enjoyed restoration of some colonial possessions. Before long they were to go on to even greater triumphs, only to come up against an unyielding Royal Navy and a reanimated British Army, whose combined efforts were in the end to give the French a drubbing from which they never really recovered.

CHAPTER TWO

A Neglected Army

The first military business after the conclusion of peace was of course the reduction of the establishment, which was begun in March 1783 by the wholesale disbandment of all newly raised regiments, with the exception of those serving in India.

SIR JOHN FORTESCUE

There were plenty of precedents for reducing the Army's size as soon as a life-and-death struggle with foreign powers – a struggle for whose result the nation had relied on this same Army together with the Royal Navy – had been concluded. It had happened when the Seven Years War was ended by the Treaty of Paris. And it now happened again when the Treaty of Versailles brought to an end the American War of Independence. Although the loss of the American colonies could be used as justification for even greater reductions, the needs for India were such that in 1783 the strength of the Army was set at roughly 50,000. Of these some 17,000 would be in Britain (plus a further 12,000 in Ireland), about 9,000 in the West Indies, 3,000 in Gibraltar and more than 6,000 in India. The Artillery would account for a further 3,000. One of the branches of the Army most badly affected by these reductions was paradoxically that part on which in the end all successful operations of war depended – the Infantry of the Line. This unhappy situation arose not only as a result of the enforced disbandment of regiments, but also of the voluntary discharge of many soldiers who could, had they so chosen, have elected to re-enlist for what the Government must have thought of as an irresistible inducement of a one-and-a-half-guinea bounty. The Recruiting Acts of 1778 and 1779, when men were so badly needed to bring the American rebels to heel, had stipulated that after three years service – or even before – the many volunteers who enlisted might take their discharge if they so chose. So many did choose that, as Fortescue has told us, many infantry regiments found themselves reduced to a mere handful of private soldiers. He reminds us that The Royal Scots, the famous First of Foot, dwindled from being 700 strong to a mere 200.

None of these worrying developments seemed to have much effect on the fortunately short-lived coalition between the wayward Fox and the discredited North. They had their eye on immediate popularity rather than the welfare and security of either the nation or the soldiers who had served it so well. It was left to William Pitt to bring order to the British Army's neglect and decline. On coming to office Pitt's great concerns were with Ireland, the reform of Parliament and finance. Foreign policy, which in the end was dependent on the readiness of the Royal Navy and the British Army, could take fourth place. Yet before long foreign policy was to take first place.

In one respect Pitt did not wholly fail in his country's preparedness to defend itself. He did not totally neglect the Royal Navy. Although some of his measures hindered, others emphatically helped. As Macaulay has pointed out, by naming his brother, The Earl of Chatham, as First Lord of the Admiralty, he ensured a certain degree of mismanagement, or to be more precise no management at all, for Chatham 'without a single qualification for high public trust . . . was kept in that great post during two years of a war in which the very existence of the state depended on the efficiency of the fleet'. Yet Chatham 'continued to doze away and trifle away the time which ought to have been devoted to the public service'. Pitt himself, of course, was a model of industry, devotion to duty and perseverance. In his first attempt to guarantee the security of the dockyards at Portsmouth and Plymouth, however, he was not successful. His argument, which was strategically indisputable, that by fortifying the dockyards, British men of war would be free to discharge their traditional and proper duty of seeking out and destroying enemy fleets, rather than remaining bottled up protecting ports, an argument most strongly supported by Admiral Lord Hood and his naval colleagues, failed to win over the Opposition, who indulged in frivolous, ignorant and irrelevant objections to the proposal. It was suggested by them that only a substantial increase in the Regular Army or the total involvement of the Militia would suffice for the manning of such defences. Pitt was obliged to hold his hand. Yet during his ten years of economy in order to restore the country's finances – before the outbreak of war – he succeeded in adding almost a hundred ships of the line to the Royal Navy's total, about one-third of these newly built, the other two-thirds by repair. The lot of the Army was to be less happy.

We have seen how the exodus of the three-year men after the American War of Independence had left many regiments at dangerously low strength. Clearly the antidote was a powerful recruiting drive, and Colonels of Regiments were instructed accordingly. Yet in both 1785 and 1786, as Fortescue has told us, recruiting parties 'might just as well have remained quietly at the headquarters of their regiments, for they found it absolutely impossible to persuade men to enter the service. Moreover, such recruits as were secured by fair means or foul were no sooner caught than they were lost again by desertion.' Ironically enough one of the regiments which was to profit from this wholesale desertion was the 60th Regiment (formerly Royal Americans), stationed more or less permanently in the West Indies and reinforced by some of these very deserters. 'Nothing is more remarkable,' observes Fortescue, 'than the splendid record of this regiment in the field, at a period when few soldiers entered it untainted by crime.' The Regiment's reputation has continued to be high right up until today even though its recruiting methods may have changed.

The trouble with recruiting, not only for the Army but for the Royal Navy too, was of course money. The pay was inadequate and the stoppages from this pay unreasonably high. At times the Navy found it impossible to man its ships, and then the Army was required to make good the deficiencies. In 1787 no fewer than eight infantry battalions were at sea carrying out the duties of Royal Marines. In 1791 the Adjutant-General, hard pressed to find 1,000 men to help man the fleet, did not know where to turn, anxiously awaiting the return of the 14th and 19th Foot (West Yorkshires and Green Howards) from the West Indies in order to lay his hands on the necessary numbers. It was essentially the inadequate pay of the private soldier, coupled with the absurd deductions from this pay – to replace worn clothing and supply himself with the proper material to present himself smartly turned out – which meant, as the Adjutant-General himself conceded, that he was unable to satisfy the common calls of hunger. Therefore he deserted.

Pitt did not initially show himself sympathetic to these genuine grievances,* until the intervention of the King, supported by General William Fawcett and Lord Barrington, did at last bring some relief to the private soldier. In 1792 a warrant allowed him something for bread and it also reduced stoppages. What this meant was that the soldier would now receive sixpence a day in pay (2.5p), which together with bread allowance and smaller deductions, would bring his total annual income to just over £12. From this would be taken nearly £8 for food and just over £3 for clothing, laundry, cleaning kit and so on, leaving him a net sum per year of 18s 10½d (94 p). Even this meagre improvement had its effect on lessening desertion and improving recruitment. Yet Fortescue's judgement of Pitt's treatment of the Army is both harsh and just:

> Surely it is a blot on any man's financial administration that the money voted for the pay of the Army should have been spent in converting soldiers into deserters, honest men into outlaws. Surely it is a grave reproach to a statesman, not less on financial than on general grounds, that with full knowledge of the condition of the private soldier (I say nothing of the seaman) he should have left him

* Although he paid an annual retaining fee for Hessians of £36,000.

to starve from 1784 to 1791, doled him out a grudging pittance in 1792, and increased his pay, under menace of mutiny, practically threefold in 1797.

One of the other ill effects of Pitt's economy was that the Army had no Commander-in-Chief, who might have been expected not only to protect its interests more diligently, but also to supervise its readiness for active service. In short there was no proper system of discipline, tactical drills, organization or training. It was fortunate therefore that in 1788 Colonel David Dundas (he later became a general) published a small book called *The Principles of Military Movement*, in which he tried to correct what he regarded as the dangerous and irregular formations adopted by the British infantry during the war in America. It was not that Dundas thought it had been wrong to employ these tactics. On the contrary, the nature of the heavily wooded country there, and the excellent marksmanship of the enemy riflemen had fully justified these dispersed and loosely controlled formations. Moreover the dearth of cavalry had further dispensed with the need for tightly packed and disciplined columns, lines and squares. All this Dundas understood. His contention was that what had served against the irregular, dispersed and independently active American forces would not do against the highly trained massed infantry of continental armies, nor when confronted with thousands of well disciplined and directed cavalry. In recommending a return to the methods of Frederick the Great, Dundas overlooked the enormous value of training light infantrymen to think for themselves, to develop cunning field craft, to be deadly marksmen, to be thoroughly flexible in their tactical thinking and practice.

Not surprisingly many of the veterans from the American war ridiculed Dundas's ideas, notably Cornwallis who described Prussian manoeuvres as the sort of thing which the worst general in England would be hooted at for attempting. Nothing, he claimed, could be more ridiculous than two lines of infantry advancing towards each other until they were six yards apart and then loosing off until they had run out of ammunition. Yet the fact was that since no standard instructions for movement in the field existed for the British infantry, and since every Regimental Colonel took it upon himself to invent his own system, it would clearly be impossible for a brigade or higher formation commander to issue any order to a group of battalions with the slightest expectation of their all doing the same thing. Some uniformity of regulation was therefore essential, and as Dundas's system received the approval of the King himself, the Duke of York and the Brigade of Guards, having been successfully tried out in Ireland, his drill-book was generally adopted. Its principal fault was that it was too inflexible, being based on eighteen separate manoeuvres, which as Fortescue wrily pointed out were 'a sad stumbling block to slow-witted officers'. Even Sir John Moore felt obliged to criticize this aspect of Dundas's book, while conceding that it had done a great deal of good. It was, of course, John Moore who, as we shall see later, was able to reintroduce the individual initiative, speed of thought and movement, and tactical dexterity of the light infantry. But Moore did not interfere with much of Dundas's teachings. Rather he was able to take the best of the Prussian system and the lastingly valuable lessons of the American War and blend them into a tactical doctrine, which gave to the Light Infantry their skirmishing and sharp-shooting skills, while at the same time preserving and enhancing the steadiness of the British redcoat which made possible so many of Wellington's victories.

Apart from these beneficial changes in tactical doctrine and drills, there were improvements in both dress and weapons for the infantry. Lighter and looser trousers and jackets were introduced for soldiers serving in the heat of India or the West Indies, together with a new hat which had both a peak and a brim, thus affording some protection from the sun. As for weapons the halberd (it was a kind of combined spear and battle-axe) finally made its exit, to be replaced by the pike, and all infantry officers would in future carry a sword. The infantry, however, were not the only soldiers for whom Dundas effected some badly needed reforms. He also introduced a new system of training for the cavalry, particularly designed to ensure better control, for the persistent fault of cavalry was that so much store was set by the fury and dash of a charge that the all-important business of rallying after the charge was neglected. It was therefore laid down that cavalry should advance towards the enemy at the trot, and gallop only when closing with their quarry. These measures were not as effective as they were designed to be and, even in the Peninsula and at Waterloo, Wellington had cause to complain of the cavalry's lack of discipline and control. They would have done well to emulate the far better drilled and directed Horse Artillery, who so often won Wellington's praise and whose first two companies were formed in 1793. It was in this year, of course, that Pitt finally saw the need to go to war with Revolutionary France, despite his initial reaction to the Revolution of 'wait and see'.

This cautious reaction of Pitt's to the tumultuous events of July 1789 was in sharp contrast to the ill-conceived rejoicing of Fox and the far-sighted warnings of Burke. Fox's pronouncement that the Bastille's fall was the greatest and best event in the history of the world was characteristic of his extravagance and, although for all men of reasonable opinion unsustainable in the light of Madame Guillotine's unquenchable thirst, yet was sustained by him. Burke, on the other hand, believing as he did that 'good order is the foundation of all good things' saw that by destroying the past, human rights would themselves be destroyed, and that the result of the Revolution would be ruthless dictatorship and bloody war. Yet Pitt refused to see it, even when the European powers started their war against Revolutionary France. Right up to the time that he decided for war, Pitt deluded himself that the European struggle was one in which Great Britain need not participate. It is scarcely surprising, therefore, that when war did come he totally failed to understand its nature and so was equally incapable of taking the measures necessary for its prosecution. We have seen how he neglected the Army in peace. Yet even when engaged in a war with a nation spurred by fanatical devotion to a new spirit of innovation, idealism and insatiable ambition, in a war which literally became a life-and-death struggle, he failed to take account of what his own country had been and still was capable of on the field of battle. Macaulay's condemnation of Pitt's management, or rather mis-management, of the country's military affairs is nothing if not thorough. He points out that the material resources available to the Prime Minister were more or less unlimited. Parliament had only to be asked for money, men and weapons and they would be provided. There was also a great store of martial tradition and experience which could be drawn upon. The men of Great Britain had frequently shown themselves to be possessed of the very qualities, both physical and moral, necessary to make good soldiers. Great generals of the past such as Marlborough, Peterborough, Clive and Wolfe had proved that leaders to command these soldiers sprang up when their services were needed. In short, Pitt had at his disposal all the ingredients to create one of the finest armies in the world. Nor was he denied the time to do so. The path on which French ambition and aspiration were set had long been made clear. Yet Pitt's policy had been such that when Britain went to war with France in 1793, its Army was totally unprepared – in numbers, in weapons, in organization, in training, in direction. It was hardly surprising therefore that it now had to undergo what Arthur Bryant called the *Years of Endurance*. We must now take a look at the Army's fortunes and misfortunes during those years.

CHAPTER THREE

Dispersion and Defeat

The English Army, under Pitt, was the laughing-stock of all Europe. It could not boast of one single brilliant exploit. It had never shown itself on the Continent but to be beaten, chased, forced to re-embark, or forced to capitulate. To take some sugar island in the West Indies, to scatter some mob of half naked Irish peasants, such were the most splendid victories won by the British troops under Pitt's auspices.

LORD MACAULAY

When Great Britain took up the sword against Revolutionary France in 1793, she was more or less doing what John Hampden did when he raised a regiment in 1642 to dispute the divine right of Charles I – throwing away the scabbard. For the fight went on for twenty-two years, and in that time the British Army was transformed from a contemptible mob into a splendid fighting force with which Wellington said that he could have gone anywhere and done anything. We have seen how Pitt's financial policy, one of strict economy, did great harm to the Army. During the period between the Treaty of Versailles and the outbreak of war with France, the Army's decline – with no Commander-in-Chief to guard its interests and the ministerial post of Secretary at War little more than a sinecure – was absolute. Its strength was pared to the bone. The military system was almost wholly corrupt. Money purchased regimental command for mere children or the debauched classes of rank. What few recruits there were were often drunk, absent or ill-disciplined. Some of the regiments at home were totally unfit for service. Less than 50,000 strong – compared with France's half a million – the British Army had less than one-third at home, and two-thirds scattered abroad, rotting in unhealthy colonies. The officers were on the whole rich, privileged, ignorant of military matters and incompetent. The men for the most part were down-and-outs, jailbirds and delinquents*, who had enlisted for drink as a last

---

* One recruit was Coleridge, who more for pecuniary (6½-guinea bounty) than patriotic reasons, joined the 15th Light Dragoons in December 1793. He was as he said 'a very indocile Equestrian', and suffered appalling saddle sores and boils. Trooper Comberbache, as he called himself, rode a horse as 'young and undisciplined' as himself, which ran off parade with him and threw him three times in one week. After an unofficial payment of 25 guineas by his brother George, Trooper Comberbache was discharged as insane in April 1794.

resort and were subject to rigid drilling, harsh discipline and unimaginative training. This was the Army which, in spite of Pitt's belated and inadequate efforts to strengthen and improve it, was shortly to show in a series of abortive attempts to argue the toss with French Revolutionary armies how useless it was. It would take the Duke of York and a number of enlightened commanders more than seven years to put it right.

When Pitt was at length convinced that war with France was necessary, not on ideological, but on strategic grounds, he declared on 1 December 1792 what many others had throughout history said before, that readiness for war was the surest way of preserving peace, and to reinforce the point both called out two-thirds of the Militia,* and summoned Parliament to meet in two weeks' time. When the House of Commons debated the matter, Fox in a characteristically capricious gesture attacked Pitt's policy and divided the House. In spite of Fox's being followed into the lobby by a few loyal supporters, the House overwhelmingly approved the Government's intention to strengthen the armed forces. Thus it was that Parliament voted in favour of increasing the Army by 17,000 soldiers and the Royal Navy by 9,000 seamen. In addition an Aliens' Bill was introduced designed to supervise closely the activities of foreign refugees. When Chauvelin, French Ambassador in London, demanded its repeal, his request was summarily rejected.

Even at this stage with King Louis XVI on trial for his life and the French Executive Council beginning to plan for the invasion of the United Netherlands – a move which would certainly bring about war with Britain – Pitt was appealing in vain to Russia to persuade the nations of Europe to mediate with France. He proposed that in return for France's withdrawing her armies and abandoning her conquests, the Great Powers would undertake neither to engage in hostilities against France nor to interfere in her internal affairs. His ideas were ill-received. Russia and Prussia were determined to aggrandize themselves at the expense of Poland; the Emperor of Austria was insisting on the restoration of the French monarchy; the French themselves were not merely unwilling to make peace – they were longing for more conflict and more conquests. On 21 January 1793 Louis XVI was executed. Three days later Danton was bellowing to the Convention that they would throw at the feet of the Kings in coalition against them the head of their own King. He urged the Convention to take the momentous step of annexing Belgium, and a week afterwards, on 1 February, the French Republic declared war on Great Britain and Holland.

Meanwhile Pitt, his peace policy in ruins, was warning the House of

* Apart from the Regular Army, Britain relied for her defence on the Militia (raised by ballot), the Volunteers (one way of avoiding Militia), Fencibles, for home defence only, like the Militia; and the Yeomanry.

Commons that there could be no compromise with the apparently insatiable territorial ambitions of France. It was clear that the French Government would not tolerate any form of government in other countries which did not conform to their own ideas of liberty, ideas which could best be defined as those of removing liberties from those opposing them. Therefore England must set its face against France's ambition and aggrandizement, for in the end France was bent on the destruction of England. 'If France is really desirous of maintaining friendship and peace with England, she must show herself disposed to renounce her views of aggression and aggrandizement, and to confine herself within her own territory without insulting other governments, without disturbing their tranquillity, without violating their rights. And unless she consents to these terms, whatever may be our wishes for peace, the final issue must be war.'

It was one thing to declare for war, another to wage it. Even the Royal Navy was not on a war footing, let alone the Army. It was true that the Navy could boast a total of 113 battleships, but in 1792 only twelve had been in commission. The problem therefore was not merely one of getting more ready for service, but of finding the seamen to sail in them. Yet although Pitt had neglected the Army (even as late as the spring of 1792 he had reduced its regular strength at home by several thousand), he had always been conscious of the need to provide money for the Navy, both building new and repairing existing ships during the ten years of financial economy following the Treaty of Versailles. Mobilization plans for the Royal Navy, therefore, not only existed, but reserves of naval stores in well-cared-for dockyards enabled these plans to be put into effect so quickly that within a month of the declaration of war, more than fifty battleships were provisioned, manned and in commission, while nearly another forty awaited only crews to render them fit for service. This rapid mobilization of British sea-power together with the decay of the French Navy – its skilled royalist officers removed, the best of its lower deck complement disbanded, ships, ports and magazines neglected – meant that Pitt would be able to base his war strategy on that so much favoured and exploited by his father – the blue water policy. By using the fleet, together with modest land forces, Pitt would aim to rob France of her colonial possessions, and so by increasing Britain's trade and profit finance the armies of Austria and Prussia to take on the common enemy on land. Not that the British Army would do nothing! On the contrary, as early as February 1793, three battalions of the Foot Guards were despatched to Holland under the command of the Duke of York to assist in the defence of that country.

Before we follow the course of this campaign, it is important to explain and understand the absurd arrangements by which the conduct of war by the British Government was to be directed. As

Professor Watson* has made clear 'the war had to be run by a committee of the king, Pitt, and Dundas,† carrying with them the rest of the cabinet'. Watson goes on to explain that Britain's military machine was not merely flawed at the top. It was flawed throughout. Not only did those directing policy not know how to deploy and employ their military resources properly. These resources, particularly as far as the Army was concerned, were themselves inadequate. The time-honoured lessons of singleness of aim and concentration of forces were forgotten. Instead was substituted diversity of aim and dispersion of forces. So that when Pitt began to frame his strategy, he tried to do far too much with too little, and ignored the master rule of military strategy – to select his primary object and then deploy his forces in such a way as to ensure the achievement of that object. Instead he devised a whole series of military ventures – negotiations with French colonials in Haiti to seize their territory; reinforcement of the Duke of York's army in Flanders; raids on the French coast in Brittany with a view to rousing the Royalists there; and an expedition to the eastern Mediterranean – any one of which might have been successfully pursued by concentrating all naval and military resources on it, but for which the strength to pursue all four simultaneously simply did not exist. 'To undertake these worldwide military campaigns', wrote Professor Watson, 'he had an available British army of only 20,000 effectives.'

Although in Flanders the Duke of York's British troops would be strengthened by some 13,000 of the King's Hanoverians and 8,000 Hessian mercenaries, whose fortunes we will shortly follow, the urgent requirement was to recruit, equip and train more British soldiers. Yet the system of recruitment was chaotic. It was true that the Militia could be mobilized for home defence, and so in theory allow the regular soldiers to be used for overseas expeditions. But the arrangement whereby men called for Militia service could pay substitutes to do this duty for them not only robbed the Militia of those who could afford to shirk their obligations, it also reduced the total manpower available for other forms of enlistment. In this way many of the potential soldiers who could have served abroad with regular battalions were restricted to home defence. There were also the demands of the Royal Navy, whose system of forcibly enlisting men by use of their unscrupulous press-gangs still further reduced the numbers who could be persuaded by bounty money, and consequent inebriety, to join the Army. Having done so, however, and having been

---

* *The Reign of George III 1760–1815*, J. Steven Watson, Oxford University Press, 1960.
† Henry Dundas, Pitt's great friend and tippling companion, held many offices: Secretary of State for War, First Commissioner for India, Treasurer of the Navy. He knew nothing of military matters but none the less, and with Pitt's support, behaved as if he were Minister of Defence in the Churchill mould.

turned into soldiers simply by being issued with a uniform, totally untrained, totally bewildered and totally unfitted for service, they were dispatched in transports to join the Duke of York's miscellaneous army of British, Hanoverian and Hessian troops under the overall command of an Austrian general, Prince Frederick of Saxe-Coburg, to see what they could do towards winning the first British campaign in Flanders.

The Flanders campaign of 1793 to 1795 was a model of how the Allies might properly have conducted war against the armies of Louis XIV, when siege and reduction of fortified towns seemed to represent the height of tactical ingenuity. It would not do against the swift and reckless manoeuvring of French revolutionary masses. Under Coburg's direction there was no boldness, no seizing of the initiative, no strategic foresight, but a dull, methodical practice of outdated and indecisive military drills, which took no account either of the new nature of warfare, or of the opportunities presented by the difficulties in which France's armies often found themselves. It was, as far as the British were concerned, redeemed only because its commanders, including the Duke of York, learned what was wrong with the Army, and learned also how not to go about making war against the French. Among those who benefited from this exercise was one of Britain's future great captains, Arthur Wellesley.

On 1 May 1793 Coburg began his ponderous advance towards the frontier between the Austrian Netherlands and France. There was very little to stop him continuing the advance across the northern plains of France, for two months earlier Dumouriez's plans to invade Holland had been defeated by the Austrians at Neewinden, and Dumouriez himself had defected to the Allies. But Coburg had no intention of exploiting such an opportunity. His progress was sluggish and uninspired, with every possible route by which the French might advance against him picketed and every strongpoint, however insignificant, reduced. By the time his army reached the frontier, spread out between Ostend and Mauberge, he decided that only the reduction of the Valenciennes and Condé frontier fortresses would enable him to continue the advance. By the end of July Valenciennes had been taken, while the Prussians who had been besieging the Rhineland city of Mainz finally succeeded in capturing it. The Duke of York's attempts to take Dunkirk with his British and Hanoverian troops, however, had been repulsed at Hoondschoote. And it was just before this time that Lazare-Marguérite Carnot, the organizer of victory, had taken a hand in the game.

Carnot was a Captain of Engineers, who had never commanded troops in battle, but had in Carlyle's extravagant language a 'cold mathematical head and silent stubbornness of will'. When in August 1793 Carnot was recalled from the *Armée du Nord* to confer with the Convention's Committee of Public Safety, France's overall position with regard to the war was hardly encouraging. As we have seen, Mainz and Valenciennes had fallen; and elsewhere in Lyons, Marseilles and the Vendée insurrection was widespread; Toulon was besieged; even Spanish troops had dared to cross the Pyrenees. The situation was desperate, yet the Allies, disunited, hesitant, self-seeking and faint-hearted, failed to take advantage of this supreme opportunity. France took two great measures to avert disaster. First, the *levée en masse*, proposed by Danton, was approved. It was virtually to prepare the nation for total war and would therefore find military employment for all national resources. In the first place every man, woman and child would be given a duty to perform – young, single men immediately to become soldiers; those a little older and married to be ready to serve in the Army; the middle-aged and elderly to manufacture weapons, run supply depots and encourage recruiting; even women and children were to be mobilized, making uniforms, nursing, and ensuring there would be a steady flow of medical dressings. Barracks would be created from buildings in public use; all the country's horses and horse furniture, no matter to whom they belonged, would be requisitioned for military or official purposes. The whole of France would be put on a war footing. But, of course, all this would take time. Meanwhile there was an urgent need for a victory, any victory, to reinforce revolutionary zeal and gain some of that all-important commodity, time. This is where Carnot's ideas came in.

He proposed to strike a blow in the north, where the Allies were still dithering, and wrest the advantage from them there. To do so would mean robbing the Revolutionary armies further east, guarding the Rhine and Moselle, but there was less danger there as Prussia seemed more concerned with making sure of her share of Poland than fighting the French. Thus he devised a plan to distract the Allied advance towards Mauberge by sending a force of some 20,000 under Houchard and Jourdan in a raid to Ostend. It was while this operation was under way that the French came into contact with the Duke of York's mixed army heading for Dunkirk, and although initially held by the British Foot Guards at Linselles, the French succeeded in overcoming the Hanoverians at Hoondschoote, so seriously threatening the Duke of York's position besieging Dunkirk that he was obliged to withdraw northwards, abandoning heavy guns and stores. It had been a lesson in the new French tactics that Carnot had introduced and which were to prove so effective. In front of the main French columns would advance a flood of *tirailleurs*, the swift, sharp-shooting skirmishers, reconnoitring the enemy's positions and disrupting them; then would come the dense, packed columns of the main body, whose sheer numbers and weight alone would make up for inferior training, and whose concentrated fervour would quickly penetrate the defenders' lines which lacked the necessary depth to slow them down and stop them. This whole concept of Carnot's – launching a single, narrow, concentrated blow against enemy defences, which being so wide and extended were weak everywhere – exactly suited the temperament and tenacity of the Revolutionary armies, and was to succeed time and time again. Moreover Carnot's overall strategy, to concentrate on one strategic objective at a time, achieve that one, and them move on to the next, was exactly in keeping with those two principles of war – singleness of aim, concentration of forces – which, as we have seen, the British forces under Pitt's direction seemed determined to eschew.

This failure to conform to the simple rules of strategy was soon to land the British in further trouble, for when a great opportunity offered itself at Toulon, they had neither the resolve nor the resources to exploit it. During the occupation, and subsequent evacuation, of Toulon by the British, two men made their entrances on history's stage; both were ever after to be remembered in the annals of war. The first was Napoleon Bonaparte, who was to occupy as a conqueror at the head of his Army almost every capital of continental Europe* and who was at length kicked out of his own country's capital by the Marshals of this same Army; the second, implacably opposed in all his thoughts and actions to the first, was Horatio Nelson, who by his courage, humanity, audacity and strategic vision won both the huzzas of the British people by his spectacular victories and at length despite his foibles, by his unswerving devotion to duty, their hearts. Nelson with HMS *Agamemnon* was with Lord Hood's Mediterranean fleet when Toulon declared its loyalty to King Louis XVII – the Dauphin – and invited Hood and his fleet to enter its strongly fortified harbour. 'What an event this has been for Lord Hood,' wrote Nelson to his wife. 'Such a one as History cannot produce its equal. That the strongest place in Europe and twenty-two sail of the line should be given up without firing a shot; it is not to be credited.' Yet although Hood sent his Royal Marines ashore, the city's defences, albeit powerful, would need some 50,000 troops to man them properly. Here at once was made clear the dilemma into which the British strategy of diversity and dispersion of effort had cast Pitt and his advisers. When Hood appealed for reinforcements, what were they to do? Reinforce Toulon, by withdrawing troops from Flanders and abandoning any idea of military adventures elsewhere? Or continue with Pitt's favourite 'blue water' policy of attacking French colonies overseas, thereby satisfying the city merchants, and necessarily forgetting all about European involvements? In any event even if the whole British Army had been concentrated and sent to Toulon – a feat impossible to bring off with the necessary speed – it would still have fallen well short of the 50,000 required. As it was Pitt tried to do everything and as a result failed to achieve anything.

* Not St Petersburg or Stockholm; nor Constantinople if it can be called European.

While the Allies dithered, Carnot acted, dealing with the threats to the Republic one by one. First he dealt with a possible infiltration over the Alps by Austrian troops, suppressing rebels in the Rhone valley and capturing Lyons. In October 1793 he again mounted an offensive in Flanders, in the east defeating the Austrians at Wattignies, and in the west by driving through Ypres and Nieuport, forcing the Duke of York's army to retire to its base at Ostend. With the Allied armies now skulking in winter quarters, Carnot was able to turn his attention to eliminating the Vendeans. 'By Christmas,' wrote Arthur Bryant, 'half the villages of the West were heaps of cinders and the fields strewn with thousands of corpses. As the blue-coated armies drove outwards like some mighty force compressed, the Jacobin bosses followed them, scotching dissension with unspeakable terror.' At the same time the great opportunity presented by Toulon had been lost for ever. Not only had Carnot put together some 35,000 troops to re-take the place, but among them in charge of the artillery was a young captain whose name was Napoleon Bonaparte.

To defend Toulon there were some British marines and soldiers, some French royalists, and Spanish and Piedmontese troops. The French attacking troops stormed and took one position after another, their artillery able to bear on the harbour itself, until their general assault on the night of 17 December broke the defences absolutely. The Spanish and Piedmontese troops ran away, and although the British fought on, their last positions were soon overcome and the following night Lord Hood ordered evacuation, taking with him as many Toulonese refugees as he could. Nelson, writing to his wife, commented on the horror of domestic wars, how grievous it was, and how every tale of the Republicans' savagery to their own people multiplied the horror. Although Hood had intended to destroy all the French ships he had captured, delegating this part of the operation to Captain Sir Sidney Smith (a rival to Nelson in dash and glory-seeking and who like Nelson was to succeed in thwarting the great Bonaparte), the incendiary parties of Spanish sailors failed in their duty. Hood had made off with four French ships of the line and some frigates, but of the twenty-seven French battleships left, only nine were burned, thus leaving a fleet to contest the British position in the Mediterranean. Nelson blamed Smith, who apart from being bold in action, was never chary of using his tongue. 'Great talkers do the least,' was Nelson's comment.

Everywhere, therefore, the British were failing in their land campaigns. George III summed up the cause by pointing out that there were too many objects to attend to, and so the forces were too weak at every point. Yet if 1793 had been a year full of hope, which was then frustrated, 1794 and 1795 were, with the exception of some victories at sea, to be a good deal worse. Even though the British expedition to the West Indies which sailed under Sir John Jervis* in November 1793, succeeded during the following year in capturing a number of French islands, the cost was appallingly heavy. During the three years to 1796 the total British casualties from fighting and yellow fever amounted to the astonishing total of 80,000, half of whom died and half were rendered unfit for service. No remote sugar island was worth such a price when the key to success against France lay not in the West Indies but on the continent of Europe. What is more, French revolutionary fervour and revolt spread to these islands themselves, when Paris made it plain that white and black men were equal. The one advantage the British did gain from it all was command of the seas and control of the Atlantic when Lord Howe defeated the French fleet off the Brittany coast on 'The Glorious First of June'.

The Royal Navy's supremacy was not matched by the Duke of York's army. He had a perpetual struggle to manage both his troops and his allies. The former were inadequate in number, ill-equipped, ill-disciplined and on the whole poorly led. The latter were unreliable, untrustworthy and usually in the wrong place at the wrong time. The campaign of 1794 was, to say the least, ill-starred. First, while vainly attempting to support the Austrians at Tourcoing, the valiant Duke found himself riding for his life to escape capture, thankful only for the breeding, pace and staying power of his horse. In July, following the French victory at Fleurus and their pursuit of the Allied armies, recapturing all the frontier fortresses, the Duke's army retreated and went on retreating, behaving with disgraceful indiscipline as they did so, until finally the campaign ended in March 1795, with a mere 6,000 effective British soldiers left, having been forced to retire through Germany to Bremen, and from there evacuated to England. Thus all Pitt's hopes of securing Flanders against the French, the very purpose for which he had gone to war in the first place, had come to nothing. Something was clearly very wrong both with Pitt's strategy and the state of the British Army. There were plenty of observers who saw what needed to be done. Among them was Captain Calvert, the Duke of York's aide-de-camp:

> We want artillerymen, we want a general officer at the head of the artillery, we want drivers and smiths, we want a commanding engineer of rank and experience – we want, at least, two out of the four brigades of mounted artillery with which his Grace of Richmond is amusing himself in England. We want a total stop put to that pernicious mode of bestowing rank on officers without even the form of recommendation, merely for raising (by means of crimps)† a certain number of men, to restore to the Army those independent and disinterested feelings and high principles which

---

* Whom we last met with Wolfe and will meet again with Nelson.
† Crimps were Army brokers.

should actuate a soldier and form the basis of military discipline of a free country.

In this last requirement Calvert was echoing Burke's plea that if the nation were to have an army that was not a base rabble and a navy that was nothing but rotten timber, it was imperative to instil into both these bodies a liberal obedience which could only spring from a deep attachment to the leaders set above them, thus ensuring a sense of the stake which each of them had in the national institution these leaders represented. Nelson was to be the supreme embodiment of such a leader. In a different way, Wellington, who took part in the disastrous Flanders campaign, quickly saw that there was nothing wrong with the British soldier if he were properly directed, but that it was the system itself – the organization, administration and command – which was at fault. The depths to which a defeated and disintegrating army could descend at the end of the Duke of York's ill-fated expedition were admirably described by Sir John Fortescue:

> Far as the eye could reach over the whitened plain were scattered gun-limbers, wagons full of baggage, stores or sick men, sutler's carts and private carriages. Bedside them lay the horses, dead; here a straggler who had staggered on to the bivouac and dropped to sleep in the arms of the frost; there a group of British and Germans round an empty rum cask; here forty English Guardsmen huddled together about a plundered wagon; there a pack-horse with a woman lying alongside it, and a baby swaddled in rags peering out of the pack with its mother's milk turned to ice upon its lips – one and all stark, frozen dead. Had the retreat lasted but three or four days longer, not a man would have escaped.

For the future Duke of Wellington, at this time Lieutenant-Colonel Arthur Wellesley, there could have been no better introduction to the business of how not to conduct operations. As Elizabeth Longford (great-great niece by marriage of Wellington's wife, Kitty Pakenham) points out in her fine biography, the young Wellesley saw all that could go wrong when command was divided, when there was no proper organization of food, clothing or supplies, when the local people were more in sympathy with the enemy than the Allies trying to protect them, when the winter climate dominated operations, and when discipline broke down in retreat. Yet his own battalion, the 33rd Foot* had behaved well, and Wellesley himself in his first action at Boxtel in September 1794 had distinguished himself by his coolness and tactical skill, ordering his infantry to hold their fire until the enemy were close and then engaging them with such disciplined musketry that they were quickly driven off. He saw, too, how excellent regiments

---

* Now The Duke of Wellington's Regiment.

could be when their officers looked after the men properly and knew what they were about. As for the general management of an army, there were few indeed who knew anything about it. The mere fact that headquarters seemed so ignorant determined Wellington always to be on the spot which mattered in person, seeing everything and doing things for himself. It was this, he later confided to Stanhope,* that was the real reason for his subsequent successful campaigns.

Before he could embark on these campaigns, however, much had to be done to reform the whole system, administration, tactics, training and command of the British Army. Fortunately, the right man was at hand to reorganize the Army, for however ill-suited the Duke of York had shown himself in command of an army in the field, as an administrator and reformer he was to prove himself imaginative, hard-working and supremely successful. This overhauling of the Army was going to be urgently necessary, for in the year following the Duke's fiasco in Flanders, the star of Napoleon Bonaparte was to begin its glittering progress across the battlefields of Europe and Egypt. The Grande Armée was to be created and make its way to most of its enemies' capitals except London. That it did not reach London too owed much to the activities of Nelson, and after Nelson had immortalized his name at Trafalgar, the other Briton, who finally brought Napoleon's career to an end, was that same Arthur Wellesley who had been learning his trade in Flanders.

* *Conversations with Wellington*, Earl Stanhope, The World's Classics, 1938 (first issued privately, 1886).

CHAPTER FOUR

Eastern Triumphs

In order to destroy England utterly, we must get possession of Egypt.
NAPOLEON BONAPARTE

Unlike the conscripted armies of Russia, Prussia and Austria with their rigid tactics and formal discipline, or the massed, ardent, seemingly invincible sansculottes of France's Directory, the British preferred a military system which made a virtue out of improvisation, variety and individuality. For those Britons for whom a scarlet coat would satisfy the demands of patriotism, penury or plumage, there was an infinity of choice. For some it might be a Yeomanry Dragoon regiment, for others the county Militia or Volunteers, for yet more the Regular Army. So successful were the recruiters in 1794, when some 40,000 men were enlisted, that other difficulties intruded. The shortage of men for the Royal Navy caused the Government to stop all Army recruiting for a time and to prevent merchant ships from leaving harbour. Moreover, this huge expansion of military forces produced its own chaotic conditions among these same forces. It was fortunate that the right man was at hand to bring some order to this chaos.

We have seen that Frederick, Duke of York, did not shine as a commander of armies in the field. Yet after the disasters in Flanders, he was in February 1795 appointed Commander-in-Chief, a position which not only soothed his wounded pride, but at which he was to show himself singularly adept. At the Horse Guards, where he was to remain for the best part of fifteen years, he showed himself to be, as Arthur Bryant put it, 'a born administrator – a hard worker with an orderly mind, a royal memory and a mastery of detail'. Having seen the Army's deficiencies while in command, he was in a uniquely qualified position to put them right. What is more he was devoted to the Army. He was able to bring it what it needed above all – order and organization. There was no doubting the courage or perseverance of many of its officers and men. The proud tradition of its regiments had been proved time and again. But the system was wrong. We have noted already the absurdity and anarchy of its recruitment. We have seen that the method of selecting those to command regiments was based on money and rank, not on experience or competence. We have observed how in the field its lack of properly directed artillery, engineers, transport or supply arrangements brought about a complete breakdown in discipline, control and effectiveness. The Duke of York's task was thus clear. It was to provide sound leadership, proper training with good equipment and an organization which would survive and triumph over the exigencies of war.

Among the reforms introduced by the new Commander-in-Chief were those designed to ensure fitness for command. By this he did not mean merely professional ability, but also that extra and indispensable responsibility of officers to care for and look after the men under them as well as to lead them in action. He therefore abolished the commissioning of infants, and although he could not abolish the system of purchase itself, he made sure that promotion by purchase was only allowed after a given period. In this way no one could become a major without having six years' experience as an officer. The youngest age for an officer to be commissioned at all was sixteen. The Duke of York also instituted a system, which has survived and prospered to this day, of confidential reports on officers' performance of their duties, so that both the Adjutant-General and a newly appointed Military Secretary could judge which officers were fit for greater responsibilities. By this method he was enabled to select officers unable to afford promotion by purchase, to higher positions by virtue of their merit alone. Later, he went further and established the Royal Military College (now Sandhurst) for training young officers, together with a Senior Department (now the Staff College) for their further education to serve on the staff.

He did not, however, confine his activities to the selection and training of officers. The whole of the field army would in the future conform to a regular programme of exercises, so that during each week regiments and battalions would practise their own particular drills, take part in brigade training and also have field-days. By these means the Duke of York slowly gave to the Army the orderliness and instruction it so badly needed. Particular attention was paid to the correct use of arms. In the cavalry, whose troopers were just as likely to chop off their own toes or their horses' ears as do any damage to the enemy, the rules and regulations for using the sword, laid down by Colonel Le Marchant (whom we shall meet later at Wellington's great Salamanca victory) were adopted and practised. In the infantry, he introduced and organized light companies with special training instructions and concentration on rapid and accurate use of the musket. In his enthusiasm for exploiting mobility and adaptability, he experimented with specially formed forces of light infantry, light cavalry and light horse artillery. Early in the 1800s, as we shall see, he was greatly assisted in this idea by Sir John Moore. But, of course, all these innovations and experiments took time. Indeed many of them were opposed by the more conservative elements of the Army. No branch was slower moving than the Ordnance Board, which controlled the all-important artillery, although the arrival of Lord Cornwallis as Master General of the Ordnance in place of the Duke of Richmond (of whom Captain Calvert spoke so scathingly) was to produce results in the end. In praising the Duke of York's work, Arthur Bryant gives him credit for bringing about a steady improvement into every branch of the Army, while Jock Haswell writes that the Duke 'turned his army into a splendid fighting force'. We must turn shortly to observing it in action, but before doing so, it will be as well to take note of what the young French artilleryman, who struck so decisive a blow to English hopes at Toulon, was doing in Italy, in France and in Egypt.

When the diminutive gunner general arrived at Nice on 27 March 1796 to take command of the Army of Italy, the four veterans awaiting him, Schérer (from whom Bonaparte was taking over), Sérurier, Augereau and Masséna, did not think much of the appointment, which they regarded as having been secured largely by intrigues of political counsels and the bed chamber. They were soon to change their minds. The new Commander-in-Chief had brought with him associates, who in their separate ways were to serve the Napoleonic legend with marked distinction – Berthier, the brilliant chief of staff; Murat, the outstandingly brave and successful cavalry leader; and Marmont, an artilleryman like Napoleon and a close friend.* Having hitched themselves to Bonaparte's star all these men, except Schérer, were to become Marshals of the Empire. When we consider that after three years of indecisive playing at warfare, which the French Revolutionary armies had been indulging in with their Austrian and Piedmontese enemies, Bonaparte was suddenly by his whirlwind tactics of rapid marching and concentration of force to turn the whole concept of warfare upside down, we may also recognize that an extraordinary talent was on parade. First there were the qualities of the man himself – a very special physique which produced unusual activity; an ability to go without sleep which enabled him to maintain this superhuman activity for weeks on end; and an eye for country (which every aspiring military commander should possess) which Bonaparte owed to his upbringing in the savage, undeveloped mountains and hills of Corsica, and with which he could gauge (as Wellington too was always trying to guess) what lay on the other side of the hill. Lastly, as a gunner, he appreciated how important it was to concentrate fire-power on to a single objective, and then, having been successful there, to switch this fire-power rapidly to the next.†

* Yet Marmont, Duke of Ragusa, betrayed Napoleon in 1814, and the French language acquired a new verb: *raguser* – to betray.
† I am indebted to Vincent Cronin's *Napoleon* (Collins, 1971) for this analysis.

These qualities do not in themselves explain how it was that
Bonaparte, beginning his campaign in April 1796 at Nice, and ending
it just over a year later sixty-five miles from Vienna, obliged the
Austrian Emperor to make peace with France and hand over the
Duchy of Milan. 'Though men knew that a change had come', wrote
A.G. Macdonnell, 'very few understood what the change was and how
the new magic was worked, either in 1796 or for years afterwards.'*
Macdonnell goes on to say that having inherited the spirit of attack,
the tradition of glory, the infantry column with a cloud of skirmishers
ahead, the sheer individualistic élan of his countrymen, Bonaparte
simply imposed on them willpower of genius, clarity of object and
furiously fast movement. Vincent Cronin goes further and points out
that he also brought a discipline of behaviour, an incentive to bravery
and a unity of command that had not previously existed in the
Revolutionary armies. All these things had prevailed with lightning
speed and extravagant results against the Austrians. How would they
fare against the British?

It was a question Napoleon was soon to ask himself, for after his
return from the Italian campaign he was appointed to command the
army against England, and early in 1798 he found himself inspecting
troops and vessels concentrated at the Channel ports with a view to
making a descent on the one country still in arms against France.
Bonaparte had already seen what British sea-power could and could
not do, at Toulon. He had heard what Jervis and Nelson had done to
the Spanish fleet at the battle of St Vincent in February 1797, when
Nelson covered himself with glory both by his tactical genius and his
personal courage. The British Army was in a small way able to share in
his use of a 'patent bridge for boarding first-rates'.† Nelson explains it:

> A soldier of the 69th Regiment‡ having broke the upper quarter-
> gallery window, jumped in, followed by myself and others, as fast as
> possible. I found the cabin doors fastened and the Spanish officers
> fired their pistols at us through the windows, but, having broke
> open the doors, the soldiers fired . . . [Nelson is referring here to the
> British soldiers with him].
>
> Having placed sentinels at the different ladders and ordered
> Captain Miller to push more men into the *San Nicolas*, I directed
> my brave fellows to board the first-rate [*San Josef*], which was done
> in a moment. When I got into her main-chains, a Spanish officer
> came upon the quarterdeck rail, without arms, and said the ship had
> surrendered.

Nelson summed it all up when he observed that 'the Dons may make

* *Napoleon and his Marshals*, Macmillan, 1950.
† This referred to Nelson's using the eighty-gun *San Nicolas* as a bridge to board the
first-rate *San Josef*.
‡ Later The Welch Regiment, now The Royal Regiment of Wales.

fine ships, but they cannot make men'. Something of the same idea with regard to French seamen no doubt crossed Bonaparte's mind when he gazed across the rough, grey waters between the Channel ports and England. The Dutch and Spanish fleets had already suffered at the hands of the Royal Navy. An attempt to land in Ireland by General Hoche some months earlier had been thwarted. It was all too chancy. Better to turn east and undertake a far less dangerous venture with infinite promises for destroying the very sinews of British power. There were many reasons for the Directory to give their approval to the revived idea of mounting an expedition against Egypt. First, it should be a picnic compared with trying to invade England – Egyptian opposition would easily be overcome, Egypt would become a French colony, and Talleyrand would reconcile Turkey to the loss of one of the Sultan's nominal possessions; second – and this was not only dear to Napoleon's heart, but was also the most likely to provoke an instant and powerful British reaction – it would be a preliminary move in the ultimate aim to strike at India. Here were two admirable strategic objectives, but the third, which was solely Napoleon's own idea, was 'to improve the lot of the natives of Egypt', that is to bring to these backward people the latest benefits in medicine, science and technology, of civilization. Not only this, but by learning too from an ancient culture and relatively unknown geographical conditions, the Army of Egypt would bring great advantages to the peoples of the country they were proposing to conquer. The reality was somewhat different.

And so Napoleon Bonaparte with his army of soldiers, scientists, artists and philosophers, sailed for Egypt in May 1798, narrowly evading Nelson's squadron en route – the reckoning would come later – and landed in Egypt. His veterans swiftly disposed of the Mamelukes, while, as their Commander-in-Chief reminded them, forty centuries looked down upon them, and in no time the conquest of Egypt was completed. But meanwhile, Nelson, whose strategic instinct was as powerful as his tactical flair, had repeated his chase to the east and this time on 1 August was rewarded with a signal from Captain Hood's *Zealous*: 'Enemy in sight'. Comments on the prospect of battle varied. Nelson himself observed that by the morrow it would be either a peerage or Westminster Abbey for himself. Some of the sailors were less lofty in their expressions. One, noting that the French fleet was composed of thirteen sail of the line, considered that they would 'hammer the rusk off ten of them, if not the whole boiling'. Another was glad of the chance to have a go at the enemy, with a prospect of prize money, for he badly needed some new rigging for Sundays. A third confirmed this and was anticipating 'a damned good cruise among the girls besides'.

Nelson's virtual annihilation of the French fleet not only brought jubilation to the Royal Navy, the British people and Emma Hamilton;

it brought something like despair to those generals still in Egypt with Napoleon, for it seemed now that they were cut off for ever from their beloved France. Napoleon himself, however, did not despair, neither then nor at any other time. He simply continued with the campaign, and after being repulsed by Sidney Smith at St Jean d'Acre – which put an end to further advances – returned to Cairo, disposed of a Turkish army which had been unwise enough to land at Aboukir, having no notion whatever of the new rules of warfare, and so consolidated his conquest of Egypt. But all this was changed, again by Sidney Smith, who had chivalrously sent his opponent a packet of the latest newspapers from Europe. It was enough to convince Napoleon that events in France required him to abandon the Army of Egypt and hasten back to Paris. There would be no going to India for him now. Had he done so, he might have crossed swords with the second British military genius, who – like the first, Horatio Nelson – would constantly hinder his insatiable ambitions and eventually play the final card in the game of bringing him down.

Wellington and Nelson, the two great arbiters of British strategy against Napoleon, met but once, and this one meeting emphasized the difference in their characters. The one, aloof, austere, infinitely patient, tirelessly vigilant, never really understood or wanted to understand the British soldier, but this did not stifle his regard for that article, nor prevent his doing what he thought best for him. What *he* thought was best for them and what they thought was best for themselves did not, of course, always coincide. The second of these two, convinced that he was destined to do great things, vain, restless, intense, egotistic, paternal, his name still the touchstone of naval excellence, seemed to have an insight into the feelings and aspirations of the lower deck that has never been equalled. We can no more hear Nelson calling his sailors the scum of the earth than we can imagine Wellington saying: 'Kiss me, Picton'. Their horizons were necessarily different. Nelson, in spite of ranging much further afield and trying his hand at diplomacy with marked success, was a sailor once and always, and had he survived Trafalgar, would, we may suppose, have quitted public life except for an occasional speech in the House of Lords, and retired to his beloved Merton. Wellington's sphere of duty was much wider. Soldier, diplomat, statesman and in the end virtual major-domo of England, he was never, and never could be, out of harness. He himself drew attention to the fact that whereas a costermonger's donkey might be allowed some rest, the Duke of Wellington was not.

Despite these differences the two men had much in common – their ardent patriotism, their simplicity, their disastrous marriages, their diverting liaisons, and their understanding, but not identical possession, of what have been called the four aces of leadership.*

* In his *From the Dreadnought to Scapa Flow* Professor Arthur Marder gives us Admiral James's definition of the three Nelsonian aces, and adds one of his own.

These were, and are, first and foremost, imagination – that is to say the gift of discarding the orthodox and thinking of something new, simple and singular in planning and directing battles; next, the ability to inspire subordinates, officers and men alike; third, the breadth of vision to confide in your juniors and make use of their ideas while acknowledging their source; last of all, and kernel of the Nelson touch, the offensive spirit. Nelson, of course, held all four aces all the time, indeed defining them was merely a question of listing his qualities. But the sheer nature of the war at sea made it much easier for him to play the third and fourth aces, while the task which Wellington undertook in the Peninsula and the Army with which he carried it out were of such a nature that it was far more difficult for him to hold, let alone play, these two cards. The first two aces he too held in full measure.

On the one occasion that the two men met, in a little anteroom in Downing Street, both waiting to see Castlereagh, Secretary of War, in September 1805, Nelson at first disgusted Wellington by his vanity and egotism, although when Nelson discovered to whom he was speaking, he soon changed his tune, and as Wellington recorded talked 'with a good sense, and a knowledge of subjects both at home and abroad, that surprised me equally and more agreeably than the first part of our interview had done; in fact he talked like an officer and a statesman ... I don't know that I ever had a conversation that interested me more'. Yet Wellington himself was not without vanity, or perhaps it was more a consciousness of being a great man and accepting the fact that others were conscious of it too. Melbourne, the last man to exaggerate, commented: 'The Duke of Wellington is amazingly sensible to attention. Nothing pleases him so much as when one asks his opinion about anything.' There was therefore much pleasure in store for him, since 'Better ask the Duke' became a phrase heard as frequently in Downing Street as it was in Buckingham Palace. It simply was a matter of course that people would consult him, just as they also made calls on his purse.

With Nelson it was very different. 'Poor man,' said his old friend, St Vincent, 'he is devoured with vanity, weakness and folly.' The fact is that in contrast to the plain, reserved, at times even humble man of duty that Wellington was, Nelson from the very beginning had something of the poet and mystic in him. 'Nelson was the poet in action,' wrote Aubrey de Selincourt, 'in his grandest moments he ceased to belong to this world and entered a realm as visionary as Shelley's.' It is this explanation which helps us to understand why it was that when he described to his captains the method by which he proposed to destroy the French fleet in 1805 – the so-called Nelson touch – many of them were overcome with emotion. It also helps us to see why busts of Nelson and Napoleon, but none of Wellington, rested on Winston Churchill's desk. It was honour that predominated in Nelson's mind, not riches. He coveted honour in the way that Hotspur and his rival, Harry, did. He even misquoted from the Crispin speech in a letter to St Vincent, substituting the word *glory* for *honour*. But acquiring honour and glory was not the only key to Nelson's character. He desired recognition as well. 'I am the child of opinion,' he wrote.

Wellington would have despised such histrionics, and cared little or nothing for the opinion of others. Perhaps it was this cool reserve, this calm straightforwardness that explains why in France, despite all that Wellington did for that country after Waterloo – being sure, as he was, that France 'would never sleep on the pillow of shame' – it was Nelson who was admired and Wellington who was unpopular. And how characteristic of Napoleon, who, the moment he heard of Nelson's pre-Trafalgar signal, ordered that every French man-of-war have inscribed on it: *La France confide que chacun fasse son devoir*! There is more to it. What could appeal more to the French than the poet in action, the perpetual seeker after glory, the man who next to doing great things loved to write of them? How could they resist a man of whom Thackeray was to make Miss Crawley say:* 'That was the most beautiful part of dear Lord Nelson's character. He went to the deuce for a woman. There *must* be good in a man who will do that.'? There was perhaps one other thing. Nelson may have thwarted Napoleon. At the moment when there seemed to be no stopping him, it was the sailor who stepped from the wings on to the centre of the stage, and did not make his exit until the sea-power of Imperial France was finally and utterly broken. This could be forgiven. But Wellington did the unforgivable. He defeated Napoleon in person. By then Wellington's character was formed, his military skill at its height. By what stages, we might ask, was this brought about?

Let us first join Colonel Wellesley at Seringapatam in 1799 in his battles against Tipu, whom Napoleon had proposed to assist in overthrowing the British in India. In writing to his brother, Lord Mornington (who had succeeded Cornwallis as Governor-General in 1797) before the battle, he had expressed his confidence that they would be masters of the city and fort before long, but he was to undergo a most chastening experience before they were. The approach to Seringapatam was screened by numerous thickets, called 'topes', and Wellesley was required to clear the Sultanpettah Tope, which had the additional hazard of being criss-crossed by numerous irrigation canals. There had been no time to reconnoitre in daylight, and when Wellesley with his 33rd Foot made an attempt to push through the enemy outposts in darkness, he and his men were unable to locate them, and suffered casualties from musket and rocket fire. So confused was the situation that he lost all control of the operation and was obliged to withdraw, only too aware of his failure. There and then he

* *Vanity Fair.*

determined that he would never in future allow an attack to be made at night on a strongly positioned enemy unless proper reconnaissance of the enemy's positions had been previously made in daylight. In the desperate assaults on Ciudad Rodrigo and Badajoz that he was subsequently to order and oversee in the Peninsular War, he kept his word. At his next attempt on the Sultanpettah Tope, Wellesley carried all before him – 'all done in high style and without loss' as his friend Colonel Close recorded – and this meant that the besieging British force could now get to grips with the relentless business of laying siege to Seringapatam in form. The result was highly satisfactory. Not only did the bombardment blow up the magazine inside Tipu's fort and clear the way for an assault, but the storming troops were led by Major-General David Baird, who had been imprisoned by Tipu's father, Hyder Ali, and kept in chains for over three years at Seringapatam itself. When on 4 May 1799 Baird led the 4,000-strong attacking force with the rousing words: 'Now, my brave fellows, follow *me* and prove yourselves worthy of the name of British soldiers!', they did do so, and within a matter of minutes had attained the breach's summit. As British reinforcements poured after the triumphant 'forlorn hope', Tipu's defending troops abandoned their positions and fled. Tipu himself, fighting bravely as became The Tiger of Mysore, was killed. 'When news of the Allies' victory reached the Governor-General,' wrote Elizabeth Longford, 'it drew from him an avalanche of congratulatory eloquence: consummate judgment, unequalled rapidity, animation, skill, humanity, honour, splendour, glory and lustre – all were theirs. In England it seemed as if the days of the great Clive had returned.' Wellesley was soon to show that they had indeed.

If British arms triumphed in India, however, they did not do so in the Netherlands. It must strike us as extraordinary that, despite the lessons of the past, the British Government was once more set upon turning the French out of the Netherlands. While it could be argued that there were plausible strategic reasons for doing so – that is, the supposed menace which a descent on Britain from the Dutch coast by hostile navies and armies might present – the real argument lay more in how to persuade potential allies to collaborate, notably Prussia and Russia. There was also the point that with the French Republican armies strung out along a huge front from the Netherlands to Genoa, the opportunity existed for British soldiers once more to set their feet upon the Continent after four years since their former expulsion. What is more, and perhaps for the first time since the outbreak of war, the Government was positively searching for some theatre in which to employ the Army. The wasteful policy of sending British soldiers to an early grave in the West Indies had been relieved by Abercromby's raising native regiments to garrison the islands. Cornwallis's liberal rule in Ireland had lessened the strain on garrison duties there. The British Army was actually seeking employment.

One imaginative proposal for this came from General James Stuart, who had so distinguished himself in helping Nelson capture the Corsican stronghold of Calvi in 1793, the action in which Nelson lost his right eye.* Five years later Stuart conquered Minorca and, with British naval supremacy in the Mediterranean once more established, proposed to the Government at home that the Army should be used to form a Mediterranean force which would strike at the enemy's southern flank. In this concept he was anticipating the kind of strategy pursued by Sir John Moore and Wellington in the Peninsula, and more than a century later by Churchill both in the Dardanelles and in Italy. What Stuart wanted to do was to launch an attack on French communications north-west of Genoa, and so cut off the Republican armies further south. It was a bold idea, wholly in keeping with the manipulation of British sea-power, and might have paid large dividends, but the Government had different plans. In June 1799 a treaty between Britain and Russia laid down conditions for their joint invasion of the Netherlands. Britain would supply both troops and the money to pay for Russian soldiers. So, despite their previous experiences of landing in the Netherlands only to be defeated and chased out again, the British Army prepared to do it again. What is more, for want of anyone more qualified or acceptable to the Government, the Duke of York was appointed to command, with that brave veteran, General Abercromby (who had little faith in the expedition) as his principal adviser and deputy.

In England there was great enthusiasm for the prospect of the redcoats – to the sight of whom the people had become accustomed by their constant drilling – having a go at the enemy. Confidence in their ability to take on and beat the despised Frenchies was widespread – among those who knew little of the matter! Even the King was carried away by his pride in watching thousands of London Volunteers and Militia march by him in Hyde Park, giving the Inns of Court Regiment the nickname 'Devil's Own' which has survived until today. The soldiers themselves were sufficiently carried away by the prospects both of action and a £10 bounty that thousands of Fencibles and Militia volunteered for overseas service. So the gaps in Regular regiments were filled up and the invasion force assembled in Kent to await the word. Pitt was so impatient to get the thing moving that, together with his Secretary for War, Dundas, he moved to Walmer Castle to supervise it all. From Abercromby, however, to his intense irritation, the Prime Minister found constant objection to what was intended. It was another example of Pitt's total inability to see that no matter how desirable a political objective might be, it could not be achieved by military means unless these means were practicable. Thus when Abercromby pointed out that the Army had no transport to move guns, stores or the wounded – 'An army,' he very reasonably

* Of this action, John Moore wrote: 'Never was so much work done by so few men,' which no doubt Churchill remembered for his tribute to the Battle of Britain pilots.

observed, 'is not a machine that can move of itself; it must have the means of moving' – Pitt dismissed such a quibble, as Arthur Bryant put it, 'as the ill-timed pedantry of an old woman in a red coat'. He seemed to think that Abercromby took pleasure in opposing whatever was proposed. None the less, shortly before the expedition sailed, a Royal Wagon Train was hurriedly put together. At first five troops, later eight, each of some seventy waggons and drivers, were made ready. It was the beginning of what later became the Royal Army Service Corps (now the Royal Corps of Transport). This illustration of Pitt's total failure to grasp the practicalities of war enables us to understand why Macaulay condemned Pitt's military administration as that of a driveller.

In this particular instance Pitt's political instincts were equally at fault. He had allowed himself to be persuaded by officials at the Foreign Office and refugees from the Netherlands sympathetic to the House of Orange that the Dutch people would rise in opposition to the French and, in conjunction with the Allied armies, turn out the hated invader. Nothing of the sort occurred. On 27 August the British fleet under Admiral Mitchell succeeded in getting Abercromby's army of 10,000 men disembarked at Den Helder, where they scattered the defending French and Dutch troops. Two days later the only real prize of the whole campaign was won by Mitchell, when he sailed his warships through the channel between Den Helder and Texel Island and captured the entire Dutch fleet at anchor. John Moore recorded that this great stroke had been achieved within a few hours with very few losses. The achievements of the soldiers were to be less striking and less permanent. One historian* has summed up the campaign by saying simply that the Allied armies advanced in drenching rain from Den Helder to the line of the Zype canal, where they stuck fast in the mud, while the Dutch people did not lift even a finger to support their supposed liberators. After a good deal of dithering and recrimination, the British Army withdrew again and was evacuated. The causes of this failure were familiar. Very few of Abercromby's soldiers had any experience of fighting. There was the normal shortage of artillery, supplies and transport. Coordination of operations between the Royal Navy and the Army did not exist. The Duke of York, who at one time had commanded an Allied army of nearly 40,000 men, was incapable of concentrating his forces to win a decisive victory. The Russians proved wholly unreliable allies. Indeed when their commander, General D'Hermann, was killed during the battle for Bergen when the French counter-attacked, the Russian troops' panic-stricken withdrawal (their former valour in taking the village of Groat notwithstanding) was in danger of deteriorating into a rout, had it not been for the gallant and steady behaviour of the Brigade of Guards and the

* J. Steven Watson. *The Reign of George III*, Oxford University Press, 1960.

British artillery. Time after time one part of the Allied army failed to reinforce another and so turn temporary advantage into decisive victory.

It happened again at the battle of Egmont. Although the Duke of York had proposed with uncharacteristic imagination and boldness that the way to break the deadlock was to mount an amphibious operation, either behind the French lines from the North Sea or by direct assault on Amsterdam itself from the Zuyder Zee, he was unable to convince either his subordinate generals, Abercromby and Dundas, or Admiral Mitchell who seemed to think that having accounted for the Dutch fleet, his participation in the affair was complete. There seemed therefore no alternative but another frontal attack on the French positions. At the end of September there were more frightful storms and rainfall, but on 2 October Abercromby attacked the French at Egmont, while Dundas was engaging them in the area of Bergen and Alkmaar. Abercromby's attempts were seriously disrupted by the French *tirailleurs*, their skirmishing sharp-shooters, who caused heavy casualties to the advancing redcoats, and to whom the British seemed to have no answer. It was a lesson not lost on Abercromby's second-in-command, Major-General John Moore, who was badly wounded in the attack. Once more there was no proper coordination between the various columns engaged. Had Abercromby known Dundas's precise situation, he might have moved his main force east, while holding the French in front, reinforced Dundas, broken through there, and rolled up the entire French position at Egmont. As it was the French commander, Brune, simply retired, leaving the British in possession of the field, but still with no proper decision.

The next engagement was further south on the general line Wyk–Kastrikum–Akersloot, but again, although Abercromby and Dundas, advancing respectively on the right and left, made good progress, in the centre a Russian column was counter-attacked by Brune, throwing the whole Allied effort into confusion. That great cavalry soldier, Lord Henry Paget*, commanding the 7th Light Dragoons, was able to restore the Russians temporarily by conducting one of those brilliant charges for which he became famous, until Abercromby moved to their assistance. But the Allied advance had been disrupted. The Duke of York, observing the battle from Alkmaar, was quite unable to control events and, when advised by his subordinates that security lay only in withdrawal, agreed to do so. One week after their attack on Egmont, the British Army – greatly to the disgust of the soldiers who rightly thought they had done well, and much to the surprise of Brune and his army – had retreated and was back in its former positions behind the Zype canal. A week later the Cabinet decided to abandon the whole campaign. One more expedition to the Netherlands had

---

* Later Earl of Uxbridge and Marquess of Anglesey.

ended in failure and evacuation. It was all very well for Pitt to take comfort from the thought that the Army had been restored to the country. The trouble was that the country had lost confidence in the Army. It would be for John Moore and Wellington to give it back. Each of them would at one time argue the toss with Bonaparte himself.

An eagle is ascendant in spirit, swift in flight, sudden in decision and ruthless in deed. How apt a symbol then was the eagle for Napoleon! What is more he was a man with nerves of steel plus a will so resolute that he could never be reconciled to surrender or compromise. He was not slow to demonstrate this willpower on his return from Egypt. Landing in France just at the time when the British Army had withdrawn to Zype, he quickly summed up the political situation and rallied those soldiers on whom he could rely absolutely – Lannes, Murat, Berthier and Marmont – so that when the time came for a *coup d'état*, the key men would be beside him. Come it did on 9 November 1799 when the Jacobin Deputies at St Cloud turned on Bonaparte in the Council Chamber, only themselves to be turned on by two generals, Lefèbvre and Murat. After Murat had invited his grenadiers to chuck the Deputies ('these blighters') out of the window, the whole thing was pretty well over, and two days later Bonaparte became one of three Consuls, dedicated to an indivisible Republic to be founded on liberty, equality and so on. Just how equal it was all going to be was made clear a month later when Bonaparte was appointed First Consul, well on the way to supreme power. It required another military victory to confirm him in his new position, and in the middle of June 1800 he won just such a victory at Marengo.

Later in his career Napoleon always wanted his generals to be lucky. At Marengo, having dispersed his forces too widely and hardly giving the Austrian commander, Melas, credit for being able to deliver a concentrated attack, the First Consul was dismayed to find his divisions being pushed back. Luckily for him, three of his subordinates saved the situation. His almost desperate plea to Desaix to bring up his infantry was quickly answered, Marmont in charge of the artillery managed to muster a battery of eighteen guns, and away to the flank were some of Kellermann's cavalry. A.G. Macdonnell's description of Bonaparte's luck is so good that it warrants inclusion here:

> The French counter-attack was, by chance, one of the most perfectly timed tactical operations by combined infantry, artillery, and cavalry in the whole history of warfare . . . For twenty minutes Marmont's battery of eighteen kept up the bombardment . . . and then Desaix went forward. Marmont managed to limber up four of his guns and went up in support. Suddenly, through the dense smoke he saw, not fifty yards in front, a battalion of Austrian grenadiers advancing in perfect formation to counter the counter-attack, and some of Desaix's men were tumbling back in confusion. Marmont, whatever his faults might be, was a quick thinker, and he

unlimbered his four guns and fired four rounds of canister at point-blank range into the compact battalion, and at that precise moment, while the Austrians were staggering under the blow, and an Austrian ammunition-wagon was exploding with a monstrous detonation, Desaix went forward with a shout, and young Kellermann came thundering down on the flank, through the mulberry-trees and the tall luxuriant vines, with a handful of heavy cavalry. A minute earlier, or three minutes later, and the thing could not have succeeded, but the timing was perfect, and North Italy was recovered in that moment for the French Republic.[*]

Napoleon could certainly not complain of a shortage of luck on this occasion. Moreover, the Austrians had not been defeated only at Marengo. The French under Moreau had beaten them at Ulm too and were occupying Munich. Everywhere, it seemed, the Austrian army had failed. The British Foreign Secretary, Grenville, was hardly flattering to his own country's army in commenting on this when he wrote that it could hardly have done worse than the Austrians. Better things, however, were in store for the redcoats further east. Although Bonaparte had left Egypt himself, he had left a French army there. It was now for the British Army to turn it out.

The year 1801 was a remarkable one. It saw the fall of Pitt, Nelson's triumph at Copenhagen, the British reconquest of Egypt, and the peace of Amiens. Early in the year Pitt's attempts to bring in a measure of Catholic Emancipation met with such hostility from the King that he laid down his office and Addington formed an administration. Before Pitt went, however, he introduced a budget which provided for greatly increased military expenditure. The Army was to be 300,000 strong (220,000 Regulars and Fencibles, 80,000 Militia) while the Royal Navy would have nearly 500 warships (over 200 ships of the line and 250 frigates). Both services were to justify the nation's confidence in them. First the Army, which in the previous year had been sailing aimlessly about in the Mediterranean, from Gibraltar to Minorca and Malta and back again to Gibraltar, was ordered to Egypt. Abercromby was in command and with him once again was Major-General John Moore, and a young colonel, who was to become another hero of the British Army, Edward Paget. In a letter to his father on the day before the British landed at Aboukir, he described the mood of grim boldness and superiority which his soldiers felt. He was sure that this feeling would carry the army through thick and thin. 'At no former period of our history did John Bull ever hold his enemy cheaper'.[†] Although Abercromby had viewed the whole affair with his

[*] *Napoleon and his Marshals*, Macmillan, 1950.
[†] About a quarter of a century later, according to William Hazlitt, there had been little change: 'John Bull is certainly a singular animal. It is the being the beast he is that has made a man of him. He must have someone to butt at; and it matters little to him whether it be friend or foe, provided only he can *run-a-muck*. He must have a grievance to solace him, a bug-bear of some sort or other to keep himself in breath; otherwise, he droops and hangs the head – he is no longer John Bull.'

customary cautious gloom, when John Moore, who had selected as his first objective a hill to the west of Aboukir Castle, landed with his first division and charged the hill with the 23rd, 28th and 40th Foot (Royal Welch Fusiliers, Gloucestershire and Lancashire Regiments), he so surprised and dismayed the defending French brigade that they took to their heels and fled, leaving their guns behind them. This gallant action enabled the rest of Abercromby's 15,000 strong army to land and dig for water. Then, on 12 March, leaving a force to block Aboukir Castle, the army set off towards Alexandria, some twelve miles away, to capture the city and port. Before we follow their fortunes further, however, we must turn to the man whose naval domination of the Mediterranean had made their expedition possible in the first place, and see what he was up to in northern waters.

Bonaparte's manipulation of the Baltic powers, Russia, Sweden and Denmark, and the formation of the Baltic League, had made it necessary for a blow to be struck there. There was but one man to strike it – Nelson. Appointed as second-in-command to the rich, timid and uxorious Admiral Sir Hyde Parker, Nelson made the running first and last. On 12 March, the same day that Abercromby began his advance to Alexandria, the fleet sailed from Yarmouth with fifteen battleships, sundry frigates, brigs and nearly 1,000 soldiers. Parker, nervous that Nelson's indomitable spirit and yearning for the offensive might unsettle him, was so touched (keeping a good table was almost as important to him as gratifying a young wife) by Nelson's gift of a splendid turbot that at last he confided in him. Not greatly to his comfort, however, for Nelson, as might be expected, was all for instant and aggressive action. His note to Parker outlined his view that 'not a moment should be lost in attacking the enemy: they will every day and every hour be stronger . . . I am of the opinion the boldest measures are the safest', struck a cord of response by its emphasis on something safe, and the whole fleet sailed through the narrows between Kronborg Castle on the Danish shore and the Swedish coast, keeping closer to the latter's silent batteries and so out of range of the Danish cannonade. With this passage accomplished on 30 March and Copenhagen now in sight, Nelson made his plan on 1 April. He would lead his ships against the moored Danish fleet and shore batteries, concentrating his fire on each target as he advanced, and so overwhelming them. The subsequent duel was what Wellington would have called 'hard pounding' and Nelson named 'warm work', but the gallantry and gunnery of the British sailors, together with Nelson's 'right to be blind sometimes' when Parker signalled him to discontinue the action – 'I really do not see the signal' – prevailed to bring about both a truce and negotiation, at which Nelson also excelled. His diplomacy, together with the assassination of the Russian Czar Paul (his successor, Alexander I, was for the time being prepared to wait and see) dissolved the Northern League by which

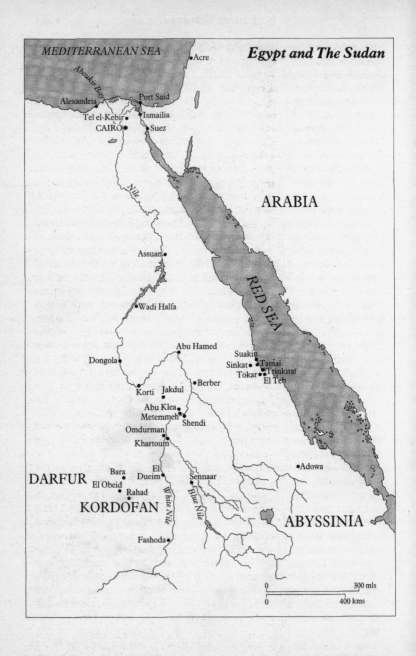

Napoleon had set such store. With this action Nelson had reinforced his reputation for impulsive tactical brilliance by showing his cool ability to exploit strategic and political opportunity. 'All agree,' wrote his old commander-in-chief, St Vincent, 'there is but one Nelson'.

More good news was on the way. We left Abercromby making his way slowly towards Alexandria. Always cautious in advance he had positioned his army some three miles east of the port, with his right flank on the sea at a ruined Roman palace and his left flank on Aboukir lake. Meanwhile General Menou,* the French commander, had marched 10,000 men from Cairo to reinforce Alexandria. So confident was he of the superiority of his troops (quite apart from his confidence in them, he had more guns, and unlike the British who had none, some 1,400 cavalry) that on 21 March he attacked Abercromby's defences before dawn, feinting on his left with the main thrust on the right. John Moore's division which received the principal blow of both French cavalry and infantry responded magnificently to the training and trust that Moore had given them. Particularly gallant were the 42nd Highlanders (The Black Watch) who, despite being broken through by cavalry, continued the fight in small groups, until reserves came forward. Also winning immortal fame that day – and the honour in perpetuity of wearing their Regimental badge on both the front and back of their headdress – were the 28th Foot (Gloucestershire Regiment) under Edward Paget's command. When engaged by infantry in front and suddenly threatened with cavalry in the rear, Paget coolly ordered his rear rank to face about and fire. The British Army showed such steadiness and skill in this battle that although losing some 1,500 men they inflicted far heavier casualties on the enemy and forced them to retire behind the walls of Alexandria before the morning was over. Moore had once more shown what a fine, intrepid leader he was, inspiring his soldiers to great deeds and showing the French veterans what fighting really was. But, alas, it was Abercromby's last battle. Wounded in the thigh during an encounter with French cavalry, he ignored his injury until the battle had been won. A week later he died, and when the news was received at home, his former fellow-commander, the Duke of York, published a General Order recalling his 'life of honour and death of glory', his insistence on discipline, his care for the troops, his perseverance and spirit, his life of action and hero's end. Under his hand and in his last battle, the British Army had shown itself as triumphant in eastern lands as the Royal Navy had in eastern waters. Alexandria fell less than a month later and the road was open for the reconquest of Egypt.

Egypt was safe. Napoleon had wanted it as a stepping-stone to India. All that was finished. And in India itself Wellesley was

---

* Menou, an ardent Bonapartist, behaved in a somewhat unrevolutionary fashion when he turned Mohammedan and married the ageing, ill-favoured daughter of the Shireef.

consolidating British supremacy. Having executed the conquest of Mysore at Seringapatam, he was next about to break the Mahratta powers at Ahmednuggur and Assaye. Although the Peace of Amiens* (March 1802-May 1803) intervened, we may follow these further eastern triumphs before returning to Europe. Ahmednuggur, the great hill-fortress on the north-west frontier of the Nizam of Hyderabad's territory, had to be seized before Wellesley could get to grips with the armies of Scindiah of Gwalior and the Bhonslah. The reduction of the fort at Ahmednuggur was a splendid achievement, and the celebrated comment on it by Gooklah, the Mahratta chief, is not merely an admirable model of brevity in summing up a battle; it illustrates too how, time after time, the British Army in India displayed an almost insolent contempt for the odds against it, and how again and again – from Clive's exploits at Arcot and Plassey to feats which were to be repeated a hundred years later at the Mutiny – a handful of determined, well-trained and well-led redcoats could rout indigenous armies many times their number. Gooklah's comment, it will be recalled, was to the effect that the English were a strange people, their General a wonderful man, in that they had come to Ahmednuggur in the morning, looked at the fortress's wall, walked over it, killed all the garrison and returned to breakfast. 'What,' he asked, 'can withstand them?'

When we consider how strong the fortress was, how solid, how high its walls and what armaments they mounted, we may understand his wonder. Ahmednuggur was built of solid stone and chunam, surrounded by a deep, dry ditch, with large circular bastions at short intervals; each bastion had three or four guns in casemated embrasures; in the terraces above were loopholes for musketry; in all the bastions housed sixty guns; an abrupt glacis covered thirty feet of the walls. We must certainly concede that it was a formidable undertaking. Yet if the taking of Ahmednuggur illustrated that the General was a wonderful man, it was to be powerfully confirmed at Assaye. What was remarkable about Assaye was not only the discrepancy between the opposing numbers engaged – 50,000 Mahratta infantry, to say nothing of countless cavalry, taken on by a mere 7,000 under Wellesley; it was also Wellesley's immediate decision to attack and his quick eye, which, without on this occasion having to guess what was on the other side of the hill, saw the way to do it. But there was more to it than this. The battles and pursuits which followed Assaye throughout the Deccan were what finished off the dissidents, brought peace to India, and allowed Wellesley to return to Europe to get on with the far more serious business awaiting him there. Wellington was never to forget or underestimate what India had done for him. He always thought of Assaye – all his Peninsular

* Sheridan called it 'a peace which all men are glad of, but no man can be proud of'.

victories and Waterloo notwithstanding – as the best thing he had done in the way of fighting. And when asked to what he owed his extraordinary stamina on the day of Waterloo itself, he replied that it had been the years of campaigning in India which had given him the robustness so indispensable to a commander of armies in the field. By the time he returned to England in 1805, his country had been at war with France again for two years.

CHAPTER FIVE

Weathering the Storm – Again

What I desire is that France should feel that Great Britain cannot be trifled with.

LORD CASTLEREAGH

During the Peace of Amiens, with Addington as Prime Minister and Pitt idling away his time at Walmer Castle, the First Consul began his calculated policy of trifling with Great Britain. So much so that Pitt's disciple, George Canning, who had already hailed his hero as the pilot that weathered the storm, once more gave it as his view that Pitt was the only man who could save the country. Yet it was Addington – amiable, conciliatory, platitudinous* Addington – who declared war on France in May 1803. What made him do it? He stood essentially for retrenchment and peace. The fact is that Napoleon pushed him too far. By the Peace of Amiens Britain was to return her overseas conquests to France – including those in India – Spain and Holland, except for Trinidad and Ceylon. Malta was to be restored to the Knights of St John of Jerusalem and British troops would be evacuated from the island. But it soon became clear that Napoleon's intention was not merely to regain those overseas territories which France had lost. He was determined to add to them and lost no time in setting about it. Louisiana, Elba and Parma were acquired by an understanding with Spain, which was wholly under the First Consul's influence. What is more, Spain assumed authority over the Malta Knights, thus threatening the independence of Malta itself. Napoleon also re-established his hold over northern Italy. The time was rapidly coming when something would have to be done. In reply, therefore, Britain neither withdrew her troops from Malta, nor restored French territories in India. Yet despite these breaches in the peace agreement, with their inherent threat of renewed hostilities, Addington's administration went on with its policy of retrenchment, notably in the armed forces.

* Addington was no orator and was surrounded by such star performers as Burke, Sheridan, Fox and Pitt.

His reduction of the Army and Royal Navy had begun within weeks of the peace treaty's being signed. There were no half measures. Pitt's income tax, introduced in order to pay for the war, was abolished, and this in turn meant that there had to be drastic cuts in the armed forces. The Army was more or less halved. Its regular strength was set at 95,000, plus 18,000 in Ireland, and a Militia of some 50,000 with half that number again in reserve. The Volunteers were disbanded. As if this were not bad enough, Addington also severely reduced the size of the Royal Navy. Instead of a hundred ships of the line in commission, there were to be a mere forty, with the consequent loss of seamen amounting to more than 50,000. Throughout this period of British military economy, Napoleon embarked on a programme of preparation for a renewal of war, and in particular the creation of a large navy which was to be as invincible as the army.

It was this challenge to British naval supremacy that turned the scales in favour of war. The French programme of naval building would mean that by 1804 they would have another 23 ships of the line in their fleet, bringing the total number of battleships to nearly seventy. Moreover, Napoleon's preparations for an invasion of Britain were already being executed. Intense activity was reported in the harbours and dockyards of the coast which stretched from the Scheldt to Biscay. Yet it was the dispute over Malta which gave rise to a final break. In February and March 1803, Lord Whitworth, British Ambassador in Paris, was treated to some spirited exchanges with the First Consul. Like all dictators faced with rational argument questioning their desired and indeed already predetermined course of action, Napoleon rapidly descended to shouting. He wanted control of Malta because of its decisive influence in mastery of the Mediterranean, and was prepared to indulge in every kind of political chicanery to secure it. The British, however, although indulgent towards certain other breaches of the Amiens agreement, were equally conscious of Malta's vital contribution to their naval strategy, and dug in their heels. When Napoleon heard that Parliament had voted funds to increase the Royal Navy by a further 10,000 men and was told by Whitworth that unless given cast-iron guarantees as to Malta's independence, the British would simply retain the island, he flew into a rage, and talked about arming and fighting.*

The arguments went on and on until at last in May 1803 it became plain to the British Government that it was impossible to enter into negotiations with Napoleon which would be at once reasonable and likely to be honoured. On 18 May, therefore, Great Britain declared

---

* 'If you arm,' he shouted, 'I shall arm too; if you fight, I will fight also.' It puts us in mind of Hitler in September 1939, yelling at the Swedish mediator, Dahlerus, 'If England wants to fight for three years, I shall fight for three years . . . and if necessary, I will fight for ten years.' Another striking parallel is the vitally important part played by Malta in both these conflicts.

war on France, greatly to Napoleon's fury, for although he wanted war, it had come too soon – before his fleet was ready to argue the toss with the Royal Navy. Never mind – the Grande Armée would compensate for his lack of ships. In commenting on how the First Consul set about the business of making the Grande Armée, A.G. Macdonnell reminds us that 'it was to be a real, full-dress, organized, trained fighting machine. Its training ground was to be the north-east coast of France, and its objective was England.' As this was to be the army that dominated Europe for the next ten years and against which the British Army – although in a relatively minor way and in a subsidiary theatre of war – was to try its mettle and prove itself, we may well pay some attention to its make-up and its personalities.

The Army of the Coasts of the Ocean, as it was called, was formidable in both numbers and quality. Nearly 200,000 strong, organized in seven corps, spread out between Hanover and Brest, subject to arduous drill and training, and commanded by the most dazzling array of corps commanders ever assembled in any army – Bernadotte, Marmont, Davout, Soult, Lannes, Ney and Augereau, all of whom were to become Marshals of the empire and against three of whom (Marmont, Soult and Ney) the future Duke of Wellington was to pit his wits and his beggars in red – almost half of this powerful army was concentrated at Dunkirk and Boulogne, waiting for the moment when the transports would be ready, the escorting battleships concentrated, and the world's greatest soldier in command of the expedition which would subdue a nation of shopkeepers once and for all. Backing up these seven corps were six divisions of the Reserve Cavalry under the flamboyant command of Joachim Murat, Napoleon's brother-in-law and the most outstanding cavalry leader of the age. Finally a division of the Imperial Guard (Napoleon became Emperor of the French in 1804) was under Bessières. This glittering array of martial talent was not destined to descend on England, however. We shall see later what it did do in one of the most astonishing campaigns ever conceived and directed by Napoleon, but for the time being the feasibility of its being able to cross the narrow strip of water between Boulogne and Dover was being frustrated by the war policy of that least warlike of Prime Ministers, Henry Addington.

Addington had none of the grand ideas of Pitt, such as sending expeditions here, there and everywhere, to capture sugar islands, retake Egypt, invade France or support a supposed rising by the Dutch. His strategy was purely defensive, although based on the striking power of the Royal Navy. Napoleon might be allowed to manipulate affairs in continental Europe; indeed there was no way of preventing his doing so. But the Royal Navy would rule the waves, encouraging and guaranteeing British trade, while blockading and stifling the enemy's ports and shipping. To counter this strategy the

French would be obliged to attempt the invasion of England. The Royal Navy would then defeat this attempt, and the war would be won. Such was Addington's idea of war. In fact, as far as the conduct of war by the British for the first five years from 1803 to 1808 went, it was surprisingly successful*, even though Addington did not remain Prime Minister for long, and Napoleon never did dare to risk crossing the channel. Yet in essence the Royal Navy removed even the threat of an invasion, while the British Army slowly and surely built itself into a force of sufficient strength and competence to chance another expedition into French-controlled territory. This time the redcoats would not instantly be defeated and obliged to retreat and re-embark. This time they would have come to stay, and they would be led by some brilliant commanders, whom Arthur Bryant christened Neptune's Generals.

Before we follow the activities of Nelson and his band of brothers, we may briefly review the way in which the British Army was pulling itself together. Addington's[†] inclination for doing things on the cheap led him into the same errors as those who in the seventeenth century had opposed the formation of a standing army. Since his idea of waging war was essentially a defensive one, all that was needed, he argued, was a large number of men in uniform, and the cheapest way of getting them would be to increase the size of the Militia and raise more Volunteers. It never occurred to him that should Napoleon's veteran troops actually land in Sussex and Kent to find themselves faced with even a large number of English yeoman and burghers who had no training, discipline or knowledge of the affairs of war, and who would probably be armed with nothing more deadly than a pike, the outcome of such a meeting was unlikely to be favourable. Nevertheless he introduced a new Militia Act which would increase by a further 25,000 the existing provision for raising some 50,000 men for home defence by ballot. The fatal flaw in this arrangement was the continued existence of the system of substitutes, under which someone chosen by ballot for the Militia could avoid service by paying up to £30 to a good-for-nothing with a healthy thirst. Since this substitute could get a bounty of only £7 12s 6d (£7.62) for joining the regular army, his choice was clear. Thus, just at the time when recruiting for Regulars was at its most urgent, a major source of manpower was denied them.

As if all this were not bad enough, the Government also exempted from the obligations to respond to a planned *levée-en-masse* to repel invasion all those who volunteered for home defence before 16 June

---

* Britain's allies, however, Russia, Austria and Prussia were defeated in battle after battle.

†Although Addington was no statesman or war leader, he lacked neither courage nor strength. As Home Secretary later he did not flinch from introducing the Six Acts to counter real revolutionary dangers. 'No man', he contended, 'was fit to be a Minister to whom it was not a matter of indifference whether he died in bed or on the scaffold.'

1803. As the patriotic enthusiasm to do so was very great and huge numbers came forward, the Government, in its haste to raise men, had robbed itself of yet another rich fund of potential redcoats, whether Regular or Militia. Worse still, so many volunteers came forward that there were no proper weapons for them and no one with the proper skills to organize, train and command them. It was yet one more illustration of that curious trait in British character when faced with the prospect of military glory. Despite an ill-concealed dislike and contempt for the ordinary soldier, the moment John Bull was presented with the prospect of trouncing some foreigner impudent enough to suppose he could set foot on British soil with impunity, then nothing would do for this same John Bull but the instant indulgence of his yearning for a red coat. When no fewer than 300,000 Volunteers had come forward in less than a week, the Government saw fit to cancel the proposed *levée-en-masse*. In August they went further and put a stop to the raising of more Volunteers in those counties where their numbers were more than six times those of the Militia. It may be imagined what confusion this appeal to and then dampening down of the nation's patriotic instincts caused. Not only this, but, as Arthur Bryant put it: 'Instead of giving the military authorities an Army, it had saddled them with an immense, amorphous force of untrained, unarmed amateurs, serving in a hotchpotch of self-governing units, each subject to rules of its own choosing and none under regular discipline'. Bryant here is voicing the criticism made at the time by William Windham (Secretary for War under Pitt, 1794–1801) who strongly advocated the need to build up the regular army rather than rely on an ill-assorted *canaille* of non-professional soldiers. Windham also anticipated future policy by recommending a system whereby soldiers signed on for a limited, rather than indefinite, period. But for the time being his pleas fell on deaf ears. By May 1804, however, his former chief, Pitt*, was back as Prime Minister, Addington having resigned over his near defeat in the House of Commons on the Irish Militia Bill. Despite the atrocious muddle initiated by Addington with regard to raising forces to defend the realm, would Pitt now benefit from the Army reforms which had begun to take effect in his former administration?

We have already touched on the Duke of York's reforms and must now turn to one particular aspect of them, which proved to be of such value to the British Army when it once more set foot on the soil of Napoleon's Europe, this time in the Peninsula. As far back as 1799 the Duke had given orders that an Experimental Rifle Corps should be formed at Shorncliffe and that fifteen regiments were to send officers and men there for special instruction in light infantry tactics. The need for doing something like this had arisen because of the Army's failure

* Pitt called Addington 'a man of little mind, of consummate vanity and of very slender abilities'.

in Holland, employing rigid drills and manoeuvres, to cope with the French combination of fast-moving, straight-shooting skirmishers, who would disrupt the British formations, so leaving them vulnerable to the massed advance of the following enemy columns. In short an antidote to the French *tirailleurs* had to be developed. Much of the subsequent direction and training of the British Army's light infantry was entrusted to that brilliant soldier and truly admirable man, Sir John Moore. If Moore had not been killed at Corunna, where we will accompany him in the next chapter, he would have rivalled Wellington himself for the accolade of Britain's greatest general since the Duke of Marlborough. We may therefore do well to examine this remarkable man more closely.

When Moore began his task at Shorncliffe in 1802, he was forty years old and had seen action all over the world, from America to Corsica, from the West Indies to Holland, from Ireland to Egypt. In command of troops at all levels he had shown that superb combination of courage, coolness, tactical dexterity and care for those under his direction. Always at the point of danger and decision, he had twice been wounded. A fine-looking man, whom everyone admired and loved, he resembled another truly great commander, Nelson, in possessing that indispensable quality – humanity. He was, says Arthur Bryant, at once realist and idealist. On the one hand his concept of what needed to be done to put things right was a model of clarity, precision and perseverance. On the other hand his sense of justice, his integrity and his passionate dedication were such that they inspired both devotion and awe. He could not bear to see a fault go unpunished in an officer that would be punished in a private soldier. He was insistent that hardship should be shared by soldier and general alike. His sense of duty was absolute. Any avoidance of some unpleasant service by means of influence was totally abhorrent to him. Yet he was able to temper the need for blind obedience to orders by giving the individual soldier the sort of training that enabled him to make the best use of his initiative, his common sense and his military skills. Napoleon once defined the three great requirements in war as accuracy, simplicity and character. Sir John Moore possessed all three to an exceptional degree.

Before Moore had been appointed by the Duke of York to supervise training at Shorncliffe much had already been achieved by two other remarkable soldiers, Colonel Coote Manningham and Lieutenant-Colonel William Stewart, who had been responsible for developing the Experimental Rifle Corps by giving special instruction in light infantry tactics, fieldcraft and shooting to the officers and men sent to them from fifteen regiments. From this modest start sprang the famous Rifle Brigade, the 95th Regiment, with green uniforms and black buttons. Although temporarily disbanded at the Peace of Amiens, they were re-formed later in 1802 and armed with the Baker rifle which had far greater range and accuracy than the smooth-bore musket. Then, together with the 43rd and 52nd Regiments and the 14th Light Dragoons, they underwent Moore's special training in disciplined initiative so successfully that his brigade became not only the finest in the Army, but a model for all others. Their first task was to help repel an expected invasion. Instead they were to win golden opinions from all sorts of people by their performance in the Peninsula. Moore summed up his own secret by commenting on his own original Regiment, the 52nd, after he had inspected them: 'It is evident that not only the soldiers but that each individual soldier knows what he has to do. Discipline is carried on without severity, the officers are attached to the men and the men to the officers.' Here Moore put his finger on the British Army's principal strength – the Regimental system. Many writers have described and analysed it, none better perhaps than Arthur Bryant:

> The unit of this Army was the Regiment, territorial and traditional; its Colours the ark of the British soldier's covenant. During a hurricane in one of the West Indian islands a private of the 46th,[*] set to guard these sacred emblems, remained at his post while the wind lifted the barrack timbers for more than a mile, and was found next day buried where he had stood. Between the regiments a strong intimate rivalry was handed down from veteran to recruit. Every corps had its peculiar history and character, the subject both of pride and banter; the 50th[†] were called the Dirty Half Hundred from their black facings, while those of the 33rd,[‡] which matched their coats, were falsely reputed by envious rivals to have been taken from them as a punishment for having lost their Colours. In camp and barracks such regimental legends – the sagas of rude and unlettered men – were sometimes a source of embarrassment; on the battlefield they became a spur to emulous courage and endurance.

Thus the tradition, the spirit, the foundation were all there. What Moore did was to build upon them. He did so by the very simple method of treating soldiers as men, not as machines. Since war put the heaviest possible demand on a man's mental and physical powers and since morale was a fundamental necessity (even Napoleon argued that in war considerations of morale made up three-quarters of the game[§]), it was up to those responsible for training soldiers to develop these qualities to the utmost. There was also the all-important requirement of self-respect and professional pride. This in turn meant that the soldiers had to understand the reasons for becoming proficient in their

[*] The Duke of Cornwall's Light Infantry
[†] The Queen's Own Royal West Kent Regiment – now The Queen's Regiment.
[‡] The Duke of Wellington's Regiment.
[§] 'A la guerre, les trois quarts sont des affaires morales.'

various tasks, so that they could then think for themselves. In applying his teaching principles Moore went back to the ancients, who had regarded physical exercise, running, swimming and competitive games as an indispensable part of their civilization. Moore wanted his soldiers to develop the virtues of sobriety and endurance, to become 'thinking fighting men', to devote their whole time to their profession, and he insisted that the officers got to know each man under their command, to lead them by example and so acquire a discipline based on mutual regard. It was William Napier who summed up what Moore was doing at Shorncliffe by saying that the soldiers' discipline was an example to the whole Army, that the officers were trained to command and that together they enjoyed pride in both their regiment and their calling. When it came to manoeuvres, everything was done under conditions as close as possible to war itself. Formal parades and military displays were abandoned in favour of reproducing the rigours of actual campaigning. Troops were doing what they should be doing and so rarely are, even today – training for war. Indeed unless they did so, there would be little purpose in taking on Napoleon's veterans.

One of the special features of light infantry training was the quick march, which allowed the body to move in an easy and natural way so that long distances could be covered without excessive fatigue. Indeed the Rifle Corps' regulations reached almost lyrical heights when they defined 'the grand principle of marching' as bringing down the feet easily without shaking the upper part of the body.* Fast marching and straight shooting had always been Michel Ney's great recipe for success on the battlefield, and it was enthusiastically echoed by Moore, who insisted that the whole purpose of their training and their subsequent activity in the field was to 'inflict death upon the enemy'. To be able to do this with the highly accurate Baker rifle demanded all sorts of skills, not only marksmanship itself, but fieldcraft, skilful use of ground, judgement of range and quick thinking. Mastery of all this would not only give the soldier great confidence in his own ability. It would make him the admired and valued member of a team, whose members would know they could rely upon each other. Another of Moore's innovation, was the recognition and reward of merit. When late in his life the Duke of Wellington was asked whether, thinking it all over, he would have done anything differently, he replied after a few moments of reflection that he would have given more praise. Moore understood this point and acted on it, by arranging for special badges, cockades and medals to be awarded to the men for particular merit and good conduct.† All that he did was based on the principles

---

* How many of us remember, from our first days on the square, the drill sergeant who by the mere act of screaming orders at us would make both our bodies, and his, shake all over?
† The Long Service and Good Conduct Medal is still awarded for 22 years' 'undetected crime'.

of common sense, humanity and recognition that the basic elements of
combat – fire and movement – were unchanged. It was fire which
actually killed or disabled the enemy; it was movement which enabled
you to out-manoeuvre the enemy and bring your fire more effectively
to bear on him. The two were wholly complementary. While one body
of troops was on the move, it would be supported and covered by
another body's fire-power. Then the process would be reversed.
Arthur Bryant (who understood all this so well, wrote about it so
majestically and in the end recorded his great admiration for the Rifle
Corps in his *Jackets of Green*) summed up what it was that Moore
achieved in language which cannot be bettered:

> A rifleman in battle was the instrument of an orchestra in which
> every change of position, whether of individual or unit, was,
> wherever possible, protected by co-ordinated fire, directed at the
> precise spot from which any interference with that movement might
> come. The Light Brigade's special system of drill was directed to this
> end.
>   At the back of every rifleman's mind Moore instilled the principle
> that the enemy was always at hand ready to strike. Whether on
> reconnaissance or protective duty, he was taught to be wary and on
> guard . . . It was the pride of a light infantryman never to be caught
> napping; of a light infantry regiment or company never to have an
> outpost or picket surprised.*

Bryant goes on to explain that by this means the British Army would in
the future benefit from having a screen of expert, reconnoitring
marksmen, well-concealed and elusive, watching and reporting on the
enemy's movements, 'each one an alert and intelligent individual
acting in close but invisible concert with his comrades'. Perhaps the
most remarkable part of Moore's achievement was that if a recruit, no
matter how bad his previous record, had something good in him, 'the
Light Brigade would sooner or later turn out a smart, well-trained,
independent fighting man with a craftsman's self-respect and skill'.
Although the rest of the Army was slow to follow Moore's example,
other regiments were left in no doubt as to the astonishingly high
quality which at length they sought to emulate.
   Yet no matter how excellent the Light Brigade might be, it could not
by itself take on the Grande Armée. It was therefore fortunate that
after the confusion caused by Addington's hasty resort to raising from
the Militia and Volunteers forces to defend the realm, the measures
introduced by Pitt, together with eventual acceptance of Windham's
proposal for limited, not indefinite, service, gradually increased the
size and quality of the Regular Army. At the time of the war's renewal
in May 1803 there were just over 100,000 Regulars; within two years

* *Years of Victory*, Collins, 1944.

the numbers had increased by a further 60,000; by the time Castlereagh became Secretary for War in the summer of 1807, the Army's strength had risen to nearly 200,000 Regulars and the new Minister was quick to increase it still further by persuading some 40,000 Militiamen to transfer to the Regular Army – persuasion in which recruiting sergeants were greatly assisted by the offer of bounties – during the following year. An army of this size could clearly indulge in some further overseas adventures, apart from helping the Royal Navy to guarantee the country's own security. It was not, however, for Pitt to initiate or enjoy such indulgence, although his war policy did lead to one great triumph which ensured that Napoleon's invasion preparations would come to naught and that Nelson's memory would be immortal.

One of Pitt's most cherished pronouncements, made on 9 November 1805, at a Lord Mayor's banquet when his health was drunk as the saviour of Europe, was to the effect that Europe was not to be saved by any one man, and that England in saving herself by her exertions would, as he trusted, save Europe by her example. It was a splendid thing to have said on a splendid occasion. Yet for those who had listened to the King's Speech in July 1804, when Pitt's intended policies were outlined to Parliament, it had been said already. For in this speech it was made plain that Pitt had come to the inescapable conclusion that although England might fight alone, only by persuading other European powers to fight too could a stop be put to France's territorial ambitions. In short Pitt was looking for 'the re-establishment of such a system in Europe' urged on by England's example 'as would rescue it from the precarious state to which it is reduced'. An effective barrier had to be raised against Napoleon's schemes of aggrandizement.

First, however, Pitt had to be sure that Napoleon could not successfully invade these islands. A distraction had to be found and as it could not be found by using British troops alone, allies were indispensable. The diplomatic moves he now initiated led to the Third Coalition against France. To start with only Russia responded to his overtures. As might be expected from the new Tsar, Alexander I, over-sensitive and opinionated as he was, and whose ambition was equalled only by his pride, any snub to his self-esteem or obstacle to his imperial aspirations was likely to arouse considerable hostility. It was scarcely surprising therefore that Napoleon's expansionist policy in the eastern Mediterranean, clashing as it did with Alexander's own designs on Constantinople, together with Napoleon's seizure of Naples and Hanover, despite anything the Tsar might have had to say about it being taken into account, had a violent effect on him. Unless France could be restrained, it was clear to Alexander that his own expansionist intentions and his own passionate wish to be thought of as a kind of *major-domo* of Europe were unlikely to come to much. All this, together with Napoleon's rash kidnapping and subsequent execution of the Duc d'Enghien, lightened the task of British diplomats in St Petersburg and resulted in the Anglo-Russian alliance being signed in May 1805.

Prussia, whose eye was still on Hanover, remained neutral, as did Austria initially. But when Napoleon had himself crowned King of Italy in May 1805, he so antagonized Austria that she joined forces with Great Britain and Russia. Allied intentions were to oblige France to remove her troops from Italy and northern Germany, and also to free Naples, the Netherlands and Switzerland. In this way, so reasoned Pitt, with France engaged from both the east and the south, Napoleon's own threat to Britain would be countered. It was all very well for the Allies to talk about threatening France from the east, in order to liberate the Netherlands and Flanders, but little could be effected even by half a million Russian soldiers paid for by English gold unless these troops were allowed to pass through Prussia. This Prussia would not permit. An alternative therefore had to be devised. The plan was to attack the French in northern Italy, using British troops from Malta and Sicily, and Russian forces which would deploy through Austria. Although neither of these threats actually developed, their mere possibility determined Napoleon to abandon his invasion plans and turn east to settle with Austria and Russia.

It was very much a last-minute decision, for as late as July 1805 the Emperor was still trying to bring about an opportunity to rush his army near Boulogne across the Channel. He knew of course that this could only be done if he could lure the bulk of the Royal Navy away from the Channel, and bring to bear there a superior force of French warships. He therefore bullied his admirals first to sail to the West Indies to attract British ships away from home waters, and then to concentrate in the Channel to win temporary superiority there and enable his transports to make the short crossing and see what mincemeat his army would make of the British militia. But in August when the Emperor heard the news of Austria's entry into the war against him, he rapidly changed his plans, broke up the camps on the coast near Calais and set the Grande Armée on an almost unbelievably rapid march right across Europe to confront the Allied armies on the Danube and in particular General Mack's 30,000 men positioned at Ulm. The speed, precision and sheer beauty of the manoeuvre were such that, as A.G. Macdonell put it: 'Within forty-five days of the quiet tents of Boulogne, Bruges, and Montreuil (distant, as the crow flies, four hundred miles from Ulm), Napoleon had laid more than 150,000 men, concentrated and co-ordinated, on the northern flank of General Mack, while Murat's cloud of horsemen in front prevented the Austrians from knowing what storm was about to burst.' It was virtually all over bar the shouting, and apart from one engagement at Elchingen, the Grande Armée simply surrounded Mack and captured his entire army. The Third Coalition's efforts on land had hardly begun auspiciously. Worse, far worse, was to come. Despite the bad weather, and in October it was very bad, despite the exhaustion of the Army and the shortage of food, Napoleon pushed on, took Vienna without a fight, succeeded in crossing the Danube by a ruse, and finally came up with the combined Austro-Russian army with the two Emperors, Alexander I of Russia and Francis II of Austria, nominally in command with Kutusov doing the thinking for them, at the Moravian village of Austerlitz. On 2 December 1805, with the sun of Austerlitz looking down on them (Napoleon had great faith in favourable omens) Marshal Soult went forward, together with Bernadotte and Oudinot, the Imperial Guard under Bessières in reserve; the vital hill in the centre of the Allied positions was taken, their centre destroyed and their left wing (like the map of Europe itself, as Pitt bitterly commented) rolled up. It was all over. Austria made peace, the Russian armies went away, the Third Coalition was at an end and Pitt had little more than a month to live.

Yet in that very October when Napoleon had been driving the Grande Armée forward, the British had been rewarded with what was perhaps the most renowned naval victory in their history, conceived and executed by their most revered admiral. It was a victory that would enable the British Army to set foot on the southern shores of Napoleon's empire more or less at will – and when necessary, as we shall see in the next chapter, to leave those shores again. When after prolonged manoeuvring, chasing, seeking and doubting, Nelson at last came up with the combined French and Spanish fleet on 21 October 1805 off Cape Trafalgar, he and his captains knew exactly what they were about. Never were Nelson's four aces of leadership to be played to better effect. His imagination in planning battles, in determining what the enemy would do under certain circumstances, his imagination in training, in dealing with the lower deck, his genius, if you like, was at its height. His ability to inspire was such that his enthusiasm and confidence animated the whole fleet, the entire nation. Every captain aspired to be a Nelson himself. They could not bear that Nelson should think ill of them. And Nelson himself, embarked at Portsmouth for the last time and observing onlookers weep, commented: 'I had their huzzas before; I have their hearts now.' As for his subordinates, never surely did such mutual confidence, trust and reliance exist between a commander and his lieutenants. Above all the fourth and last ace, the offensive spirit, was the very apotheosis of all that Nelson stood for – his absolutely overriding determination to win, to annihilate the French fleet, by bringing about what he called 'a pell-mell battle' by tactics which would 'surprise and confound the enemy'. When Nelson explained to his subordinate commanders the tactics which he would employ when he encountered the French, the so-called Nelson touch, they were so moved and electrified by the

sheer beauty of the idea – 'It was new – it was singular – it was simple
. . . It must succeed' – that some of them actually wept.

It did succeed, of course, brilliantly and devastatingly. As Nelson lay
dying in the cockpit of *Victory* and Hardy congratulated him on his
success, saying he was sure that fourteen or fifteen enemy ships had
surrendered, Nelson replied that it was well but that he had bargained
for twenty. In fact of the thirty-three enemy ships engaged, eighteen
were captured on the day of the battle, four were taken two weeks
later, and the remaining eleven which reached Cadiz never put to sea
again to fight. It was indeed a victory of annihilation, and its
consequences were not only to remove once and for all any possibility
of a French army's invading Britain, but to give Britain and its army a
further opportunity to fight the French on the Continent. By now
perhaps even Napoleon had come to understand what it was that
Castlereagh so desired – a recognition that Great Britain could not be
trifled with, certainly not at sea. Before long it would become clear that
on land too, her army, although to start with trifling in numbers, was
not to be despised in quality.

Pitt did not live to see it. Three months after Nelson's death, the
great Prime Minister himself died. On the day following, 24 January
1806, there appeared a notice in *The Times* which attempted to do
justice to his achievements:

> This great man, for such he has been considered even by the parties
> who opposed him, had not exceeded his forty-eighth year, a period,
> when the body and mind are frequently in a very high state of
> activity and enjoyment.
>
> We shall speak of him with the truth and the freedom of history;
> and in that spirit, we are ready to acknowledge the splendour of his
> talents, the powers of his eloquence, and his indefatigable attention
> to the objects of his Administration.
>
> He began his career with a prematurity of talent, which has no
> example, and in a time of difficulty, which required the most
> determined resolution, the utmost vigour of exertion, and a mind of
> the most potent grasp, and unbounded comprehension; he not only
> possessed them all, but applied them with incomparable energy and
> effect, to the advantage of his country.

Thus two of the great English adversaries of the Emperor Napoleon
were down. Nelson's memory – 'the darling of the British navy, whose
death has plunged a whole nation into the deepest grief' – would be
immortal. Pitt, like Nelson, a triumphant weatherer of storms, had
before his death rolled up the map of Europe for ten years. Now,
during the decade to come, two soldiers would step from the wings on
to history's stage and take up further the challenge against Napoleon.
One would die the death he had always wanted on the field of battle.
The other would survive war to become a 'Pillar of State'. Both, in

leading British armies, did much to determine what the map of Europe would look like at the end of this same decade.

CHAPTER SIX

Corunna

Slowly and sadly we laid him down,
From the field of his fame fresh and gory;
We carved not a line, and we raised not a stone,
But we left him alone with his glory.

CHARLES WOLFE

After Pitt's death Grenville formed what was called the 'Ministry of All the Talents'. Alas, talent was in short supply and the one man, Fox, who had plenty of it and as Foreign Secretary, in contrast to his capricious behaviour in opposition, showed himself sensible and steady in office, died in September 1806. In its obituary *The Times*, despite its anti-Whig tendencies praised Fox's greatness:

> He possessed in an high degree the talent which distinguishes man, and the genius that elevates him; nor was he without a portion of that virtue which is superior to them both. As Mr. Burke has observed, and when he was in intimate friendship with him, his faults, though they might tarnish the lustre, and sometimes impede the march of his abilities, were not formed to extinguish the fire of great virtues. In his faults, there was no mixture of deceit, of hypocrisy, of pride or ferocity, or complexional despotism, or want of feeling for the distresses of mankind.
>
> In short, Mr. Fox was among the distinguished characters which nature seems to have prepared and ripened to become the ornaments of the present reign.
>
> We lament that the country is deprived of such a man. He had done much towards laying the first stone of the Temple of Peace; and much do we wish, if wishing were not the vainest of all things, that he had lived to see it rise into strength, and to promise duration, that it might have been at once his record and his tomb.

In fact while Fox was for his short time in office, his attempts to end the war had quickly been disillusioned by his realizing that it was not possible to negotiate a secure peace with Napoleon. Austerlitz had simply enlarged his appetite, and soon he would be at war again with Prussia, Russia and Spain. The conflict in Spain would at last give the British Army an opportunity to do something useful. As if in anticipation of it, Windham, Secretary for War, had eventually been successful in introducing his ideas about recruiting, notably enlistment for shorter periods and higher pay on re-engagement. He had even abolished the system of substitutes for the Militia, establishing instead a scheme for giving some military instruction to every man in the country. It was unfortunate that the implementation of these necessary measures did not match the ideas themselves. A totally different military matter, that of allowing Roman Catholics to hold commissions in the Army as high as Colonel's rank – *in England*, as well as in Ireland itself – met with such opposition from King George III that the Whig government fell in March 1807, and the Duke of Portland formed an administration with Eldon, Perceval, Castlereagh (Secretary for War), Hawkesbury (later Lord Liverpool) and, as Foreign Secretary, the brilliantly clever, intriguing and never wholly trusted George Canning. Meanwhile the war was going badly. Napoleon had been making hay of Britain's European allies and had issued his Berlin Decree designed to prevent any ship sailing from Britain or her colonies from docking at any port under French control.

In September 1806 Prussia, no doubt with memories of the great Frederick in mind, had been unwise enough to declare war on France. On 14 October at Jena and Auerstädt, they were to discover just how unwise it had been to take on the Grande Armée when, despite mistakes by Lannes, Ney, Bernadotte and even the Emperor himself, the iron Davout and his corps of 27,000 took on 60,000 Prussians on the right wing at Auerstädt and held them until Napoleon could rectify his blunder of misappreciating where the bulk of the Prussian army was. But it was the pursuit which followed that illustrated strikingly what Napoleon's idea about war really was.* As A.G. Macdonnell has reminded us, the Napoleonic concept was that whereas the battle itself was to be thought of as the breaking of the crest of a wave, it was the flood which swept irresistibly after it that was the real victory. The classic example of this was what happened after Jena and Auerstädt:

> Napoleon hurled his army northwards in the greatest sustained pursuit in history. The pursuit is sometimes called the Pursuit of the Three Marshals, because Murat, Bernadotte, and Soult were in at the death.
>
> On November 6th Blücher surrendered in Lübeck, and the mighty machine of Frederick the Great had vanished. There was not a single man, horse, or gun left. Twenty-three days had done the entire trick, and Murat wrote to the Emperor that the fighting was over for lack of opponents.

* It was said that of all the Marshals, only Davout understood what Napoleon was up to.

So fell the Prussian Army, and Napoleon symbolically removed the sword of Frederick from the tomb in Potsdam.*

Totally decisive pursuit like this is rarely achieved. In the Second World War, although the German Army and its *Blitzkrieg* tactics brought it off in Poland, France and in the early days of the Russian campaign, for the Allied armies it was almost unknown. It could be said that at Beda Fomm, O'Connor had successfully pursued the Italian 10th Army and liquidated it. No such claim could be made after the battle of El Alamein. There was no pursuit in the Napoleonic sense. It was a dull and measured following up. The same might be said of the battle for Normandy, in that after Allied failure at Arnhem, the Germans under Field Marshal Model made a remarkable recovery and imposed a kind of stalemate in the West – even launching a counter-offensive in December 1944.

Military events during the early part of Portland's administration were hardly calculated to inspire much confidence in its ability to wage war. Although in the summer of 1806 Sidney Smith's fleet and John Stuart's army of some 5,000 men landed in Calabria and gave the French a lesson in what steady British infantrymen could do, so small a force was unable to stay there and returned to Sicily. In South America Admiral Home Popham (who had made a vitally important strategic contribution by re-capturing the Cape of Good Hope) proceeded to take Buenos Aires with the aid of General Beresford and 1,500 redcoats, only to lose it again when the local inhabitants rebelled. This loss did not, however, deter the British Government from trying again a year later, and in June 1807, General Whitelocke with the best part of 8,000 soldiers attacked Buenos Aires, suffering such heavy casualties that he withdrew again. The policy of getting at Napoleon by attacking his allies' colonial possessions was not paying many dividends, while in Europe itself all Britain's potential partners had either, like Austria and Prussia, been disposed of already, or, like Russia, were about to be. It is true that the Russian army gave the Grande Armée a shock at Eylau, when as Napoleon himself put it: 'The Russians have done us great harm'. Indeed the situation was saved only by the intervention of perhaps the most colourful cavalryman of all time:

> 100,000 men of the two armies watched one of the most famous spectacles in the whole history of warfare, when ninety squadrons of the Reserve Cavalry galloped across the snow to attack unbroken infantry and artillery, with Murat himself at their head, wearing his gold-embroidered uniform, his ostrich-feathers in his hat, with his saddle over a great leopard-skin, and carrying a gold-headed cane in his hand.†

---

* But as he stood there, Napoleon said to his Marshals: 'Hats off, gentlemen – if he were alive we should not be here'.
† Macdonnell, *Napoleon and his Marshals*.

Eylau had been fought in February 1807. Four months later, at Friedland, Napoleon destroyed the Russian Army, and the Treaty of Tilsit followed, with the two Emperors, Alexander and Napoleon entering into a pact designed to bring about the destruction of Great Britain. Yet the shadows were beginning to lengthen over the Napoleonic legend and already murmurings for peace and bread were being heard in the ranks of the Grande Armée. Before long the shadows would lengthen further. As part of their pact, Alexander and Napoleon intended to bully Sweden and Denmark to join their ban on English ships, and to dominate Portugal. Britain's response in the north was to seize the Danish fleet, and to attempt to bolster up Sweden by sending Sir John Moore there with 12,000 soldiers. Even before Moore could land, Sweden's King Gustavus, who was mad, had taken it into his head to attack Norway and try to arrest Moore, who escaped and returned to England with nothing achieved. Elsewhere, however, and as a result of Napoleon's misappreciation of the Iberian peoples, Moore was to achieve much.

Napoleon's resolve to subdue Portugal had profound consequences. In the first place Portugal's oldest ally, England, succeeded in persuading the Regent to quit Lisbon, sail to Brazil with the all-important Portuguese fleet, and await events. Second, it gave to the British an opportunity to exploit with her sea-power and a relatively small army an abundance of ports and thus points of entry to a country whose nature was ideal for innumerable and fanatical guerrillas to multiply many times the effect which this same small army was able to make on numerically superior French forces. Third, it gave them another ally, whose initial resistance to Napoleon's arrogant assumption of the right to dictate events turned gradually into a burning, unquenchable hostility which devoured untold thousands of French soldiers – the Spanish people. In writing of a totally different and much earlier war,* Macaulay summed up the difficulties which the Grande Armée was going to encounter in Spain. He pointed out that whereas it was easy for an army to overrun Spain, it was immeasurably hard to conquer the people there. However contemptible might be the resistance put up by her regular army, once this had been brushed aside, a different sort of resistance, energetic, tenacious and per-severant, sprang up instead. Her armies might be ill-disciplined rabbles, but her rabbles had the habit of acquiring a formidably martial spirit.

The soldier, as compared with other soldiers, is deficient in military qualities; but the peasant has as much of those qualities as the soldier. In no country have such strong fortresses been taken by surprise: in no country have unfortified towns made so furious and obstinate a resistance to great armies. War in Spain has, from the

* War of the Succession in Spain.

days of the Romans, had a character of its own; it is a fire which cannot be raked out; it burns fiercely under the embers; and long after it has, to all seeming, been extinguished, bursts forth more violently than ever.

It was into this country and against these people that Napoleon was shortly to launch his armies.

He did not, however, make war on Spain to start with. He began by bullying those in charge of Spanish affairs to allow General Junot and the so-called Corps of Observation of the Gironde passage through Spain on their way to teach Portugal a lesson. At the same time Napoleon was aware that sooner or later it would be necessary to teach Spain a lesson too. It may be doubted whether history can boast a more miserable or unattractive quartet than that which was either nominally or actually at the head of Spain's government in the early part of the nineteenth century: King Charles IV, footling, imbecile, with a passion only for hunting; his ill-favoured, strong-minded, sexually voracious, adulterous wife, Maria Luisa; their heir Ferdinand, hideous, tubby, dull, bigoted and tyrannical; and the Spanish Minister, Manuel Godoy, coarse, venal, the Queen's favourite and virtual ruler of Spain. It was Godoy who had roused Napoleon's ire by issuing a proclamation shortly before the battle of Jena – seizing what he thought of as a chance to assert Spain's position while the Grande Armée was engaged elsewhere – calling on his people to come forward *en masse* to fight an unnamed enemy. The trouble was that his proclamation specified an increase in the size of the army, with special pleas for more horses. No mention was made of a need to set to rights the Spanish navy which had never recovered from Trafalgar. All this made it somewhat difficult for Godoy to assure Napoleon after Prussia's collapse that the enemy he had had in mind was the British, not the French. For the time being, Napoleon let it go. He had already made up his mind that Spain was to enjoy the benefits of French control, but the imposition of this control could not only wait a while, but best be cloaked by arranging with Spain for the passage of French troops through their country to occupy Portugal and so complete the process of closing European ports to British trade.

Thus in October 1807 Junot entered Spain with some 24,000 men, and six weeks later with his numbers reduced to a mere 1,500 and by this time without any horses or guns or any hope of being able to fight a battle, found himself at Lisbon, which instantly surrendered. During the next six months Napoleon dispatched army after army across the Pyrenees. They were supposedly further Corps of Observation, yet slowly, surreptitiously, they occupied northern Spain, Barcelona, Madrid and the frontier fortresses. Having persuaded King Charles IV and his heir, Ferdinand, to come to Bayonne in April 1808, Napoleon had them seized, then bullied Charles into abdication, and after Murat had put down a rising by the Madrid mob with ruthless efficiency, convinced Ferdinand too that abdication was a choice preferable to death. It seemed that Spain, with Napoleon's elder brother, Joseph, as their new King (Murat, who had hoped for the crown, went off to Naples instead) and Portugal were now mere provinces of Imperial France. It was an illusion.

During all this time there had been no declaration of war, but in May 1808 the people of Spain took up arms against the French. All over the country – Asturias, Galicia and Old Castile in the north, Aragon, Valencia and Murcia in the east, Andalusia in the south and Estremadura in the west – everywhere the peasants and the Spanish army declared war on the invader. The French had over 100,000 soldiers in Spain, yet the remnants of their fleet in Cadiz were obliged to surrender, they were unable to wrest Saragossa from the hands of the rebel Spaniards, and worst of all in July 1808, General Dupont with his army of 17,000 surrendered at Baylen. Both in Portugal and in Spain the French armies were losing control. Now surely the time had arrived for the British Army to take a hand in the game. When the Spanish uprising began, the youngest lieutenant-general in the Army, Wellesley, was preparing to set off for Spanish America from Cork with 9,000 men to assist the Venezuelan revolutionary, General Miranda, in his intended rising against Spain* – at this time still thought to be France's ally. But the latest news from Spain changed the destination of Wellesley and his men. He himself had observed that rather than go all the way to South America, surely a much sounder way to 'alarm' Napoleon, whose armies were dispersed all over Europe, would be to strike at him nearer home. The Government thought the same and with the encouragement of both Spanish and Portuguese emissaries, it was decided to despatch Wellesley and his small army to the Peninsula. At a dinner shortly before his departure the future Duke of Wellington made some profoundly prescient points about his future campaigning:

> Why, to say the truth, I am thinking of the French that I am going to fight: I have not seen them since the campaign in Flanders, when they were capital soldiers, and a dozen years of victory under Buonaparte must have made them better still. They have besides, it seems, a new system of strategy which has out-manoeuvred and overwhelmed all the armies of Europe. 'Tis enough to make one thoughtful; but no matter.
>
> My die is cast, they may overwhelm me, but I don't think they will out-manoeuvre me. First, because I am not afraid of them, as everybody else seems to be; and secondly, because if what I hear of their system of manoeuvre is true, I think it is a false one against

---

* This was all part of Canning's notion of calling the New World into existence to redress the balance of the Old.

steady troops. I suspect all the continental armies were more than
half beaten before the battle was begun – I, at least, will not be
frightened beforehand.*

He was shortly able to demonstrate the soundness of his ideas at his
first Peninsular battle, Vimeiro. Having arrived at Corunna on 20 July
1808 and conferred with the Galician Junta there (the Spaniards did
not relish the presence of *any* foreign troops on their soil) Wellesley
accepted their suggestion that the best course of action would be to
support an uprising in northern Portugal in order to mount an
offensive against Junot. Continuing ahead of his troops, therefore, he
went on to Oporto, arriving there on 24 July. After discussions with
the Junta there and with Admiral Cotton, who was in command of the
blockading fleet, he decided to land his army at Mondego Bay, about
eighty miles north of Lisbon and far enough away from Junot's army
to avoid his interfering with disembarkation and concentration.
Wellesley's small army of some 9,000 men was reinforced by a further
4,000 under General Spencer and by 2,000 Portuguese troops. It was
also planned that a further substantial addition of 10,000 soldiers
commanded by Sir John Moore (after his abortive attempt to bolster
Sweden) should arrive before operations should get under way. Junot
thought otherwise and was determined to engage the British while
they were still relatively weak. As if Wellesley's shortage of fighting
soldiers were not a sufficient disadvantage, he had also heard from
Castlereagh the unwelcome news that he was not to remain in overall
command for long, but that it would pass first to General Sir Harry
Burrard (who had no experience of commanding large forces in the
field and later was relegated to doing what he could do – commanding
the Guards in London), then to General Sir Hew Dalrymple (another
elderly incompetent and Governor of Gibraltar). The Government's
absurd reasoning behind these ridiculous jugglings was that they did
not wish Sir John Moore to be in overall command simply because he
had not hesitated to criticize the Government's military strategy.
Therefore, someone senior to Moore had to be dispatched. Wellesley
accepted his disappointment with characteristic common sense, and
determined to get on with the business without waiting for those who
would supersede him, hoping indeed to beat Junot before any of them
arrived.

Accordingly he ordered his army to land, reminding the troops that
Portugal was a country friendly to His Majesty and that therefore their
customary crimes of stealing both the goods of the men and the virtue
of the women were to be deprecated. To the Portuguese themselves he
proclaimed that the time had come to rescue their country and restore
their lawful Prince. By 8 August the landings had been effected, and
two days later Wellesley began his advance towards Lisbon. Mean-

Croker Papers.

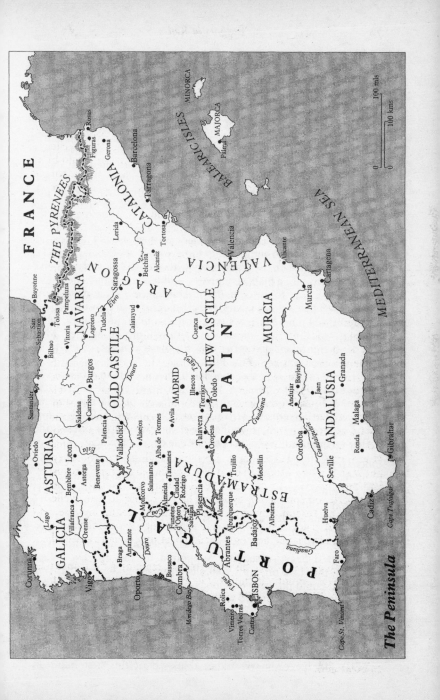

The Peninsula

while Junot had dispatched General Laborde with some 4,000 troops to delay the British and after some preliminary skirmishing – during which the 60th and 95th Rifles not only showed how well they had learned Moore's lesson of skilful fire and movement, but actually charged the rearguard enemy position – the two armies met for the first battle of the Peninsular War at Roliça. Wellesley, aware that a second French force under General Loison was marching to reinforce Laborde, was determined to strike at once and as he had three times Laborde's number, intended to make a showing to the front, while outflanking Roliça by columns to left and right of the French positions. Colonel Leslie has told us how the British Army looked just before its first engagement in Portugal on the morning of 17 August 1808:

> Arms piled and the men occupied as they usually are on all occasions of a morning halt – some sitting on their knapsacks, others stretched on the grass, many with a morsel of cold meat on a ration biscuit for a plate in one hand, with a clasp-knife in the other, all doing justice to the contents of their haversacks, and not a few with their heads thrown back and canteens at their mouths, eagerly gulping down his Majesty's grog or the wine of the country, while others, whiffing their pipes, were jestingly promising their comrades better billets and softer beds for the next night, or repeating the valorous war-cry of the Portuguese.
>
> There was more in this condensed formation than a casual halt required. A close observer would have noticed the silence and anxious looks of the several general officers of brigades, and the repeated departure and arrival of staff-officers and aides-de-camp, and he would have known that the enemy was not far distant, and that an important event was on the eve of taking place.

Indeed it was. Wellesley sent 5,000 men under Ferguson to the east, or right, flank of the French and his Portuguese troops to the other flank, while he himself was in the centre with the main body. Laborde, seeing the threat to his flanks, withdrew behind the village of Roliça to a stronger position. It was then that the 29th Regiment (Worcesters) under their gallant, but somewhat rash, Colonel Lake prematurely advanced to the top of the hill where the French main position was, and suffered heavy casualties. Supported by the 9th Foot (East Norfolks) they held on, until Wellesley, realizing that the outflanking movement could not now develop, advanced in the centre, preceded by the invaluable 60th and 95th in their jackets of green. Laborde retired and as the British had not enough cavalry to pursue, the battle was over. It had not been decisive. Wellesley's next encounter with the French would be more so, even though it was to be marred by the timidity of his superior officers.

What did the ordinary soldier think about this first battle in

Portugal? Let us first accompany a bugler of the 71st Foot who remembered coming up against the French on the heights of Roliça when his regiment was under the command of General Craufurd (Black Bob of the Light Brigade). He recalled moving forward as part of the main advance, first inclining to the left, then to the right, engaged by enemy cannon, but nevertheless pushing the French back. It was very hot and they were all thirsty, but stories that the French had poisoned the water abounded. As he and his comrades reached the heights, they saw many dead soldiers, both British and French. They observed with interest the way in which the local Portuguese dragged the dead bodies of French soldiers away to strip them naked, and saw too how the enemy wounded pleaded with the British both for protection from the Portuguese and for water. They advanced further against the retiring enemy and were left in possession of the field. There was little more to do that day than make camp and talk over what they had seen and felt. It is curious how the private soldier often remembers not the fury of an engagement, but rather the less dramatic incidents. Wellesley, on the other hand, described it more colourfully as a desperate action – he had never seen such fighting.

Next day he had to deal with two reinforcements, the one, some 4,000 men in their transports off the coast decidedly welcome; the other, General Sir Harry Burrard decidedly not. He moved his army to Vimeiro on the river Maceira to cover the disembarkation of the reinforcing brigade, and himself went to confer with Burrard aboard the frigate *Brazen*. Their ideas as to what should now be done differed widely, Wellesley all for a bold and swift advance to Mafra and so to outflank Junot's army at Torres Vedras, Burrard all for caution, remaining concentrated at Maceira Bay and awaiting the arrival of Sir John Moore and his 12,000 soldiers. In the event it was neither of these British generals who determined the next move. It was Junot. Junot had some 13,000 troops and twenty-four guns, having left about half that number to keep an eye on Lisbon and guard his communications to the east, an entirely adequate force, he believed, to push a bunch of amateurs back into the sea. His intention was to engage the British first with his *tirailleurs* and artillery, and then finish off the job with his columns of grenadiers and the cavalry. Wellesley had been expecting the enemy to approach from the south, and when at nine o'clock on the morning of 21 August it became clear from rising dust that Junot was actually coming from the east, he was obliged to make some rapid redispositions. On the ridge to the north and east of Vimeiro he placed his main force and, except for the Portuguese and one British brigade further west, the rest of his army on a hill to the south of Vimeiro. His infantry were behind the crests on the reverse slope with orders to wait until the last moment before opening fire; his twelve guns further forward; and in order to deal with the French *tirailleurs*, his own light infantry skirmishers were posted at the foot of the hills. It was a typical

Wellesley defensive tactic, and as it was often to do in the future, it succeeded completely.

A few hours were enough to do the business. The French columns advancing with customary courage and *élan* were subjected to a varied but continuous series of shot and shell, first the rifle fire of the skirmishing light infantry, then artillery (including for the first time bursting 'Shrapnel'), and last the deadly musketry of the thin lines of British infantry, who because of their deployment in two lines were able to pour a devastating hail of bullets into both the head and flanks of the French columns. When these columns began to halt and break up, they were faced with British bayonets charging at them. It was hardly surprising that they broke and ran. Such was the nature of the fighting both at Vimeiro Hill and the ridge north of the village. Many regiments distinguished themselves that day – the 29th, who had suffered at Roliça, the 40th (Somersets), and the 71st and 91st Highlanders (Highland Light Infantry; Argyll and Sutherland High-landers) were among them. The cavalry, in the shape of some sixty 20th Light Dragoons, displayed all the dash expected of them, but none of the control required, and did little damage except to themselves. Wellesley was often to complain with reason about the cavalry's inability to preserve the iron discipline which could make them so valuable and effective. But he had won the day; the enemy had lost fifteen of their twenty-three guns, had almost 2,000 casualties, and were fleeing. It was still only noon. If ever there were a moment to turn a French retreat into utter rout by pursuit, it was now, and it was just this course of action that Wellesley pressed on General Burrard, who had arrived on the battlefield earlier but happily had not interfered with his subordinate's direction of affairs. But when Wellesley urged him to agree that while the army's left-hand body should pursue the French, and the right-hand body, which had not been in action, make for Torres Vedras, 'Betty' Burrard demurred. Better wait for Sir John Moore. Enough had been done. Wellesley was so disgusted that he commented to his officers that they might as well go off and shoot partridges.

Vimeiro was the first of Wellesley's defensive actions in the Peninsula, and it was a pattern often to be repeated. Let us now see how it appeared to the redcoats and greenjackets. Our bugler friend in the 71st Foot was cleaning himself up ready for Divine Service when the drums and bugles called them to arms. The French were advancing. The Colonel gave orders to fall in and moved his regiment to confront two advancing enemy columns. Orders to prime, load and lie down followed, which was just as well for the French artillery was sending over plenty of shot and shell, allowing our bugler the opportunity to reflect on his ill-preparedness to leave this world. The Major then reported that lots of musket balls were flying about. Next the 71st were told to advance. They did so, moving towards the French columns and noting how fine they looked. The Colonel gave orders not to fire until they were nearer the enemy. Soon they were near enough, both sides fired, the enemy turned and made off, pursued by the cheering 71st, who reached the top of the crest, halted, piled arms and began to see what was in the knapsacks left lying there by the retreating French. After a pause the French reappeared, charging forward, cheering and shooting. Several of the Regiment were wounded, including our bugler. Then the 71st charged the enemy, with a wounded piper encouraging them. This time the enemy had gone, not to return. Wellesley rode up and was given three cheers. The battle was over and they all marched back to camp.

Rifleman Harris of the 95th who was in the skirmishing line at the start of the battle recalled a sharp encounter with French grenadiers – 'all fine-looking young men, wearing red shoulder-knots and tremendous-looking moustaches'. They swarmed down on the Rifles, raining on them a shower of bullets, which were returned with interest, but the 95th were so outnumbered that they were obliged to resort to their 'firing and retiring' tactics, ably supported from behind by their sister regiments of light infantry, the 43rd and 52nd, who were eager to charge 'Boney's Invincibles'. They were, however, restrained by General Fane, who, praising their performance, made it clear that he did not want them to advance yet. One of Harris's comrades gave the General a green feather, taken from a French *tirailleur's* cap, which Fane stuck into his own cocked hat, shortly after giving the order to charge.

Down came the whole line, through a tremendous fire of cannon and musketry – and dreadful was the slaughter, as they rushed onwards. As they came up with us, we sprang to our feet, gave one hearty cheer, and charged along with them, treading over our own dead and wounded, who lay in the front. The 50th were next to us as we went, and I recollect, as I said, the firmness of that regiment in the charge. They appeared like a wall of iron. The enemy turned and fled, the cavalry dashing after them as they went off.

Such were Harris's recollections of the battle of Vimeiro. We shall meet this great Rifleman again. If Wellesley's superior officers had had the same fighting spirit as some of his private soldiers, Vimeiro might have been an even greater victory.

Burrard's timidity had been bad enough. When Sir Hew (Dowager) Dalrymple arrived on the day following the battle and took over command, he was agreeably surprised to find that the French – in the form of Junot's emissary, General Kellermann – wanted an armistice. This suited Dalrymple admirably, and Wellesley, realizing as he did that 'the old gentleman' was as incapable of commanding an army as he was of taking advice from a subordinate, was disinclined to kick up a fuss. The Convention of Cintra, which was concluded on 30 August

1808, arranged for the evacuation of the French Army from Portugal, and for them to be taken with their arms and equipment to a French port in British transports. The news was received with dismay in England, where the previous dispatches announcing Wellesley's victory at Vimeiro had caused jubilation. It seemed that the long years of defeat were at last over, and that the British redcoats had shown themselves to be inferior to none. Inevitably, success was exaggerated and there was talk of Junot's absolute capitulation and British entry into Lisbon. So that when the actual terms of the Cintra Convention were known, they could hardly be believed. It looked as if victory had simply been thrown away. The politicians, of course, blamed the soldiers, including Wellesley, whose signature was also on the document, although in the end it was Dalrymple (of whom it was said that 'humiliation' would in future be spelt with a 'hew') who bore the principal responsibility. Wellesley would return to show once more that the French system of manoeuvre was a false one against steady British infantry. But before he did so, Napoleon himself was to play a part in the affair, a part he played with exceptional energy and enthusiasm when he heard that the elusive English leopards under the generalship of Sir John Moore were at last within his grasp.

That it was high time for the Emperor to turn his attention to the Peninsula was made clear not only by Junot's failure in Portugal, but by the success of Spanish arms against the hated invader. At the time of the Convention of Cintra only 60,000 French troops remained in Spain and they were all north of the Ebro, in Navarre and Barcelona. Madrid had been retaken by General Castaños, Saragossa was firmly in Spanish hands, King Joseph had retired to Vitoria, and to the British Government an opportunity not to be missed presented itself. It was for the British Army to support the Spaniards and destroy the French position once and for all. Any such idea was founded on a total misunderstanding of what the Spanish people were actually like, on ignorance of their total incapacity for concerted action, the rivalry of the various Juntas, the utter lack of discipline or perseverance, their readiness to put off anything that had to be done today until some indeterminate tomorrow, above all of acceptance of the sheer unlikelihood that a mob of unruly, ill-armed peasants could prevail against the veteran French troops led by generals of unrivalled experience and valour – all these considerations meant that, far from the British Army's being in a position to finish off the business quickly, it would take them the best part of six years.

Nevertheless, Sir John Moore, now in Portugal with some 30,000 troops was given his orders early in October 1808. His task was to go to northern Spain with 20,000 soldiers (leaving the rest to secure Portugal) either by sea or land to give his support to the Spanish armies. He was to be reinforced by a further 17,000 under General Baird. Moore would shortly have something to do for it was also in

October 1808 that Napoleon, leaving some 40,000 soldiers in Germany to watch the Austrians, set the rest of the Grande Armée on the road to Spain. Early in November he was himself in Vitoria and about to launch the campaign which he believed would put an end to Spanish resistance and give him a chance to get at the British Army. We may perhaps examine the intentions of these two Commanders-in-Chief before we see what actually happened. First Napoleon, sticking to his principle that what was needed in war was simplicity, devised his very straightforward plan of driving with greatly concentrated force – he had nearly 200,000 men at his disposal – through the Spanish centre, then dividing his army into three, one on either flank to deal with each Spanish army to the right and left, the third to drive south and take Madrid. After that he would move on to Portugal and deal with the British.

Sir John Moore's charter was clear: 'His Majesty, having determined to employ not less then 30,000 infantry and 5,000 cavalry in the North of Spain, to cooperate with the Spanish armies in the expulsion of the French from that Kingdom, has been graciously pleased to entrust to you the Command-in-Chief of this force.' The difficulty was how to do it. In the first place he had only 20,000 men until he was joined by Baird's additional 17,000, who had not yet even arrived in the country; second, convinced as he was that Napoleon would shortly attack the Spanish armies, he was obliged to move fast if he were to render them any assistance at all; next, the 5,000 cavalry under Lord Paget would not reach Corunna until mid-November; and last, he had no knowledge of the mountain roads over which he would have to advance, no maps and no pre-positioned stores of provisions and ammunition. If ever there were a classic example of war being an option of difficulties, it was in the task now facing Moore. None the less he made the decision to march his army to Salamanca in order to join with Baird in Castile and so be in a position to support the Spanish. Faulty information about roads caused him to dispatch his heavy artillery by a different route, when on 16 October he set off from Queluz to march his army through the Portuguese mountains, making for the Spanish frontier and Ciudad Rodrigo.

When, about a month later, having passed through Ciudad Rodrigo on 13 November, he discovered at Salamanca on the 15th that the situation had dramatically changed, he found himself in a most unenviable position. Napoleon had already smashed the Spanish centre, the French had occupied Valladolid, and Moore was in danger of being overwhelmed by the enemy before he could link up with Baird at Lugo, Paget at Corunna or Hope with his artillery a hundred miles to the south.

Happily, Napoleon's concern with his grand design, together with lingering Spanish resistance on the Ebro, prevented this. Having taken

Madrid on 4 December, the Emperor prepared to advance towards Portugal to eliminate the British, whom he believed still to be there. Soult at Carrion de los Condes was guarding the western flank of his communications with France. Thus Moore, given a breathing space, was able to concentrate his army near Salamanca and now mustered some 30,000 troops with over sixty guns and the cavalry. He decided to strike at Soult and threaten Napoleon's communications by moving on Burgos. When Napoleon heard what was happening on 22 December, he once more showed what could be done when he pulled on his long boots. In his classic *History of the Peninsular War*, Sir Charles Oman described his reaction:

> Napoleon acted with a sudden and spasmodic energy which was never surpassed in any of his earlier campaigns. He hurled on to Moore's track not only the central reserve at Madrid, but troops gathered in from all directions, till he had set at least 80,000 men on the march, to encompass the British corps which had so hardily thrown itself upon his communications. Moore had been perfectly right when he stated his belief that the sight of the redcoats within reach would stir the Emperor up to such wrath, that he would abandon every other enterprise and rush upon them with every available man.

Napoleon claimed that he was the boldest general that ever lived, yet we must concede that Moore showed how bold a British general could be when he took this step of placing his relatively tiny force astride the French communications knowing that an army many times the size of his own could be turned against him. Moore could not persist in his bid against Soult once he knew that the Emperor was after him. There was no alternative but to retreat – to Corunna where the British fleet could do what it had so frequently done before and would do again, evacuate a British army on the run. Yet this retreat was a kind of victory, a Dunkirk 132 years earlier.

Before Moore was obliged to order the retreat, having given his orders for an attack across the Carrion on Soult's positions, the army's spirits had been high. Although Moore recognized the danger into which he might be leading his men, he was determined to show the world that the British were doing all they could to support the Spanish cause. The columns set off on Christmas Eve, regiments cheering as they did so, 'every heart beating high, every breast buoyant for victory'. Alas, it was not to be so for long, since during that very evening Moore received information that caused him instantly to countermand the advance orders in favour of a retreat to Astorga, then over the Cantabrian Mountains to Lugo and Corunna. The news he had received from his patrols was that Napoleon had recrossed the Guadarramas and that his leading cavalry were already at Palencia, a mere twenty miles from Carrion. To continue that advance would be to invite encirclement and destruction.

Orders to halt and retrace their steps were greeted by the redcoats with anger and dismay. Their former high spirits were dashed into gloom and grumbles. The retreat was to last nearly three weeks (the army reaching Corunna on 11 January 1809) over a distance of some 230 miles, with roads of slush and ice and a dearth of villages where firewood and food might be obtained. Throughout, the army would be impeded by disintegrating hordes of the so-called Spanish Army and harassed by pursuing Frenchmen. It was marked by the most gallant, steady and professional behaviour of some regiments, and by the disgraceful ill-discipline, drunkenness and pillage of others. The whole story has been incomparably narrated by Arthur Bryant,* who pointed out that the task facing Moore was daunting indeed – not only to get across the river Esla and gain the relative security of the mountains north of Astorga before he was cut off by Napoleon wearing his long boots, but during the process to keep his army under disciplined control. He could risk neither conducting a deliberate fighting withdrawal only to find himself surrounded, nor pushing his men too fast and too far only to find his command disintegrating. It was true that he had some fine regiments, trained by himself, on which he could rely absolutely, but it was equally true that with long and vulnerable lines of communication and supply, it would require superhuman efforts of leadership and discipline to maintain the morale of the entire army.

There were some splendid actions fought before the British had retired beyond Astorga. The Reserve Division under Edward Paget, the Light Brigade, whose commander, Robert Craufurd seemed to thrive on danger and difficulty, the cavalry with the incomparable Lord Paget at its head – all fought with magnificent skill and courage while the rest of the army made their way west and then north. In an encounter with Chasseurs of the Imperial Guard at the Esla near Benavente, the 10th Hussars together with a Hussar regiment of the German Legion charged and engaged so successfully that they accounted for one-third of the French cavalry and captured their commander, General Lefebvre-Desnoëttes. Yet the Esla bridges were not destroyed and it was still touch and go as to whether Moore would evade the French attempt to encircle him. When he reached Astorga on 30 December, therefore, Moore sent Craufurd and the Light Brigade to secure his southern flank by making for Vigo. Not only the danger of encirclement faced Moore, however, but starvation too, for Astorga had but two days' provisions. The retreat therefore continued and with it the army's further demoralization. At Bembibre dreadful scenes of plunder, disorder and drunken orgy were enacted, and

* *Years of Victory*, Collins, 1944.

stragglers from the retiring British columns received no mercy from the avenging French cavalry in pursuit.

By 1 January 1809 it was clear to Napoleon at Astorga that Moore had now succeeded in evading his grasp, and this combined with news from Paris about intrigue against him and Austria's re-arming persuaded him to hand command over to Soult and return at once to Paris. He had achieved neither of his aims – the Spanish revolt had not been suppressed, and both the British Army and Lisbon had thus far escaped his Eagles. Meanwhile the still retreating, reduced British army, now about 25,000, had reached Villafranca, where further acts of gross ill-discipline took place. At last and still some hundred miles from Corunna, there was food and wine in plenty. Soldiers simply brushed aside the commissaries and took what they liked – biscuits, salt meat, rum and wine – wagons were broken up for firewood, all pretence of control, of belonging to well-ordered fighting formations seemed to have disappeared. It took the arrival of Moore himself to set things partially to rights. Harsh measures, including summary hangings and shootings, did something to restore order, and the army set off east again for Lugo. Even Paget's Reserve Division, still acting as rearguard, had had its troubles and at Cacabelos, to the east of Villafranca, Paget was obliged to punish plunderers by flogging, and had condemned two culprits to death, when it was reported that the French were approaching. His offer to spare them if they all promised to reform was greeted with cheers, and moments later they proved themselves against the French cavalry. Particularly prominent in the action were Moore's old regiment, the 52nd, the Light Company of the 28th Foot (The Gloucesters) and the 95th (Rifle Brigade), one of whose marksmen, Rifleman Tom Plunket brought down one of the most dashing and tactically brilliant Hussar officers of the Emperor's light cavalry, General Colbert.

The worst part of the retreat was yet to come, that of the main body to Lugo and the southern flankguard to Vigo, and for this ordeal we will accompany two of the private soldiers who took part in it, first our bugler friend of the 71st Foot. He recalls descending Snow Mountain on New Year's Day, the roads deep in mud from melting snow. It was so dark that he falls into the side of the road and cannot climb out again until he has laid down his firelock. Recovering it and his shoes and unable to move because of being so deep in the mud, still only seventeen years old, he finds himself weeping. Then, catching up with the Regiment, he gets a little sleep after washing his clothes and shoes, before they move on again between two mountains, with a steep precipice on one side with a river at the bottom, into which guns and ammunition are being thrown to lighten the soldiers' loads. Shots go off, killing exhausted cavalry and artillery horses. He has to remove his shoes and proceeds more slowly barefoot, again catching up with the Regiment in time to eat some potatoes which the Colonel has bought, but the men have to pay for. Another two days' march and at last they reach Lugo. The French are close behind so they are posted behind a wall at night, in drenching rain, thunder and lightning. They huddle under blankets, but get little sleep. Daylight sees both sides foraging for something to eat and ignoring each other while this urgent matter is dealt with. The Colonel rides off, finds a field of turnips, tells the men to collect themselves some, fires are kindled, flour issued, dumplings boiled and eaten, clothes dried. Then the French come forward again, supported by their artillery, the British soldiers take cover, fire back, the French retire. So another day passes, night falls, beef is served out, but before they can cook it, orders come to fall in and start the march to Corunna.

Further south the Light Brigade under Craufurd was having its own problems and at one point it was made clear why the Riflemen feared, as well as liked, their Brigade Commander, for he could, as Harris recorded, 'be terrible when insubordination showed itself in the ranks'. On discovering that two men had strayed from the main body he ordered an instant drumhead court martial and sentenced them to a hundred lashes each. When another man in the ranks grumbled that Craufurd would do better to get them something to eat rather than harass them, Craufurd, mistaking who it was that had spoken, knocked down his neighbour, and rewarded further complaints with further punishment. He was, of course, determined to maintain discipline at a time when any laxity could have proved disastrous. His own example was inspiring, for instead of riding his horse when they resumed the march, he marched all night on foot, and Harris recalled that next morning like the rest of them, their commander's 'hair, beard and eyebrows were covered with frost as if he had grown white with age'. The worst part of the whole retreat, Harris wrote, was the frightful load of their knapsacks. The agony of bleeding feet, the discomfort of dysentery caused by devouring bad food – these could be borne, but many men died, he believed, from the sheer weight they were obliged to carry, men who would otherwise have survived the retreat. Harris himself regarded the knapsack as his bitterest enemy. 'I felt it press me to the earth almost at times, and more than once felt as if I should die under its deadly embrace'. It would have been better, he thought, to have abandoned them early on in the withdrawal if such loss would have saved 'the poor fellows who, as it was, died strapped to them on the road'.*

Although Moore halted his army at Lugo on 6 January and prepared to do battle with the pursuing French, a decision which instantly put heart into the men, the enemy did not oblige, and for shortage of food alone, the retreat continued in icy downpours, the army no longer organized in regiments and formations, but a mere

* *Recollections of Rifleman Harris*, ed. Curling, London, 1848.

mass of marching men. When on 11 January, however, with the sun shining and food more plentiful, the sea was at last sighted, spirits rose, and under Moore's direction the army marched into Corunna with some semblance of regimental order and pride. As by this time, he had insufficient infantry to man the dominating heights which commanded the town, Moore was obliged to base his defences on the low hills closer in which were, of course, completely overlooked by the heights further south. Aided by the townspeople in digging trenches and delivering ammunition, able also to re-equip his soldiers from the stores in Corunna, relieved by the arrival of the transports, 110 ships, escorted by a squadron of battleships and given a little time by Soult's slow progress in bringing up his reserves and heavy artillery, Moore prepared for the battle of Corunna. By 15 January the French occupied the heights overlooking the town, and both artillery duels and exchanges between sharpshooters took place. But the real battle was on the following day. It was essentially an infantry engagement, for Moore had already embarked the cavalry who would be ineffectual on the rocky ground. At the same time the French artillery was greatly superior, as Moore had also embarked most of his guns. We may catch sight of the Commander-in-Chief by recalling the striking portrait of him given us by Charles Napier, commanding the 50th Foot, as Moore rides up to see how the French attack on the British centre is proceeding:

> He came at speed and pulled up so sharp and close he seemed to have alighted from the air; man and horse looking at the approaching foe with an intenseness that seemed to concentrate all feeling in their eyes. The sudden stop of the animal, a cream-coloured one with black tail and mane, had cast the latter streaming forward; its ears were pushed out like horns, while its eyes flashed fire, and it snorted loudly with expanding nostrils, expressing terror, astonishment and muscular exertion. My first thought was, it will be away like the wind! but then I looked at the rider, and the horse was forgotten. Thrown on its haunches the animal came, sliding and dashing the dirt up with its fore feet, thus bending the general forward almost to its neck. But his head was thrown back and his look more keenly piercing then I ever saw it. He glanced to the right and left, and then fixed his eyes intently on the enemy's advancing column, at the same time grasping the reins with both his hands and pressing the horse firmly with his knees: his body thus seemed to deal with the animal while his mind was intent on the enemy: and his aspect was one of searching intentness beyond the power of words to describe.

Further French attacks on the British centre – which Soult had wrongly judged to be the extent of their positions to the north (the British right) – enabled Moore both to reinforce his divisions there, and then bring into action against the French left Major-General Fraser's division, while his Reserve carried all before them in their assault on the main French artillery battery. This was the turning point of the battle, and it was at this moment too that Moore was struck by a cannon ball which took away his left shoulder, exposed his lungs and left his arm hanging by a thread of flesh. Removed from the field, suffering intense pain with great fortitude, murmuring that he had always wished to die this way, and, like Nelson, hoping that England would be satisfied and do him justice, Sir John Moore died and was buried darkly at dead of night with his martial cloak around him. Sir John Hope, now in command, for Baird had also been wounded, was able to embark the army. The French attack had been broken and the local people manned the ramparts while 1,500 redcoats under Beresford and Hill stayed behind to ensure the safe embarkation of the wounded. It was over.

It was not given to Moore to lead a British army to great victories. Yet he had given the army itself a priceless gift, that of confidence in itself and those who followed him in command were to reap the fruits of that gift. Indeed Moore himself in his final dispatch to Castlereagh two days before the battle of Corunna had made the point that although the army's behaviour during the retreat had been infamous, yet he was wholly confident of his troops' courage, for whenever there was the chance of a fight, they had responded with instant and absolute devotion to duty. Moreover the retreat itself had been achieved under the most trying conditions, and ill-discipline and disgraceful conduct notwithstanding, neither a gun nor a colour had been lost. Of Moore's original 30,000 men, 24,000 had been successfully withdrawn. The British may not have carved a line nor raised a stone to Sir John Moore, but Marshal Soult, who had a great penchant for building monuments, erected an impressive column to the memory of his opponent, and whenever Moore is written or spoken of today, far from being left alone with his glory, we share it with him. Many regiments of the British Army have *Corunna* as one of their battle honours – regiments of the Guards, Light Infantry, Highlanders, Fusiliers, Gloucesters, Staffordshires, Duke of Wellington's and many others. That they have it at all is owing to the boldness and leadership of Sir John Moore.

Apart from all this the strategic consequences of his campaign were profound. Napoleon had *not* cleared up the Spanish question. Moore's interference had not only stopped the French from advancing to Lisbon and crushing Portuguese resistance. In southern Spain also remnants of the Spanish Army and the guerrillas had been given a breathing space. It was true that Napoleon had left Spain for other reasons. It was true too that the whole of Moore's campaign could be regarded as yet one more example of the British Army's venturing on to Continental soil only to retreat once more to the sea and be taken away by the Royal Navy. But the British Army was to return and their activities in the Peninsula together with those of the native guerrillas were to form a kind of cancer in the flank of Napoleon's Europe which, not dealing him a mortal blow, did much to eat up the strength of the Grande Armée when it was much more urgently needed elsewhere. It would be for Castlereagh and Wellington (but not the Duke of York who had been obliged to resign his position as Commander-in-Chief of the Army in January 1809 because of his mistress's sales of military promotions and other favours) to plan the next moves.

CHAPTER SEVEN

The Fabian General

> The affairs of the Peninsula always seem to have the same appearance, the appearance of being lost. The contest, however, continues.
>
> LORD WELLINGTON

When he was required to give strategic guidance to his political masters, Wellesley set an example which would have been well followed by some of those who were subsequently called upon to do the like. We can hardly see his countenancing such ill-fated expeditions as those of Salonica and Gallipoli in the First World War, or Norway and the Aegean Islands in the Second. Unlike some soldiers, he did not allow the recalcitrance and unreliability of allies or the stubbornness and caprice of Whitehall (he did not go short of such irritants) to move him from his purpose or distort his tactical judgement. How enviable a position, therefore, Castlereagh was in to get such solidly sensible opinions as were expressed in Wellesley's memorandum of 7 March 1809 on the problems and practicability of raising an army in Portugal, reinforcing it with a British one, and maintaining them there. He made it plain that in his opinion Portugal could be defended, whatever might happen in Spain. Certain conditions, however, would be necessary – a British army of at least 20,000 with 4,000 cavalry, a re-formed Portuguese army, and for the time being the large French forces in Spain being kept occupied by the Spaniards. Once these conditions could be met, whoever was to be put in command, together with his staff, should go out there. Castlereagh was in no doubt about the strategic soundness of sending another expeditionary force or about the man to command it – Wellesley. His instructions were that his primary concern was the defence of Portugal and that any question of cooperating with the Spanish armies, should he decide it to be advantageous, would require the British Government's authority before being undertaken.

In Wellesley's memorandum, which had such a powerful effect in setting the whole Peninsular campaign in motion, there is no evasion of difficulties, no rash promise of success, no grandiloquence, but a straightforward survey of the military advantages which might accrue from such a course, and, above all, a firm statement that 'if you should adopt this plan, you must send everything from England – arms, ammunition, clothing and accoutrements, ordnance, flour, oats, etc . . .'. He moves with practised facility from matters of grand strategy to everyday affairs of administration. At about the same time as this memorandum was being pressed on the Government by Castlereagh, Dundas, the Commander-in-Chief, (who had succeeded the Duke of York) was being pressed to raise sufficient troops to attack Walcheren and Flushing, where French ships of the line were in commission and more were being built. The general shortage of troops, however (of roughly 200,000 effectives, a little less than half were serving overseas in the Mediterranean, West Indies, India and other colonies), together with plans for the Peninsula decided the Cabinet to postpone the Walcheren expedition until the summer.

On 22 April 1809 Wellesley landed at Lisbon. He would have some 20,000 British soldiers, 3,000 of the King's German Legion, and 16,000 Portuguese under Beresford. Several French armies were in a position to threaten him – Soult at Oporto to the north had over 20,000, Victor at Medellin, about 50 miles east of Badajoz, had 25,000, and at Ciudad Rodrigo with 6,000 men was General Lapisse. Elsewhere in Spain the French armies totalled 200,000. Thus Wellesley's position on the face of it was hardly such that he could anticipate resounding victories or great achievement. Yet to take this view is to misunderstand the nature of the Peninsular War. A. G. Macdonnell made a similar error when in a memorable, but not impartial, estimate of Wellesley's task in the Peninsula, he declared it to be the easiest one that had ever faced a general. With a mercenary army, assured intelligence, a population wholly hostile to his enemy, abundant supplies, interior lines, and command of the sea, he had according to Macdonnell 'the game in his hands, and yet it took him nearly six years to advance from Lisbon to the Pyrenees'. This estimate totally overlooks the point made by Liddell Hart that to treat the Peninsular War, as many British historians are tempted to do, as a series of battles fought by Wellesley against the French is to ignore the fact that 'Wellington's battles were perhaps the least effective part of his operations . . . The overwhelming majority of the losses which drained the French strength, and their morale still more, was due to the operations of the guerrillas, and of Wellesley himself, in harrying the French and in making the countryside a desert where the French stayed only to starve.' It is this aspect of the campaign which enables us to understand why Wellesley was so ready to retreat when he deemed it strategically necessary, falling back as he did on secure communications, a firm base and assured supplies, while imposing on the pursuing French armies precisely the opposite conditions.

As long as this is clearly appreciated, it will be permissible and indeed proper for us to concentrate on Wellesley's actual battles, for it is the work and achievements of the British Army that principally concern us here. In doing so we may conveniently divide the campaign into three parts: first up to the time Wellesley defeated Masséna at Bussaco in 1810 and was then bundled back to the lines of Torres Vedras; next when he cut up Marmont at Salamanca in 1812 and took Madrid, only to retire again after a repulse at Burgos; last when in 1813 he advanced a third time and for once was not required to 'know when to retreat and to dare to do so'.

Wellesley was neither dismayed by the numbers of French forces which could threaten him nor slow in taking action to deal with these forces one by one before they could combine against him. His first objective was Soult at Oporto. What now happened was the first of many Peninsular instances when Wellesley, although often called the Fabian general, displayed a boldness in attack which quite belied this qualification. Concentrating his main force of some 18,000 troops, principally British, at Coimbra, half way between Lisbon and Oporto, and dispatching Beresford with a Portuguese corps to secure his right flank, while leaving another force to watch the Tagus in case Victor should advance, Wellesley moved off on 7 May and four days later had reached the banks of the Douro just south of Oporto. Not for the first time Soult then under-estimated his opponent, believing that the Douro itself provided quite enough protection against the threat of an attack across the river. But Wellesley having found both a crossing place concealed from enemy observation and the necessary barges and boats to ferry his people across, rapidly threw three battalions of infantry, including the 3rd Foot (The Buffs) and two squadrons of the 14th Light Dragoons over the river to occupy positions on the northern bank. A well-sited British battery took heavy toll of the French counter-attack, and when Wellesley reinforced his success by sending the Brigade of Guards and the 29th Foot across the river to assault the town of Oporto itself, the game was finished and Soult withdrew his troops to the east. The French were further harassed as they withdrew by a gallant charge of the 14th Light Dragoons, but no pursuit was possible with so small a force at Wellesley's disposal. There was, however, a further dividend in that Beresford's right flanking move had effectively cut off Soult's main route to Spain. He was therefore obliged to retire north to Galicia over appalling roads and mountains, leaving his guns and wagons behind. Moreover the revenge taken on stragglers from the French Army by the Portuguese was terrible. Crucifixion and castration were common. But Soult and three-quarters of his men escaped. As Wellesley pointed out to Castlereagh, an army without guns, baggage or transport could move more quickly than one still possessing these assets. Besides, he had heard that Victor was advancing into eastern Portugal, and therefore reconcentrated his army at Abrantes. Once again he had cleared a

French army out of Portugal. Next he would have to deal with Victor. This would mean broadening his campaign into Spain, which in turn would demand cooperating with the Spanish Army.

Before doing so Wellesley received news of most welcome reinforcements, including the famous Light Brigade and the Royal Horse Artillery's Chestnut Troop. By late June he was ready to move his army of some 20,000 into Spain to join up with 30,000 ill-disciplined and ill-equipped Spaniards under General Cuesta. The idea was that together they would destroy Victor's army of 23,000 now withdrawing to Talavera. Quite apart from his Spanish allies, about whom he was to have ample cause to complain, Wellesley was by no means content with the behaviour of his own redcoats, who because of a shortage of supplies (itself caused by delays in money arriving from England) and of pay were inclined to help themselves. Such pillaging infuriated the Commander-in-Chief who described them as a rabble, capable of any outrage, liable to dissolve into disorder as readily after success as after failure. The truth was that the British soldier was only at his best in action, and so he was to prove once more in the furious fighting that took place at Talavera.

The British Army, having assembled at Plasencia, moved on from there on 16 July 1809, joining General Cuesta (described by one Rifleman as a deformed lump of pride, ignorance and treachery) and his mob of siesta- cigarillo- and garlic-loving peasants. Six days later the allied armies were at Talavera, and made contact with Victor's outposts. At this point the Allies had twice as many men as the French, but Cuesta's obstinate refusal to move robbed Wellesley, impatient to attack and entreating him to do so, of the opportunity to overwhelm Victor. Yet after Victor had sensibly moved east towards Madrid, Cuesta sent his ill-assorted troops in pursuit. They did not pursue for long. Meeting a hugely reinforced French army now totalling about 46,000 (for Victor had been joined by Sebastiani's corps and much of the Madrid garrison at Torrijos) they instantly became the pursued, and after Wellesley's intervention took up positions on the right flank of the Allied Talavera defences, with the British in the centre and on the left. Wellesley's position was by no means enviable. The Spaniards could not be relied upon, and he had only some 20,000 of his own troops, many of whom were not battle-hardened, to resist an assault by over 40,000 French veterans.

The battle of Talavera on 28 July was an excellent illustration of what Wellington (after the victory he was elevated to the peerage as a Viscount) later described as the French moving forward in the old style, in columns, and being driven off in the old style, that is by the British infantry firing volley after volley at them from their positions in line and then charging with the bayonet. For the thin red lines waiting to the north of the town, the sight of Victor's army at dawn that morning, column after column concentrated before them, with regiments of cavalry behind and hundreds of skirmishers in front, must have been daunting indeed. As the French cannonade began however, the British, as was their way, lay down under the cover of the crest in front of them, then as the enemy columns neared the summit, stood up and poured their deadly volleys into the packed French ranks before them. As the French faltered, the British charged, and after half an hour the enemy had had enough and were driven back across the Portina brook. The first phase of the battle was over.

In the afternoon, after another tremendous bombardment by eighty guns, the French troops came forward again, this time directed against both the British right and centre. It was in the centre that a serious crisis developed, for after repulsing one attack, Sherbrooke's 1st Division pursued its attackers too far, and was itself pushed aside by the French reserve columns which threatened to break through the British centre. Then, daunted by the magnificent behaviour of the British Reserve Brigade commanded by General Mackenzie, the advancing French faltered and were further dismayed by the return to the fight of the re-formed 1st Division and by the 48th Foot's attack on the enemy's right flank. No sooner had the British centre been saved than a further threat developed to their left, which if not checked could have outflanked the whole British line. Wellesley at once ordered the cavalry brigades of Anson and Fane forward to counter this move, and they together with Spanish horse artillery succeeded both in checking the enemy infantry and dispersing their supporting cavalry. By this time it was late afternoon, and when King Joseph, who had accompanied Victor, heard of another Spanish force advancing from the south towards Madrid, bearing in mind too that Cuesta's force had not been engaged, he decided that enough was enough, overruling Victor who wished to continue the battle. The entire French army withdrew. Next morning it was clear to Wellesley and his men that although they had lost about 5,000 men, the French had lost 2,000 more than this, and had left seventeen guns behind. What is more the Light Brigade, with its three incomparable regiments, 43rd, 52nd and 95th, plus the Chestnut Troop, after a march, fast even by their standards, of more than forty miles in less than a day, marched on to the bloody and scarred battlefield with General Craufurd at their head. Never can Wellington have been more glad to see them.

But we will now leave the victor of Talavera for a while and see what was happening elsewhere. While Wellington was doing what he could to help with the Grande Armée's dissipation in Spain, the Emperor was doing even better in Austria. In May 1809 he lost 20,000 men at the battle of Aspern-Essling (losing too the brilliant and brave Marshal Lannes), and although Napoleon defeated the Austrians at Wagram two months later and occupied Vienna once more, French invincibility was again being called into question, and with the loss also of another young cavalry leader, Lasalle, darling of the light cavalry, it was clear that the shadows over the Napoleonic legend were lengthening still further. Not that Napoleon was alone at this time in demonstrating military ineptitude. The British were repeating their trick of sending expeditions to the Low Countries in order to fiddle about there ineffectually and then withdraw again. On this occasion it was the postponed descent on the Scheldt.

The appointment of dithering incompetents to command military enterprises requiring speed, decisiveness and sound judgement was not the prerogative of any particular British sovereign or government. It seemed to be a favoured pastime of many.* But perhaps George III and Portland excelled themselves in choosing the Earl of Chatham – who was renowned mainly for indolence, inactivity and unpunctuality (the 'late' Lord Chatham) – to command the Walcheren expedition. Although involving 40,000 troops and thirty-five ships of the line (the fleet was commanded by Sir Richard Strachan) it achieved virtually nothing except to write off about half the troops involved because of the unhealthy climate and complete lack of medical stores. The idea was to capture Antwerp at a time when Napoleon was distracted in Austria, but in the event the expedition did not sail until Austria was once again suing for peace after Wagram, and when it reached the Scheldt, it did little more than capture Flushing after two weeks' siege, during which time the defences of Antwerp were put in good order. Chatham and Strachan decided that an attack on Antwerp would be too risky, so half the troops returned to England in September, and the rest remained to rot at Walcheren. Half-hearted attempts to fortify Flushing were soon abandoned and in December the familiar finale of evacuation drew an end to the sorry story, which is usually remembered by the anonymous ballad:

> Great Chatham with his sabre drawn
> Stood waiting for Sir Richard Strachan;
> Sir Richard, longing to be at'em,
> Stood waiting for the Earl of Chatham.

The disappointment and resentment caused by this fiasco had profound political consequences. The running dispute between Castlereagh and Canning exploded in a duel, Portland fell ill and soon died, Perceval became Prime Minister of an administration which excluded both Canning and Castlereagh (Lord Wellesley, Wellington's brother, became Foreign Secretary; Lord Liverpool went to the War Office) and the King was shortly to go mad, this time permanently, so that in 1810, Prinny, the First Gentleman of Europe, darling of the Whigs whom he instantly abandoned, at last became Regent.

---

* We shall have many opportunities to observe similarly ill-judged selections for high command. We need only think of Elphinstone in the Afghan War of 1842; Raglan and Lucan, to say nothing of Cardigan, in the Crimean War; and Chelmsford in the Zulu War to see how frequent an occurrence it was. We shall meet these gentlemen later.

Perhaps the saddest reflection which can be made about the ill-fated Walcheren expedition is to consider what excellent use Wellington could have made of such resources, which would have more than doubled the size of his army, had they been sent to the Peninsula instead. As it was, even with his limited numbers, he was doing pretty well.

Liverpool was a good choice as War Minister for he had great faith in the Peninsular campaign's strategic value and in Wellington's ability to conduct it. He therefore readily agreed to Wellington's request for further reinforcements to bring his army up to the minimum of 30,000 which he regarded as essential for successfully defending Portugal. After Talavera the situation had changed dramatically. Wellington had retired once more to Portugal, Napoleon's peace with Austria had released huge numbers of soldiers for the business of conquering Spain (and Soult soon set about it in Andalusia), while Masséna, much against his wishes, had been appointed to command the Army of Portugal, and with 70,000 men was required by the Emperor to turn Wellington out once and for all. That he totally failed to do so is explained by the special conditions which existed in Spain and Portugal, nearly all of them helping the British and obstructing the French. No matter how many times the Spanish armies were defeated, their towns sacked, their guerrilla leaders hanged, the Spanish people went on with their fanatical and merciless resistance. This meant that the various French Marshals in different parts of the country had no idea what their fellow Marshals were doing. No coordination of their activities was possible. Unless escorted by hundreds of cavalrymen, messengers from one general to another simply did not get through. The French commanders were starved of information. 'Each valley, each outpost, each town', wrote A. G. Macdonnell, 'was entirely cut off from its neighbours by the fanatical peasants with their knives and their ambuscades.' Wellington on the other hand was constantly supplied with information about French movements. There was also the question of supplies. The maxim that in Spain a small army is defeated and a large army starves was true enough as far as the large French army was concerned. But the small British army had not been defeated and would not be. A further reason for this was that in October 1809 Wellington had given orders that with the greatest possible secrecy three great defensive lines were to be constructed north of Lisbon, the celebrated Lines of Torres Vedras. The Commander-in-Chief was leaving nothing to chance. Either these defences would stop the French short in their tracks, or they would impose the necessary delay on them, should a re-embarkation of his army become unavoidable.

Masséna arrived at Salamanca in May 1810, with the fiery Michel Ney as his second-in-command. Their first task was to capture the frontier fortresses of Ciudad Rodrigo and Almeida and open the roads to Portugal. Wellington was determined to delay their advance as long as possible in order to gather the harvest and complete his defensive preparations further south. Ciudad Rodrigo held out until July, while Craufurd's Light Division continued to harass the French and force them to deploy as they advanced towards Almeida. But Craufurd was unwise enough to try the game once too often, despite a warning from Wellington not to dally in open country, when Ney realized that he had but a light rearguard in front of him and attacked with his whole corps including cavalry. It was then that the Light Division showed what it was made of. Putting into practice all that Moore had taught them, fighting in small groups, shooting, moving back covered by another group, those matchless regiments the 43rd, 52nd and 95th enabled their horse artillery to make for the one bridge over the river Coa. Yet they were nearly overwhelmed by Ney's men, and only a furious counter-attack by the 52nd saved many of them from being cut off before they could cross the bridge. Craufurd lost several hundred, including some thirty officers, of his precious men, although this loss was partially redeemed by their accounting for 500 of Ney's people as they tried to capture the bridge. It was characteristic of Wellington that he shielded Craufurd from blame, accepting the responsibility himself. Almeida held out until late August, then it was time for the British to fall back on their prepared positions. Before reaching the Lines of Torres Vedras, however, Masséna was to get a taste of what the British redcoats could do. At Bussaco it was the same story all over again, the French gallantly pressing forward to take the ground on which the long lines of British infantry were positioned, and being met by artillery and steady rifle fire, then being charged by seemingly unstoppable men. We may perhaps follow the fortunes of two battalions – the 88th Foot, the famous Connaught Rangers, and our old friends, the 52nd.

Because Wellington's line was lengthy, there were inevitable gaps, and when one division of Reynier's Corps succeeded in the morning mists of 26 September in reaching the crest of the hill between two battalions of Picton's 3rd Division, the Connaught Rangers, who had a reputation of being magnificent fighters and equally excellent at plunder, were left in no doubt by their colonel, Wallace, what was expected of them. Having told them to mind what they were about and to pay attention, he made it clear that when they came face to face with those French rascals, they were to drive them down the hill. 'Don't give the false touch but push home to the muzzle!' Sure enough, Wallace's rapid action and his soldiers' furious courage, well supported as they were by the fire of artillery and a Portuguese battalion, pushed the intruding French down the slope again. In another action further to the north of the British position, a similar sort of shock was awaiting the men of Ney's Corps. Arthur Bryant has depicted it incomparably well:

A few hundred yards to the left Craufurd was standing at the edge of the hill watching the Rifles and the Portuguese contesting every foot of ground with Loison's column. Yet it was not on the skirmishers of the 95th and the 1st Cacadores among the heathery boulders below that Craufurd was relying. Drawn up in the sunken roadway behind him, out of sight of the enemy, were the eighteen hundred bayonets of the 43rd and 52nd. Just as the French drums were beating for the final charge and their officers, capering up and down like madmen, were waving their hats on their swords and urging their men to rush the last twenty yards and seize Ross's guns on the skyline, Craufurd turned to the two famous regiments lying behind him and shouted, in a high, screaming voice that cleft the uproar, 'Now 52nd, revenge the death of Sir John Moore!' With a great cheer the men rushed forward and poured such a fire from the crest into the astonished French that the whole six thousand were dashed in a few minutes to the bottom.

Masséna lost between four and five thousand men in the battle of Bussaco, the British about one-quarter of that amount. Yet Wellington knew, despite his successful demonstration of what the British Army could do, that he must withdraw further, leaving behind him scorched earth as far as was possible. He was able, because of his superior knowledge of the country, to keep ahead of the French, and able also to rely on his cavalry and the Rifle Brigade to conduct a proper rearguard action, until his army was able to take up its positions behind the barrier, of which most of them were ignorant, of the impregnable Lines of Torres Vedras. It was for just this sort of strategic withdrawal that Wellington earned himself the reputation of being a Fabian general. But after all, as he himself put it: 'Britain has but one Army, so we had better look after it.' Yet, as we shall see, when the opportunity offered itself, he could be devastatingly bold and swift in the attack.

So well had the secret of Torres Vedras been kept that when the French came up against the defences in October 1810, they were totally nonplussed. Masséna had been given to understand by Portuguese collaborators that south of Coimbra the country would be open, rolling and free of serious obstacles. Now he was confronted with a series of elaborate defences with redoubts, earthworks and trenches, bristling with guns and established on a range of mountains. What cover might have existed before in approaching the defences had been destroyed, so that any attack would be exposed to appalling cross-fire. The way forward was further barred by marshes, defiles, palisades and parapets. Furthermore the whole thing was in immense depth. Every route to Lisbon was covered by guns, and the Royal Navy's ships were on either flank, both at sea and on the Tagus. Masséna's irritation at not being informed boiled over when excuses were made about not knowing what Wellington had been doing. '*Que diable*', he declared, '*il n'a pas construit ces montagnes*.' When Ney, 'Bravest of the Brave', took a look at the defences, he for once refused to mount an attack on them. They could hardly have been paid a higher compliment. The young French cavalryman, de Rocca of the 2nd Hussars, summed up the French army's dilemma in these words: 'Before them was a wall of brass; behind them the region of famine'. In making this comment de Rocca demonstrated how fruitful Wellington's strategy had been, for Masséna's Army of Portugal simply sat down in front of the Lines of Torres Vedras, and suffered. It suffered still more when it retreated to Spain.

Masséna hung grimly on throughout the winter, achieving little except Wellington's surprise and admiration that any army could survive for so long. Indeed it was only by further arousing the hatred of the Portuguese that the French soldiers were able to obtain provisions at all, indulging in what was called *la chasse aux hommes*, the hunting down of local peasants and then subjecting them to such ill-treatment that whatever concealed food there was, was handed over. Such a policy did not make for easy times ahead when in March 1811 and despite Ney's plea for an offensive, Masséna gave orders for retreat into Spain. Wellington's withdrawal from Spain to Portugal had been bad enough, but at least his lines of communication had been secure, his defences prepared and his reserve of supplies plentiful. No such conditions favoured the French in their retreat to Spain. It was a nightmare for soldiers and local inhabitants alike. Sir William Napier's stark description gives us the flavour of it:

> Every horror that could make war hideous attended this retreat. Distress, conflagrations, death, in all modes from wounds, from fatigue, from water, from the flames, from starvation! On all sides unlimited violence, unlimited vengeance. I myself saw a peasant hounding on his dog to devour the dead and dying, and the spirit of cruelty smote even the brute creation; for the French general, to lessen encumbrances, ordered beasts of burden to be destroyed, and the inhuman fellow charged with the execution hamstringed five hundred asses and left them to starve; they were so found by the British, and the mute, sad expression of pain and grief visible in the poor creatures' looks excited a strange fury in the soldiers: no quarter would have been given at that time: humane feelings would have thus led direct to cruelty. But all passions are akin to madness.*

It was not only on animals that the French soldiers wreaked vengeance for the murder of their stragglers by the guerrillas. Unspeakable atrocities were committed by them in Portuguese villages. One British soldier writing about it later recorded that he had never seen such

* *History of the War in the Peninsula.*

wanton destruction – in houses everything had been cut in pieces, smashed, torn up or torn down. One room contained human bodies half-consumed by fire, their scorched faces bearing expressions of extreme horror. 'In a bag lying at the upper end of the apartment was the dead body of a young child, who had been strangled: the cord was still tight about its little neck'.*

Yet the French paid a heavy price. Pursued by Wellington's advance guard and making for his bases at the frontier forts of Almeida and Ciudad Rodrigo Masséna's army struggled over the mountainous tracks of central Portugal, crossing into Spain at last early in April. He had lost over 25,000 men, nearly 6,000 horses, munitions, baggage and transport. Yet he still held Almeida, Badajoz and Ciudad Rodrigo. Wellington would need them all before he could carry the fight once more into Spain. Before he set about it, he and his army had been heartened by the news that the Duke of York had been reinstated as Commander-in-Chief at home, replacing the rigidly bureaucratic Dundas. In all his dealings Wellington was an essentially practical man, who in the day-to-day administration of his army was meticulous in his attention to detail. Campaigning as he did in a country where everything had to be supplied, mostly from England, before he could undertake any manoeuvres, it was hardly surprising. Indeed to some extent, Bagehot's estimate of a great soldier fitted Wellington well. Having rejected the idea of a general's being a romantic creature, fanciful about a female or a Sovereign, Bagehot depicted him as quiet and grave, surrounded by maps and charts, exact in calculations, a master tactician immersed in detail, eschewing all forms of eloquence and grand gestures, thinking – and here Bagehot was specific in his attribution 'as the Duke of Wellington was said to do, *most* of the shoes of his soldiers'. Wellington certainly did think of his soldiers' shoes, but there was far more to him than that. He was above all a master of the battlefield. What irritated him so much was to be bombarded with reams of useless paper. He pointed out to Liverpool that if he were to answer all the drivelling letters written to him, he would have no time for campaigning. Furthermore he was determined to ensure that those officers under his command would have comparable freedom to get on with their first duty, 'which is and always has been so to train the private men under his command that they may without question beat any force opposed to them in the field'. Thus the re-appointment of the Duke of York, who had already done so much to improve and simplify the Army's administration, was especially welcome to Wellington.

Since his supplies must for the time being come across Portugal, his next task was to clear the French from the frontier forts and, sending Spencer (who commanded the 1st Division) to invest Almeida, he went

---

* *The Eventful Life of a Soldier*, J. Donaldson (94th Foot), Edinburgh, 1827.

to confer with Beresford, who was still in command of the Portuguese Army, as to how they might best get on with the capture of Badajoz. But while doing so he received news that Masséna had reorganized his army and with nearly 47,000 troops, including almost 5,000 cavalry (the British were still short of cavalry) and some forty guns was making for Almeida to take on the numerically inferior British Army there. The result was the battle of Fuentes de Oñore fought on 11 May 1811, at which Wellington came closer to defeat than ever before, as his right flank was open and extremely vulnerable to cavalry. Once again the Light Division with Craufurd, supported by British and German dragoons and hussars, distinguished itself in repelling French attacks, while Bull's Troop of the Royal Horse Artillery did magnificent work. Masséna's main attack on the British front near the village itself was a desperate affair, with hand-to-hand fighting, another charge by our friends the Connaught Rangers, and the village streets chock-full of dead soldiers. But the British line held. Masséna withdrew and did not renew his attacks. He had lost over 2,000 men and after two days of martial display in front of the British lines, he moved his army back to Salamanca. Masséna had fought his last battle, and was soon to leave Salamanca for France, consoled by awarding himself all his back pay from money which had arrived for the army, and consoled too by his young mistress, who had accompanied him throughout the campaign dressed – when she had her clothes on – in the uniform of an officer of light dragoons. The Marshal who came to replace him was Marmont, Napoleon's gunner friend, and a great organizer. He had a remarkable effect on the somewhat demoralized Army of Portugal. He got rid of troublesome senior officers, giving command of divisions to younger men, he had great care for all the soldiers, and by hard work and enthusiasm he transformed the morale of his army. So quickly did his methods take effect that before long he was manoeuvring against Wellington.

Wellington had not been at his best at Fuentes de Oñore and observed later that 'if Boney had been there we should have been beaten'. Nevertheless the British Army had once again demonstrated that it was the only one which could stand up to and repel a set-piece attack by the French. One of his comments on the affair, when he appealed to the Government for money to re-house some of the local inhabitants, was characteristic of his eloquent economy of words when making a report. Having been the scene of a battle, he commented drily, the village had not been greatly improved. Although his purpose in fighting the battle at all – to ensure that his siege of Almeida was not relieved by the French – had been achieved, he was not pleased by the subsequent escape of the enemy's garrison there and later link-up with Masséna, which had occurred because of negligence by his own officers. Not for the first time he complained that unless he were present himself everywhere, things would go wrong. This concern, however, could not be said to extend to the battle of Albuera, fought on 16 May 1811 by Beresford, who had been trying to reduce Badajoz, against Soult's relieving force. Battle was joined before Wellington himself could get there. Beresford had some 37,000 men, made up of 12,000 Portuguese, 15,000 Spanish and 10,000 British, and he had concentrated his force east of Badajoz by the village of Albuera. The battle itself was a brutal and bloody slogging match, distinguished by the British infantry's refusal to contemplate defeat. It was here that the 57th Foot (Middlesex) won their immortal title of 'The Diehards', and where Cole's 4th Division finally tipped the scales by attacking the flank of the advancing French. William Napier's record of it defies comparison:

> Such a gallant line issuing from the midst of the smoke, and rapidly separating itself from the confused and broken multitude, startled the enemy's heavy masses, which were increasing and pressing onwards to an assured victory; they wavered, hesitated, and then vomiting forth a storm of fire, hastily endeavoured to enlarge their front, while a fearful discharge of grape from all their artillery whistled through the British ranks ... the Fusilier battalions, struck by the iron tempest, reeled, and staggered like sinking ships. But suddenly and sternly recovering, they closed on their terrible enemies, and then was seen with what a strength and majesty the British soldier fights. In vain did Soult, by voice and gesture, animate his Frenchmen; in vain did the hardiest veterans, extricating themselves from the crowded columns, sacrifice their lives to gain time for the mass to open out on such a fair field; in vain did the mass itself bear up, and fiercely striving, fire indiscriminately upon friends and foes while the horsemen hovering on the flank threatened to charge the advancing line. Nothing could stop that astonishing infantry.

In a battle which lasted seven hours, the casualties were appalling, so much so that each side believed it had been defeated. Yet the British remained in command of the battlefield. Two-thirds of the 6,500 British infantry engaged had fallen. Soult had lost almost 7,000 men, and angrily recorded that there was no beating British troops, in spite of their generals. 'I always thought they were bad soldiers; now I am sure of it. I had turned their right, pierced their centre and everywhere victory was mine, but they did not know how to run.' Once again the British had shown the French that their system of manoeuvre against steady troops was false. Yet Beresford too had been so shaken by the Allied casualties (both Spanish and Portuguese troops fought bravely) that Wellington on catching up with him was obliged to re-draft the dispatch so that Albuera could be hailed as a victory rather than a defeat. But of even greater concern to Wellington was that his army could not continue to afford the scale of casualties suffered at Albuera, and at the same time resume the offensive which is what he was now resolved to do.

He was, however, obliged to wait until 1812 before doing so, for although he took personal command of the Badajoz siege, his lack of an adequate siege train, together with the news that Soult and Marmont were marching against him, forced a further withdrawal, this time across the Agueda to cantonments at Sabugal. For once the Marshals decided not to pursue the English leopards. Former attempts to do so in winter had resulted in grievous loss to their armies by lack of supplies and an abundance of guerrilla action. The French made no further effort to conquer Portugal. The campaign of 1811 therefore ended with Wellington in winter quarters and in possession of only one frontier fort, Almeida. To take the war into Spain, he would require to storm and take the other two – Ciudad Rodrigo and Badajoz. Until the New Year he could rest his army, demand supplies from home and in particular insist on a siege train for his planned offensive. In December he at last had what he needed. Furthermore, support from home would continue, for the Prince Regent had made it clear that he intended to stick to the existing Government, however much he might dislike Perceval. The return of Castlereagh as Foreign Secretary (Wellesley had resigned) would give Wellington another staunch ally in the Government. It could hardly be said that the French Marshals in Spain were enjoying the same sort of support from Napoleon, who would constantly issue orders to them which took no account of the actual situation on the ground, no matter if it had to do with communications (because he himself had only advanced and retired over the main routes of Spain, he thought all Spanish roads were similar), the weather, state of supplies or the enemy. He kept insisting to Marmont, for example, that the British army was not in a position to take the field at the very time when Wellington was about to resume the offensive. Marmont himself wrote later that in the early part of 1812 the Emperor 'was living in a non-existent world, created by his own imagination'. He was making pictures which conformed not to reality, but his own desires. One of Marmont's fellow commanders, General Thiébault, made a similar point when he objected that you could not direct a war from a distance of three or four hundred leagues (that is, about 1,000 miles). In any case, whatever absurd orders Napoleon might be giving to the Marshals in Spain, he would before long be wholly absorbed in the final absurdity – the march on Moscow.

Meanwhile Wellington, aware that Marmont had been obliged to dispatch troops to Valencia, set his army forward on the road to Ciudad Rodrigo. He began his advance on the first day of 1812, in the middle of winter, the cold so intense that some soldiers died of it, but by 7 January he had invested the fortress, and the following night the San Francisco redoubt was captured by a few hundred men of the

Light Division under Colonel Colborne in a night attack so swift and silent that the French garrison was overwhelmed almost before they knew an attack was in progress. Digging entrenchments for the main assault began immediately, and when Wellington heard that Marmont was preparing to march to relieve the fortress, he ordered a bombardment which made two breaches in the defences. On the night of 9 January Picton's 3rd Division and Craufurd's Light Division led the assault. The troops' behaviour both before and during the assault was magnificent; after they had gained the town it was disgraceful. An observer of the leading assault party of the Light Division remembered seeing quiet determination written on their faces, as if they knew both how serious and how important a business had been entrusted to them. Greeting a friend or comrade here and there, they marched by and 'there was an indescribable *something* about them'. Comparable enthusiasm greeted Picton's words of encouragement to his men, when he told them that he had no intention of expending powder. They would do it with cold iron. When the moment of the assault came, the storming parties suffered severely as the French fired musket balls and grape-shot at those leading the attack. The incomparable Craufurd was himself killed as the Light Division went forward. Another general, Mackinnon, directing the 3rd Division's assault, was killed when a French magazine exploded. In those days generals led from the front. Yet half an hour sufficed to do the business. The Governor of Ciudad Rodrigo surrendered to an officer of the Light Division, but for the inhabitants the worst part of the night was still to come. After the appalling effects of a hail of bullets, shells and canister, not simply killing their comrades, but blowing them to pieces, in the sheer excitement and elation which their victory brought them, blood-stained and scorched, ragingly thirsty, the British redcoats became temporarily uncontrollable, all discipline gone, mad for drink and plunder. 'Guided by the baser inhabitants and the light of blazing houses', wrote Arthur Bryant, 'they quickly found what they sought. For the rest of the night, until the light of dawn enabled the harassed provost marshals to restore order, Ciudad Rodrigo became a hell on earth, where officers, hoarse from shouting, drew their swords on their own men in an attempt to save the persons of terrified citizens and where packs of drunken soldiers ran from house to house in diabolical rage. Few lives were lost but the town was completely sacked.' What really mattered, however, was that another frontier fortress was in British hands. Now Wellington could turn his attention to Badajoz.

Badajoz! the very name is like a knell, conjuring up visions of entrenchments, breaches, ramparts and storming parties; ditches, ladders, Forlorn Hopes going forward, only to be blasted to bloody smithereens; attack after attack repulsed; Wellington, aware of appalling losses, yet still no success at the breaches, and at length under desperate strain calling off the attack at the very time when, although he was unaware of it, a subsidiary assault had succeeded; the French defenders retiring when their positions are threatened from the rear; Badajoz falling to the British, and then two days and nights of drinking, looting, raping, killing – not to be stopped or restrained by officers, the provost marshals or any other authority, until on the third day fresh troops are marched in, the gallows erected and order at last restored. What sort of army had it become after nearly four years of campaigning that could rise to such heights of gallant endeavour and heroic perseverance and then after achieving the well-nigh impossible, plunge to a nadir of unspeakable depravity and uncontrollable ill-discipline?

It had become an extraordinary mixture of fighting talent and individual eccentricity. Its men were hardened, bronzed, foul-mouthed, eager for a fight, full of coarse humour, persistently on the scrounge, insatiable in their appetite for liquor, yet curiously tender in their concern for a wounded enemy or an ill-treated peasant. Confident of their superiority over Johnny Crapaud, fiercely proud of Regiment, moved still by love of country, they would in the heat of battle rush upon the French with patriotic cries like 'Hurrah for old England'. They were, of course, well commanded. Those officers who had found campaigning under such uncomfortable conditions a bit too much for them had long since returned home, their Commander-in-Chief acknowledging with icy contempt that business or restoration of health demanded this return. But these were the exceptions. In general the regimental officers represented all that was best in both Hotspur and Prince Hal. They scorned dishonour, were truthful, fearless and straightforward, led from the front, and although full of fun and ever ready for a lark, were imbued with a deep sense of Christian duty. It was not for recognition or applause or show, and certainly not for gain, that they fought so well and endured such hardships – usually with a joke on their lips – but to be true to themselves, and never to let down their comrades or their regiment. To have gone home on sick leave, even when it was justifiable, would have seemed to them a betrayal. Together these rough, plundering, jesting, hard and coolly confident men, officered, as Wellington put it, by gentlemen 'who have something more at stake than a reputation for military smartness' made a team which had shed all the rigid drills, so abhorred by Sir John Moore, and had acquired the very adaptability and individuality which he had advocated and instilled into his Corps of Riflemen. But now, Moore's ideas, which had proved so triumphant in practice, had been adopted by the whole Army.

Wellington himself, although on the whole well served by his subordinate commanders, was not slow to find fault with them when he deemed it necessary. He was understandably concerned to ensure that the reins of command remained in his own hands. 'Sir Thomas Picton,' said the Duke on one occasion, 'I sent for you to hear my orders, not to receive yours.' Too often, alas, his instructions were disregarded. There is a pleasing irony in his letters and dispatches when commenting on these matters. 'Nobody in the British Army,' he wrote to Colonel Torrens, the Military Secretary, 'ever reads an order or regulation in any manner but as an amusing novel, and the consequence is, that when complicated arrangements are to be carried into execution, every gentleman proceeds according to his own fancy; and then, when the arrangement fails (as it must if the order is not strictly obeyed), they come upon me to set matters to rights; and thus my labour is increased tenfold.' As for regimental officers it was clear that the army's discipline depended on their diligence, and these officers were responsible for ensuring that orders received by them were carried out to the letter. It was not enough simply to pass the orders on. It was essential personally to see them executed. One of Wellington's great qualities as a Commander-in-Chief was that his orders were invariably clear. They did not permit of misunderstanding. It was therefore particularly necessary that they were obeyed. Again his playful irony creeps in when he observes to Villiers, British Minister at Lisbon, that 'the foundation of all military plans is compounded of the situation of one's own troops, those of the allies, and those of the enemy: but if I cannot be certain even of my own, it is impossible for me to form, much less to execute, any military plan.' We may allow ourselves also wholly to endorse his expectation that whatever a man's right to form and retain his own opinion, when he came into the army, it was his, Wellington's, opinion that mattered and determined what was to be done.

Yet for all his observations about the army's shortcomings, Wellington knew that he could rely on them to fight. At Badajoz he would put them to the test as never before. The army's great strength still lay, of course, in its regiments. Arthur Bryant wrote:

> Pride in the continuing regiment – the personal individual loyalty which each private felt towards his corps gave to the British soldier a moral strength which the student and administrator ought never to under-estimate. It enabled him to stand firm and fight forward when men without it, however brave, would have failed. To let down the regiment, to be unworthy of the men of old who had marched under the same colours, to be untrue to the comrades who had shared the same loyalties, hardships and perils were things that the least-tutored, humblest soldier would not do.

And what regiments they were that now prepared for the assault on Badajoz! Perhaps most renowned of all were those of the Light Division – the 95th green-jacketed Rifles, with their brothers in arms, the redcoated 43rd and 52nd; yet in company with this élite band were the majestic and incomparably disciplined Foot Guards, the regiments of Fusiliers, the wild Connaught Rangers and the staunch Highlanders, together with all the infantry Line regiments, upon whom Wellington was to rely time and time again, never in vain.

On the night of 6 April 1812 the Light Division and the 4th Division stormed the south-eastern breaches, while Picton's 3rd Division would attempt to take the castle to the north of the city and Leith's 5th Division would demonstrate on the north-west side and try to take the San Vincente bastion. As we have seen, it was not the main assault on the breaches that gave Badajoz to Wellington, but diversionary attacks elsewhere. When we hear what it was like to storm the French defences from a soldier who was there,* we may understand why attempt after attempt on the breaches failed:

> Hundreds fell, dropping at every discharge which maddened the living; the cheer was for ever on, on, with screams of vengeance and a fury determined to win the town; the rear pushed the foremost into the sword-blades to make a bridge of their bodies rather than be frustrated. Slaughter, tumult and disorder continued; no command could be heard, the wounded struggling to free themselves from under the bleeding bodies of their dead comrades; the enemy's guns within a few yards at every fire opening a bloody lane amongst our people, who closed up and, with shouts of terror as the lava burned them up, pressed on to destruction – officers, starting forward with an heroic impulse, carried on their men to the yawning breach and glittering steel, which still belched out flames of scorching death.

For three hours it went on, until at about midnight Wellington called off the assault. Even as the orders to withdraw were going out, he received the news that Picton's 3rd Division had succeeded in scaling the cliffs and capturing the castle. In doing so his Division lost one-third of its attacking strength, among them Colonel Ridge of the 5th Fusiliers, of whom Napier wrote that although many men died that night amidst much glory, no man died with more glory than he. Together with Picton's success, the 5th Division under Leith entered the town at San Vincente, and with such British strength in their rear, the French garrison surrendered. It was all over except for the ghastly business of drinking, looting, raping, murdering – a fiendish sack of the town, lightened only by Captain Harry Smith's rescue, wooing of and subsequent marriage to Juanita Maria de los Dolores de Leon.†

Taking Badajoz had cost Wellington 5,000 men. Of these no fewer than 3,500 had been from his precious Light and 4th Divisions, the cream of his army. In his dispatch to Liverpool, Wellington recorded

---

* *Rough Notes by an Old Soldier*, G. Bell, 2 Vols, Day, 1867.
† Who will always be remembered not only for herself, but for the town, Ladysmith, named after her when her husband was Governor of the Cape, and which was besieged by the Boers in 1899, and relieved by Buller in the following year – Winston Churchill, of course, there in full Yeomanry fig.

that the fortress's capture had illustrated such gallantry in the troops as had never before been displayed, but he added his anxious hope that he would never again be obliged to put them to such a test. He had known that it would mean losing some of his best officers and men, yet it had been necessary because he still lacked a proper corps of sappers and miners – a deficiency which he urged Liverpool to make good without delay. Despite these losses, however, he soon took the offensive into Spain, first to deal with Marmont. While he and the French Marshal were manoeuvring against each other, Perceval, the Prime Minister, had been assassinated and been succeeded by Liverpool, thus ensuring continuity of Government policy and of support for Wellington. It was at this time too, June 1812, that Napoleon set the Grande Armée on the road to Moscow, thereby bringing about its destruction. If the British Army had in its small way been multiplying the Emperor's difficulties by fighting in the Peninsula, the Emperor was now about to make the British Army's task there much easier. That this was so owed much to Czar Alexander I's refusal to be intimidated. When faced with the seemingly invincible armies of Napoleon, he was not dismayed. In spite of them, he declared, in spite of the world's greatest captain, the most valiant lieutenants, *space* was a barrier, and by leaving his defence to the climate, he might yet have the last word. He did indeed have the last word, for six months later Napoleon was back in Paris, having lost half a million men. He had achieved nothing. Yet Russia was once more an ally of England.

Napoleon was still driving his diminishing, doomed army to the east in July 1812, when Wellington – whose battles up to this time had been largely defensive, infantry affairs – showed that given the opportunity he could be quick, bold and decisive in the offensive and employ cavalry with devastating effect. He was fortunate that for this next battle his Heavy Cavalry Brigade was commanded by Major General Le Marchant, whom we last met with his publication about Sword Exercise. On 22 July Wellington and Marmont were manoeuvring their armies south-east of Salamanca, when Marmont, unaware of his enemy's full strength because some British divisions were concealed behind hills, extended his left wing too far. As soon as Wellington saw it, he moved forward the 3rd Division under his brother-in-law, Pakenham, with Le Marchant's Heavy Cavalry Brigade in support. So effective were the combined infantry and cavalry attacks that Wellington, in a rare observation of congratulation for the cavalry, told Cotton (the overall cavalry commander) that he had never seen anything so beautiful in his life. The battle was lost and won in half an hour. Marmont himself was wounded early on in the action. The French lost 14,000 men, the British about one-third of this number. Napier waxed eloquent on the subject of Le Marchant's charge:

As they passed the left of the Third Division Le Marchant's heavy horsemen, flanked by Anson's light cavalry, broke forth at full speed, and the next instant twelve hundred French infantry, though formed in several lines, were trampled down with a terrible clamour and disturbance. Bewildered and blinded, they cast away their arms and ran through the openings of the British squadrons stooping and demanding quarter, while the dragoons, big men on big horses, rode onward smiting with their long glittering swords in uncontrollable power, and the Third Division followed at speed, shouting as the French masses fell in succession before this dreadful charge.

Le Marchant was killed for, as always, he was in the lead. Apart from French casualties, the British had further triumphed by capturing twenty guns and two Eagles. Wellington always thought of it as one of his greatest victories. The road to Madrid was now open and he took it. Yet although he entered the capital, hailed as a liberator, and then took his army north to Burgos, hoping that if Spanish guerrillas could keep the French in Andalusia and Catalonia quiet, he could capture Burgos, cut off French supplies, isolate their various armies and so end the campaign, he was to be disappointed. Burgos held out, the French rallied and threatened Madrid and Wellington had no choice but to retire, reconcentrate his Army, and once more retreat through Salamanca and Ciudad Rodrigo to Portugal – much to the chagrin of the soldiers, who could not understand why it was necessary, their spirits not being improved by the appalling November weather and severe shortage of food. The Army lost 4,000 stragglers, while thousands more died from fever and disease. Nearly one-third of Wellington's entire force was suffering some form of sickness. The whole affair was not greatly helped by the Commander-in-Chief's putting blame on to regimental officers for failing to do their duty and maintain proper discipline. His harsh condemnation was deeply resented by these same officers who could hardly be held responsible for an acute lack of clothing, boots and food. How, some of them asked, could they deserve censure for privations suffered by the army because of faulty staff work causing supply-trains to be in the wrong place? Yet although Wellington's disappointment and that of his army at not finishing off the campaign in 1812 and at having to bear the humiliation of one more retreat, one more winter in Portugal may be comprehended, his strategy had already borne great fruits. Victory was at hand. The French were still hard put to coordinate their activities, had found no answer to defeat the Spanish guerrillas or the British Army, had suffered huge losses of men, weapons and supplies. Spain had turned into a cancer for the Grande Armée, which took its dreadful toll just as surely as the Russian winter and Russian armies.

In 1812 the British Army was in action not only in the Peninsula, but in America too. The United States' President Madison had found sufficient grievances against Britain, mostly maritime, to persuade both the House of Representatives and the Senate that war should be declared. It was, in June. On land the war was waged principally either side of the frontier with Canada, resulting in successes and advances by both sides, but it was inconclusive. Dashing naval actions were equally so. At the end of 1814, with the Peninsular War over (many of Wellington's veterans were then sent to fight there), peace came. Britain and the United States had far more to gain from each other by trade than by war. Even before this peace was concluded, the struggle with France itself had come to an end. Napoleon was not turned off his throne by Wellington, but rather by Blücher's armies appearing at the gates of Paris. Moscow may have destroyed the Grande Armée, yet on his return Napoleon instantly set about creating another. Only a few months after the end of the Russian campaign, in April 1813, Napoleon was in personal command of nearly one-quarter of a million soldiers on the Elbe and Weser, while in Spain there were still 200,000 fighting men. As A. G. Macdonnell observed: 'What a country! And what a man!' Yet this time the Allies were too much for him, and in spite of some brilliant defensive actions at Lützen and Bautzen, even the Emperor admitted that his game was going wrong, his star setting. The Allies were growing in numbers and confidence, and the news of Wellington's victory at Vitoria in June 1813 spurred them to take the field once more. Wellington had left Portugal for the last time at the end of May, and advancing rapidly to Salamanca, Valladolid and Burgos, outflanking the French and forcing them to retire, he at length came up with an enemy force of some 65,000 commanded by Napoleon's brother, Joseph (his principal military adviser, Marshal Jourdan having wisely retired to bed when he heard of Joseph's decision to stand and fight in the position chosen). Wellington with 80,000 made light work of it. 'After a series of tentative skirmishes,' says A. G. Macdonnell, 'Joseph found that the English left wing was closing round behind him, whereupon the entire French Army bolted across the mountains to Pampeluna, leaving behind them 151 out of 153 guns, a million pounds sterling, and all the thousands of wagon-loads of loot which six years of steady and skilful looting had accumulated.' Soult took over in Spain and although there were still a few battles to fight, the Peninsular campaign was virtually over. Further north the battle of Leipzig destroyed Napoleon's last army in October 1813, and the Allied armies closed in inexorably on France. By early April 1814, when Wellington fought his last battle of the campaign at Toulouse, even Napoleon's Marshals had had enough, for the Allies were now at the gates of Paris, and when Ney made it clear that the army would obey, not the Emperor, but its generals, even the greatest genius of the age saw that the game was finally up, and abdicated.

Before we rejoin both Napoleon and Wellington on the battlefield of
Waterloo, we may perhaps note one tribute made to Wellington and
the British Army in the Peninsula by the French Marshal Bugeaud. He
is describing the effect of the British infantry's tactics against an
advancing French column:

> As the column moved forward some men hoisted their shakos on
> their musket, the quick-step became a run; the ranks began to be
> mixed up; the men's agitation became tumultuous, many soldiers
> began to fire as they ran. And all the while the red English line, still
> silent and motionless, even when we were only 300 yards away,
> seemed to take no notice of the storm which was about to break on
> it . . . At this moment of painful expectation the English line would
> make a quarter-turn, the muskets were going up to the 'ready'. An
> indefinable sensation nailed to the spot many of our men, who
> halted and began to open a wavering fire. The enemy's return, a
> volley of simultaneous precision and deadly effect, crashed upon us
> like a thunderbolt. Decimated by it we reeled together . . . Then
> three formidable *Hurrahs*! terminated the long silence of our
> adversaries. With the third they were down upon us, pressing us
> into disorderly retreat.

Rarely could there have been a more categorical endorsement of
Wellington's contention that the French system of tactical manoeuvre
was a false one against steady troops. Napoleon would have done well
to pay attention to what some of his Marshals had to tell him about the
performance of British soldiers and their Fabian general, but the
Emperor was incapable of accepting unpalatable advice and made the
error of grossly under-estimating Wellington. In fact Wellington had
achieved all that he had set himself to do in the Peninsula. He had
successfully defended Portugal; he had cooperated with the Spanish
Army and assisted the guerrillas to hold down and account for huge
numbers of French soldiers; he had defeated Marshal after Marshal,
and despite the need to retreat all too frequently, much to the disgust
of his army, his strategy had in the end paid great dividends. He had
moreover won the complete confidence of his subordinate commanders and the private soldiers.

Of course, Wellington was commissariat minded. Having learned
his lessons of command in a desert, he had to be. Of course, he was
occupied with detail. Having an oft-changing and not always
experienced staff, he was bound to be. Of course, he was a cautious
tactician. Having only one small army, facing many larger French
ones, he could not afford a single serious reverse. He may have
condemned his army for ill-discipline at times, called them infamous
and the scum of the earth, but he also had infinite confidence in his
men, took great pride in their understanding each other, and could
hardly have awarded them higher praise when he said of his Peninsular

Army that with it he could have gone anywhere and done anything. When Disraeli claimed that Wellington left his country a great legacy – the contemplation of his character – he might have added the perusal of his dispatches. For, being models of candour, industry and common sense, they are the key to his character. On another occasion Disraeli described parts of them as the best reading he had ever come across, and even the Duke himself, the first man to eschew all forms of humbug, was, on reading some of them over, 'surprised to find them so good – they are as good as I could write now. They show the same attention to details – to the pursuit of all means, however small, that could promote success.' In this last phrase he puts his finger on one of his own finest attributes. Nothing was too much trouble for him. It was also very much to be noted that in his dispatches, as Lemoinne pointed out in a contribution to the *Journal des Débats*, 'the word *glory* never occurs, but always the word *duty*'. If we were required to choose one word to epitomize Wellington's character, it would of course be – duty.

One duty which Wellington took especially seriously was that of improving the lot of the ordinary soldier. We find him writing to Lord Liverpool with that agreeable coalition of common sense and irony: 'I beg only to mention that the soldiers cannot cook their food unless they have camp-kettles.' Eventually he was successful in getting their needs seen to. Before undertaking his final, decisive Peninsular campaign of 1813, his army's deficiencies in equipment had largely been made good – tents were issued, portable tin kettles, three pairs of shoes for every soldier with a spare pair of soles and heels in his knapsack. It was not just a question of keeping the instrument of his military policy in good running order (the prime duty of any commander), but also genuine concern for the welfare of his troops, as illustrated by his anger with General Murillo, when he heard that his Spanish ally was complaining about lack of supplies: 'How could he have the heart to make his unfortunate troops march without shoes or bread?' Yet in his great history of the Peninsular War, Oman was critical of Wellington in that although, according to Oman, he won his troops' confidence, he never gained their affection. This accusation is hardly borne out by Kincaid of the 95th Rifles: 'We anxiously longed for the return of Lord Wellington . . . as we would rather see his long nose in the fight than a reinforcement of ten thousand men any day . . . I'll venture to say that there was not a bosom in that army that did not beat more lightly, when it heard the joyful news of his arrival.' Even more telling are the cries of a private soldier: 'Whore's ar Arthur' and 'Aw wish he wor here.'

These sentiments hardly conjure up the picture of a cold, hard man who cared nothing for his soldiers. Indeed they thought of him with both respect and affection. He was, of course, a realist as to what sort of men they were, and their sometime ill-discipline provoked in him harsh words about them. But we find him saying too: 'I know of no point more important than closely to attend to the comfort of the soldier: let him be well clothed, sheltered and fed. How should he fight, poor fellow! if he has, besides risking his life, to struggle with unnecessary hardships . . .' and he adds a tip, with which most Commanding Officers in today's Army would agree: 'One ought to look sharp after the young officers, and be very indulgent to the soldier.' Ten years after his fighting days were over, Wellington told Croker that 'in our later campaigns and especially when we crossed the Pyrenees there never was an army in the world in better spirits, better order or better discipline. We had mended in discipline every campaign until at last I hope we were pretty near perfect.' There is no greater historian of the British Army than Fortescue, yet Fortescue in stating that Wellington was above all a patriot and that he took over the Army as an instrument for saving his country is surely mistaken when he added that 'when his purpose was fulfilled, he threw the instrument aside without compunction, having no further use for it'. Before we reach a final judgement here, we must see what use he put it to in the last and most celebrated of his victories.

CHAPTER EIGHT

A Damned Serious Business

Those Scots Greys, those Horse Guards, those regiments of Maitland and
Mitchell, that infantry of Pack and Kempt, that cavalry of Ponsonby and
Somerset, those Highlanders playing the pibroch under the shower of
grape-shot, those battalions of Ryland, those utterly raw recruits, who
hardly knew how to handle a musket holding their own against Essling's
and Rivoli's old troops, – that is what was grand.

VICTOR HUGO

During the very last weeks of Wellington's campaign in March 1814
as his advance guard reached Bordeaux, the inhabitants there
expressed themselves in favour of a Bourbon restoration. This was the
very sign that the British Foreign Secretary, Castlereagh – whose great
aim was to set up in France a government which would be stable and
would survive – had been waiting for. As was customary with the
British, in victory they were magnanimous, and Castlereagh was
determined, not to punish France, but to produce a settlement which
France itself would regard as just and therefore could be made to
work. Talleyrand had made it clear that the only alternative to
Bonaparte was the Bourbon Louis XVIII. When Czar Alexander I
suggested that Bernadotte (who had betrayed Napoleon by leading
Sweden's armies against him) might succeed to the throne, Talleyrand
had dismissed the idea by pointing out that if the French wanted a
soldier for the job, they still had the finest one in the world. Yet
Alexander was in agreement with Castlereagh about the need to check
Prussia in her desire for vengeance. Thus a Provisional Treaty of Paris
signed in April 1814* which settled Napoleon's immediate future
(Elba, title of Emperor, with adequate incomes for himself, Marie
Louise and Josephine) was followed at the end of May by a Treaty
signed by Louis XVIII, giving France her 1792 boundaries and
restoring most of her colonies. There was to be no indemnity. France
had been treated with great generosity. A further stipulation of the

* Signed: for France by Caulaincourt (Napoleon's last Foreign Secretary), Marshal
Macdonald, Marshal Ney; for Austria by Metternich; Russia by Nesselrode; Prussia
by Hardenberg; Great Britain by Castlereagh.

Treaty was that 'All the Powers engaged on either side in the present war shall, within the space of two months, send plenipotentiaries to Vienna for the purpose of regulating in General Congress the arrangements which are to complete the provision of the present treaty.' Having thus come to terms with a defeated enemy, the Allies had agreed to confer at the Congress of Vienna, and it is there in September 1814 that we may observe the peace-makers in all their glittering splendour in the company of one who was there, the Prince de Ligne.

Having noted the endless procession of fêtes and balls (*Le Congrès ne marche pas; il danse*) amidst the cries for peace, justice, balance of power and indemnity, de Ligne, as a mere looker-on, requires as indemnity only a new hat as he has worn his present one out doffing it to sovereigns whom he meets at every street corner. He sees the Emperor Alexander, a figure of graceful, martial appearance, and notes the tall dignity of the Prussian King; his own Emperor, Francis II of Austria, is dressed in a stiff Venetian suit which cannot hide his affability; the Kings of Bavaria, Denmark and Württemberg are there, together with the latter's son 'whose affection for the Grand Duchess of Oldenburg has brought him to the Congress, rather than the settlement of public business that will soon be his own'. Everywhere there are titles, princes, archdukes, reigning monarchs. The only untitled ones are Englishmen and they are distinguished 'by the richness of their clothes'. Apart from the crowned heads of Europe there were the statesmen: Metternich, principal manager of the Congress; Hardenberg of Prussia; Nesselrode, spokesman for the Czar; Talleyrand, whose patience and diplomacy were to do so much for France; Castlereagh, who was accompanied by Wellington. The territorial greed of Russia and Prussia, who coveted Poland and Saxony respectively, was balanced by the manoeuvring of Castlereagh and Metternich, who succeeded in obtaining the admission of France on an equal footing with the other Great Powers. In the end Poland was partitioned and Prussia gained parts of Saxony and the Rhineland, but Castlereagh was satisfied that France was bordered by powerful states, and in February 1815 he returned to England, leaving Wellington in Vienna. On 1 March Napoleon, who had escaped from Elba, landed at Cannes.

It was hardly to be wondered at that Napoleon so easily resumed his place at the head of the French people, for, as A. G. Macdonnell put it 'during the first Restoration the Bourbons contrived to make themselves distrusted, despised and detested in an incredibly short space of time'. One of their principal blunders was their handling of the affairs of the army. Napoleon's Imperial Guard may at times have been employed on duties of ceremonial display. But they had earned the right for such occasional relaxation on a score of battlefields and in countless actions of unmatched valour. When they were turned out of

Paris to make room for several thousand silken-clad youths of the Household Corps (revived from the days of Louis XIV – in his day they did at least fight) who were more at home in a drawing-room than on a field of battle, they were justified in echoing Hotspur – 'for he made me mad / To see him shine so brisk, and smell so sweet, / And talk so like a waiting-gentlewoman / Of guns, and drums, and wounds . . .'. It had to be remembered too that almost all Frenchmen had served in Napoleon's campaigns. They might welcome the peace, they might even condemn the Emperor's insatiable ambition, but they still took immense pride in his and their country's military glory. To have appointed Dupont – the general who so enraged Napoleon in the early days of the Peninsular War by capitulating at Baylen – as Minister of War showed how remarkably stupid Louis XVIII could be.

Circumstances like the lavish distribution of the Legion of Honour to comfortably fat civilian nobodies or the award of a new military decoration, the Order of St Louis, to young pink-faced popinjays who had never seen a shot fired in anger, were hardly calculated to excite the admiration of those thousands of Grande Armée veterans returning from captivity or dismissed on half-pay. Indeed those still serving in the ranks of the army, when being numbered by their officers, would call out: '*Quinze, seize, dix-sept, gros cochon, dix-neuf!*' It was all very well for the *émigré* noblemen to sneer at the unprepossessing appearance of some of Napoleon's marshals as they mixed with them in the royal drawing-rooms, or for the reinstated ladies of the Court to snub the marshals' wives, but the real feeling of the country was made plain in January 1815, when General Excelmans, one of Napoleon's dashing cavalry leaders, was acquitted by a military court on a charge of insubordination amidst acclamations of delighted approval from the very same French people who had been so willing to see the back of Napoleon only nine months earlier.

Meanwhile Napoleon himself was watching and waiting. On 13 February 1815 a felucca from the Gulf of Spezzia arrived in Elba, carrying a devoted follower of the Emperor, Fleury de Chaboulon. He had brought with him a message from Maret, Duc de Bassano, who had been Napoleon's Foreign Minister and was a man noted for caution. 'Come back,' the message said, 'the Bourbons cannot last. There will be a rising. If you do not come, it will be the Duc d'Orléans. The people want you. The Army loves you still, and is unhappy. Come and rescue France from misfortune.' It was timely, for one of the few men who might have thwarted Napoleon's plans to return to France, Colonel Neil Campbell, British Commissioner, charged with the task of keeping an eye on him, left Elba for Italy on 16 February. Ten days later the Emperor sailed in the *Inconstant* together with six other vessels. Accompanying him were between 600 and 700 of the Old Guard, about 100 Polish lancers, some 300 volunteers from Corsica and Elba, plus members of the Imperial staff. On 1 March, having evaded the Royal Navy brig *Partridge* with Campbell on board, and having deceived the French brig *Zéphyr* as to their destination, the tiny flotilla appeared off Cap d'Antibes. 'At one in the afternoon the landing began,' wrote Vincent Cronin, 'a thousand men against the whole of France'. Napoleon had prepared three proclamations; one to the French people calling upon them to dismiss the Bourbon King and his government who had betrayed their promises and France's glory; one to the Old Guard to address to all their former comrades in arms, bidding them return to their duty; the third an appeal to the Grande Armée itself:

> The eagle with the tricolour will fly from steeple to steeple until it reaches the pinnacles of Notre Dame. Then you may show your scars, your medals. And in your fading years your countrymen will gather round and give you all the glory you deserve. You will tell them the tales of your great deeds, you will proudly say: 'Yes, I was there. I was one of the Grand Army that marched into Vienna, twice – into Rome, Berlin, Madrid, and Moscow, and at last redeemed our own beloved Paris from the shame of foreign conquerors, when we brought back peace and honour to France.'

Peace! It was the promise of peace that was all-important, and in the first of his proclamations Napoleon had pledged himself to abandon all ideas of conquest and to devote his efforts to the welfare of France. The reception awaiting him was mixed. The Marshals were faced with a grave dilemma. They had received all their honours from Napoleon's hands. Now they were enjoying them under the Bourbons. They had had enough of war. Yet to be on the wrong side would mean they could lose everything. Masséna, commanding in the south, took somewhat half-hearted measures to intercept and apprehend his former master, aware that they were unlikely to succeed, and when he heard that Napoleon had reached Paris, went there himself with the main purpose of explaining that he was too unwell to take the field again. Ney had a more difficult time as he was actually in command of the Royal Grenadiers, had sworn loyalty to Louis XVIII and had set off for Lyons. But at Lyons neither the King's brother, the Comte d'Artois, nor Marshal Macdonald had been able to persuade their troops to echo their own cry of '*Vive le Roi!*' There was no response. The Comte d'Artois and Macdonald hurriedly left, and on 10 March Napoleon entered Lyons. All the troops that so far had been sent to stop him had been overcome by the sheer magic of the man in his grey overcoat and black bicorne. Ney too, after agonizing over his divided loyalties, succumbed and joined the Emperor on 14 March. Two days later Louis XVIII made a futile attempt to put some backbone into the two Assemblies of Peers and Deputies by suggesting that there could be no better way of ending his life than in defence of his country. His suggestion was enthusiastically endorsed, but this did not prevent any of them from bolting on the night of 19 March. The following evening the Emperor of the French entered the Tuileries. As he himself noted it was the will of the people that had done it, and it was this will that he had understood and acted upon.

The reaction of Allied leaders at Vienna was immediate and uncompromising. Their joint declaration, inspired principally by Talleyrand, branded Bonaparte as an outlaw and an enemy of the world's peace. The four powers – England, Austria, Russia and Prussia – would each put into the field an army of 150,000 men. They would be kept under arms until 'Bonaparte should have been rendered absolutely incapable of stirring up further trouble'. All Napoleon's efforts to make his peaceful intentions clear, including urgent and personally penned approaches to Metternich and the Prince Regent, were rejected out of hand. It was to be war.

There would be no shortage of troops for Napoleon to make war. In addition to the 200,000-strong army which he had taken over from the Bourbon king, he had succeeded in raising half as many again. There was also the National Guard, some 200,000 strong, to secure French cities. Nearly all the soldiers were, of course, veterans of previous campaigns. 'Their morale,' Vincent Cronin tells us, 'was higher than that of any army since at least 1809. The troops were determined to wipe out the shame of their defection the previous year, and Allied spies reported their almost frenzied enthusiasm for the Emperor.' This enthusiasm did not extend to all the Marshals. There were but a few of the old hands who accompanied him or supported him for his last campaign. Mortier was with him, of course; Soult had joined him (despite his former allegiance to Louis); Suchet had been made a Corps Commander;* the iron, uncompromising Davout had accepted the Ministry of War and set about the business of putting the army in order; Ney had not yet been forgiven for his former promise to Louis XVIII to apprehend Napoleon; Murat, King of Naples, had been unwise enough, on hearing of his brother-in-law's landing in France, to play the turncoat and attack his Austrian friends with Neapolitan troops, who inevitably ran away, leaving Murat to escape ignominiously to Toulon. Had Murat behaved more judiciously and been appointed to command the cavalry at Waterloo, he would not have thrown it away in fruitless charges against unbroken and unbreakable British redcoats. Marmont had abandoned his oldest friend; Berthier was at Bamberg, torn with doubts; Macdonald and Victor stuck to the Bourbons; Masséna took refuge in ill-health. It could hardly be said that the Emperor would have the benefit of his first team for his last endeavour. There was, however, one new Marshal, Grouchy, who had served in Italy, Spain and Russia, to

---

* But was not at Waterloo, having taken command in Italy.

whom Napoleon awarded his baton in April 1815. For all the use Grouchy was at Waterloo, the Emperor might just as well have saved himself the trouble.

Although all four powers had pledged themselves to take the field against France, by June 1815 only two armies had assembled in Belgium – the Prussians under Blücher had some 113,000 men holding the frontier from the Ardennes to Charleroi, while the Duke of Wellington with a mixed force of British, Dutch, Hanoverian and Brunswicker troops totalling about 70,000 was positioned between Mons and the coast. Very few of Wellington's veteran Peninsular men were with him, as the bulk of them were in America, in overseas garrisons or on their way home in transports. Of his roughly 24,000 British troops, only about half had been with him in Portugal and Spain, but amongst them he had regiments of the Guards, High-landers, the renowned 52nd and 95th, some splendid Horse and Field Artillery, and he was strong in cavalry, including the Household regiments and the Union Brigade all under the finest cavalry leader in the British Army, Lord Uxbridge. Wellington could also rely on the King's German Legion. He would be able to position his British battalions both in the most vital areas and to bolster those of his less experienced Allies. The battle of Waterloo has been described so often by so many that we will not reiterate all its twists and turns here, but rather see very broadly what happened, examine more closely some of the British Army's activities, and contrast various judgements of it made by those entitled to express an opinion.

On 15 June having humbugged Wellington by the speed of his concentration and the secrecy of his advance, Napoleon crossed the Sambre, drove a wedge between Wellington's and Blücher's armies, and on 16 June proceeded to maul, but not destroy, the Prussians at Ligny. Although Wellington had hastened to come to the Prussians' support by occupying the important cross-roads at Quatre Bras (where Pack's Highland Brigade greatly distinguished itself in resisting Ney's* attacks, as did too the famous 28th Foot,† the Gloucesters), as soon as he knew that Blücher had withdrawn towards Wavre, he was obliged to conform and during the night of 17 June, with the British cavalry under Uxbridge brilliantly conducting the rearguard, estab-lished his army astride the road to Brussels on the ridge south of the village of Waterloo and the forest of Soignes. Two substantial farms, which were to play key roles in the forthcoming battle – La Haye Sainte on the Brussels road and the Château de Hougoumont, about one mile to the west and slightly south – reinforced his line, which measured about three and a half miles. As usual Wellington had

---

* Napoleon had given Ney command of the First and Second Corps, plus the Heavy Cavalry.
† One of Lady Butler's celebrated paintings depicts the 28th Regiment at Quatre Bras.

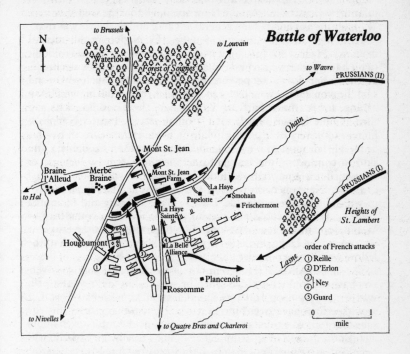

Battle of Waterloo

N

to Brussels

to Louvain

to Wavre

PRUSSIANS (II)

Waterloo

Forest of Soignes

Ohain

Mont St. Jean

PRUSSIANS (I)

Braine l'Alleud   Merbe Braine

Mont St. Jean Farm.

La Haye

Smohain

Heights of St. Lambert

to Hal

Papelotte   Frischermont

La Haye Sainte

Hougoumont

La Belle Alliance

order of French attacks
① Reille
② D'Erlon
③ } Ney
④
⑤ Guard

Lasne

Plancenoit

Rossomme

0   1

mile

to Nivelles

to Quatre Bras and Charleroi

deployed his troops on a crest, behind which they would be able to shelter from the enemy's artillery.

At eleven o'clock on the morning of 18 June, the battle began and had, as John Keegan in his uniquely thorough account of it has explained,* five phases. First came the struggle for Hougoumont which went on all day, was intended to draw Wellington's reserves away from his centre, but instead ate up French reserves; second was d'Erlon's attack on the British centre, which started about one o'clock and was checked by Picton's counter-attack, then dispersed by the British cavalry; thirdly at about four o'clock in the afternoon the French cavalry was despatched by Ney to break the British line to the west of d'Erlon's attempt, and these too were stopped by British infantry and artillery; next at about six o'clock Ney, this time with infantry, and having taken La Haye Sainte, nearly penetrated the Allied line, but was halted by Wellington's moving reinforcements to the threatened position; finally, with the Prussians now closing on his right flank, Napoleon launched the Imperial Guard just east of

* *The Face of Battle*, Jonathan Cape, 1976.

Hougoumont. This last effort was so heavily engaged by British infantry volleys, both from the front and flank that the Guard retired. Wellington gave orders for a general advance and the battle was over.

There was therefore no manoeuvring by Napoleon, no tactical dexterity. He had not thought it necessary, and when warned by Soult (who had good reason to know) about the British Army's steadiness and its commander's competence, he simply dismissed such advice and said the whole thing would be a picnic. He therefore did no more than arrange for his massed artillery to bombard the Allied positions and then mount frontal attack after frontal attack. Indeed Napoleon himself took very little part until late on in the tactical direction of his army. He left most of it to Ney, and Ney, despite all his bravery and skill in conducting the rearguard action after Moscow, was never renowned for imagination. Indeed during the whole of this last campaign Ney was never to show the coolness and steady judgement of which he had been capable. It was all fire and fury and frustrated rage. Such things could not prevail against the calm confidence of Wellington and his redcoats. Indeed on observing what the Emperor was up to, the Duke dismissed it with the laconic comment that 'the fellow was a mere pounder after all'.

The importance of Hougoumont is emphasized, perhaps over-emphasized, by Victor Hugo when he writes that the conquest of it was one of Napoleon's dreams, and that could he but have seized it, it would perhaps have given him the world. He also exaggerates when he says that four companies of English Guards held out for seven hours against the attacks of an army, for although initially the Château was defended by four light companies of the Coldstream and Scots Guards, it was reinforced by a further four Coldstream companies. But the point is that Napoleon's initial attack had not only failed to take Hougoumont or bypass it. His brother, Prince Jerome, was allowing a diversionary objective to become a main one by pouring more and more troops into the battle at the very time when the main French attack on the British centre was to get under way. The battle for Hougoumont was a desperate affair, prompting Wellington's subsequent comment that 'no troops could have held Hougoumont but British, and only the best of them'. Victor Hugo recorded that the divisions of Foy, Guilleminot and Bachelu hurled themselves at it, nearly all Reille's corps was employed but miscarried, Bauduin's brigade failed to breach the north, Soye's brigade could do no more than begin to make a breach to the south. It was like a fortress:

> The English barricaded themselves in it; the French made their way in, but could not stand their ground . . . The château served for a keep, the chapel for a block-house. There men exterminated each other. The French, fired on from every point — from behind the walls, from the summits of the garrets, from the depths of the

cellars, through all the casements, through all the air-holes, through every crack in the stones – fetched faggots and set fire to walls and men; the reply to the grape-shot was a conflagration.

The English, concluded Hugo, behaved admirably. Yet failure to capture Hougoumont did not divert Napoleon from launching his main attack, preceded by a massive bombardment from eighty guns. Although its intensity surprised even some of Wellington's veterans, his customarily skilful siting of infantry protected them. Next came the four divisions of d'Erlon's Corps, some 16,000 men in their normal columns, preceded by *tirailleurs* and making straight for the centre of the Allied line. Their appearance was sufficiently awesome for a Belgian contingent to take to their heels and disappear into the Forest of Soignes, but when the French columns came up against Kempt's brigade deployed by Picton, it was a different matter, in fact the same old story as had happened so often in the Peninsula – the steady British regiments, 28th, 32nd, 79th Highlanders and 95th Rifles holding their fire until the densely packed enemy columns were a mere cricket pitch length away and then pouring the most deadly, disciplined volley into them. It was enough to stop the French in their tracks, but alas the brave, colourful Picton had been killed by a bullet which penetrated his famous beaver hat and struck his forehead. Further to the British left two more of d'Erlon's columns had been met by Pack's Highlanders, which, weakened by its former losses at Quatre Bras, was being pushed back, and it was then that Uxbridge with two brigades of heavy cavalry took a decisive hand in the game.

Uxbridge had under his hand the Household Brigade (1st and 2nd Life Guards, The Blues, 1st Dragoon Guards) commanded by Lord Edward Somerset and the Union Brigade (Royals, Scots Greys, Inniskillings) commanded by Sir William Ponsonby. Of all these regiments only the Royals had been in the Peninsula, but for all that their horse mastership was excellent and they had been well positioned in the hollow of a reverse slope protected from artillery bombardment. Officers of The Blues had done particularly well that morning with a breakfast consisting of gin and biscuits. When Uxbridge saw the situation of Pack's brigade, he did not hesitate. 'I immediately galloped to the heavy cavalry and ordered the Household to form line, passed on to Sir W. Ponsonby, told him to wheel into line when the other brigade did. I instantly returned to the Household Brigade and put the whole in motion. I led the advance.' The charge was both a triumphant success and a tragic disaster, for having sent d'Erlon's divisions into disintegrating flight, the British horsemen – renowned for dash, but never for disciplined control – pursued their enemy too far, and blown and scattered were themselves subjected to furious counter-attacks by the fresh and numerous French cavalry, who accounted for half of Uxbridge's regiments. De Lacy Evans, who was serving as Ponsonby's extra aide-de-camp, has described it all:

Our brigade came up to one hundred yards of the little sunken road and hedge. We waited there until the head of the column had just crossed the road. The enemy had just then redoubled their cannon fire. The column had very little fire to give and must have lost many of its officers in coming up, was fired into close with impunity by stragglers of our infantry. The division under Sir T. Picton was successful, but had I think been obliged to yield. The enemy fled as a flock of sheep quite at the mercy of our dragoons. Our men were quite out of hand. It was quite evident that the enemy reserves of cavalry would soon take advantage of our disorder. Anticipating this I rode back to Sir James Kempt to ask him to advance and cover our retreat. he told me he would advance a couple of hundred yards, but could not quit the position. I galloped back to Sir William. The dragoons were in the same disorder. The French continued to advance on our left. We were helpless against their attack, those whose horses were best, or least blown, got away. Poor Sir William (killed by a lancer when his horse had foundered) might have been spared to his country had he been better mounted. Myself, I was on a powerful, nearly thoroughbred, bay gelding. He received a sabre wound from the eye to the mouth. I changed him for a brown mare which was soon shot. The bay soon recovered.*

As if one spectacular example of the misuse of cavalry were not enough, there was shortly to be another, for while the Hougoumont struggle continued, and d'Erlon attempted to re-form his divisions, another intense artillery bombardment by the French caused Wellington to withdraw his infantry under the cover of the ridge's reverse slope, and Ney, interpreting this move as a general retirement by the British line, sent forward 5,000 of his heavy cavalry to sweep the ridge clear and so bring about the victory which had evaded him hitherto. To attack unbroken infantry with cavalry alone was to break all the rules of war, and it was soon to be shown, as Ney's regiments of cuirassiers came up against the battalion squares of redcoats, with Horse Artillery batteries deployed between them and the British cavalry behind, what an enormous price they were to pay for so unconventional a manoeuvre. Not only did the Horse Artillery's nine-pounders†, loaded with round-shot and case-shot, take terrible toll of the French cavalry leading ranks, but the British and Hanoverian squares, unintimidated by the glittering array of lancers and cuirassiers who could do little damage when faced with endless ranks of bayonets, kept their discipline and when ordered to fire, brought down great numbers of horses and men. Wellington's reply to a question put to him much later as to whether the cuirassiers had not

---

* Quoted by G. N. Wood in *Army Quarterly*, January 1976.
† Boldly and brilliantly handled by Captain Mercer who later wrote a thrilling account of the battle.

come up very well, was that they had 'gone down very well too'. For two hours Ney's attacks persisted in spite of appalling losses. 'Throughout this time and during the bombardments which preceded each assault,' wrote Arthur Bryant, 'the British infantry patiently endured their fate. They seemed in their steady squares to be rooted to the ground.' Hard pounding was what Wellington called it, and inevitably each square contained its wounded, some suffering terribly from limbs shot off or amputated, yet suffering almost always in silence. 'It was a point of pride with Englishmen of all classes to take punishment without murmuring. Their stoicism was equalled by that of the French cavalry, who won the ungrudging admiration of the entire British army.'

There were now but two phases of the battle left, the first of which and the crisis of the whole affair was at hand. It was six o'clock and the Emperor was left in no doubt that the Prussians were approaching. He therefore took personal command of the battle. It was already too late. Nevertheless, he made an effort to win at the eleventh hour. There was still no sign of Grouchy and his 33,000 men, who had been detached after Ligny to finish off the Prussians, but there were ominous signs that the Prussians were getting ever nearer to the battlefield. Protecting his right flank from this threat with battalions of the Imperial Guard, he ordered Ney to take La Haye Sainte and renew his attempt to break the British centre. Ney thereupon attacked with infantry and cavalry, assisted by further devastating artillery bombardments (more hard pounding) – Napoleon was not an artilleryman for nothing – succeeded in capturing La Haye Sainte and nearly penetrated the British line. But Wellington, calm as ever, always at the crucial position, took command in the threatened sector and steadily reinforced it. The thinning red line held on, while the Prussians approached ever nearer. At about seven o'clock in a final throw of the dice, the Emperor ordered forward the Old Guard, himself encouraging them on. Waiting for them were Maitland's 1st Guards who checked their advance, and then Colborne with his 52nd Regiment, showing tactical initiative and boldness of the first order, advanced to the flank of Napoleon's Imperial Guard and subjected them to shatteringly deadly, accurate volleys. Wellington then ordered a general advance; under this, and the arrival of Blücher and his Prussians, the French army disintegrated. In the closing moments of the battle Uxbridge, riding by Wellington's side, was hit in the leg by a shell. He was renowned enough already. As 1st Marquis of Anglesey, 'One-Leg', he became even better known.

It had been 'a damned serious business' all right, with Allied losses of about 50,000. Although in his dispatch to Lord Bathurst, War Minister, written on 19 June, Wellington made little reference to it, it was clear from the fact that this dispatch was smudged by the Duke's own tears, how upset he was by the huge losses, particularly his staff and those close to him – 'I have lost nearly all my friends'. It had been a near run thing, and Wellington was right in suggesting that it would not have been done if he had not been there. For who else would in the first place have chosen the position at Mont St Jean, have handled his relatively weak army with such tactical skill, have exercised so tight a grip on crisis after crisis, and have been able to inspire such steadfast courage and endurance not only from the British regiments, but those of the Allies as well? Yet 'nothing except a battle lost can be half so melancholy as a battle won'. The result, however, was peace in Europe for forty years and the departure of Napoleon for St Helena where he set about the business of re-writing history and glorifying his own legend.

History no doubt was made to be written and re-written, and the affair of Waterloo has had its fair share. A. G. Macdonnell calls it a story of blunders and puts the blame for Napoleon's defeat squarely on the shoulders of three Marshals, Ney, Soult and Grouchy. Grouchy marched his 30,000 men about without engaging the enemy at all and ignored the classic requirement of marching to the sound of guns; Soult did nothing to stem the tide of mistakes, which as Chief of Staff was his especial responsibility; and Ney, according to Macdonnell, lost the battle by his ill-tempered countermanding of Napoleon's order on 16 June to send up d'Erlon's Corps to Ligny so that he, the Emperor, could have destroyed Blücher's army rather than simply maul it about and push it back. Had this been done, so Macdonnell asserts, Grouchy would never have been dispatched to follow up the Prussians and so Napoleon would have had an extra 30,000 men to dispose of Wellington. But as John Keegan reminds us in his remarkable *The Face of Battle* (a strange title, for what he gives us is not what battles look like, but what they *are* like) whenever that distinguished biographer of Wellington, Jac Weller, comes across 'if' or 'had' in a story about Waterloo, he flinches. One of the most revealing comments made by Keegan himself in his study of the battle is what it was that Wellington meant to imply when he observed that it had been won on the playing-fields of Eton. He suggests that it was the coolness, endurance, striving to excel, and aimed-at goals inexplicable outside the world of game-playing which somehow gave the British officers an extra hold on their men's loyalty, discipline and sense of honour, which the French officers, their bravery and dedication notwithstanding, could not match. Keegan might have added that there was another spell-binding influence at work, which gave the British officer and soldier together a unique strength and determination – the regimental spirit.

As might be expected, Victor Hugo's summing up of the whole business is more extravagant. He calls Waterloo the strangest encounter in history, for Napoleon and Wellington are such opposites.

On one side, precision, foresight, geometry, prudence, all assured retreat, reserves spared, with an obstinate coolness, an imperturbable method, strategy which takes advantage of the ground, tactics which preserve the equilibrium of battalions, carnage executed according to rule, war regulated, watch in hand, nothing voluntarily left to chance, the ancient classic courage, absolute regularity; on the other, intuition, divination, military strangeness, superhuman instinct, a flaming glance, an indescribable something which gazes like an eagle, and strikes like lightning, a prodigious art in disdainful impetuosity, all the mysteries of a profound soul, association with destiny.

A strange encounter indeed and one in the end determined, as Hugo reminds us, by the chance that Napoleon waited for Grouchy in vain, while Wellington's waiting for Blücher was at length rewarded. One of Hugo's more curious references is to Byron (who himself depicted Waterloo in *Childe Harold* – 'Battle's magnificently stern array!') as being a greater man than Wellington, and to whom another writer* compared Napoleon himself: 'Above all, he [Byron] was, next to Napoleon, the only man in western Europe to command the attention of every intellectual he encountered, and almost everyone else he didn't.'

Perhaps we may leave the last word but one to Stendhal, another depictor of Waterloo, who observed: 'From noon until three o'clock, we had an excellent view of all that can be seen of a battle – i.e. nothing at all.' Wellington himself put forward a similar sentiment when he likened the history of a battle to that of a ball. Everyone could recall with sharp clarity details here and there, at this time and at that, but few or none could comprehend or describe the whole. Waterloo ensured that the British Army would not be engaged again on a battlefield in Europe for almost forty years, when one of Wellington's aides-de-camp at that battle, Lord Fitzroy Somerset, would be in command and would show from the way he managed the Army that he had comprehended nothing of what it was that The Duke had been demonstrating as to how high command should be exercised. Well before this, however, even though there was little for the redcoats to do in Europe, there was plenty for them to undertake in wars further afield.

*A Single Summer with L. B., Derek Marlowe, Jonathan Cape, 1969.

The attitude of the British taxpayer towards the regular army is amply demonstrated by this cartoon, *circa* 1816.

CHAPTER NINE

Peace in Europe:
Various Wars Elsewhere

There's 'er nick on the cavalry 'orses,
There's 'er mark on the medical stores –
An' 'er troopers you'll find with a fair wind be'ind
That takes us to various wars.

RUDYARD KIPLING

It was characteristic of the British attitude towards the Army that three days after the battle of Waterloo, in a House of Commons debate about flogging, the Secretary for War, Palmerston (he held this office from 1809 to 1828) should have spoken against a motion raised by the Honourable Henry Bennet and Sir Francis Burdett opposing flogging.* They had pointed out to the House that in 1814 more than 18,000 men had been flogged, and that although severe punishment might be necessary in the Army, surely there were other methods than that of treating the soldier like a beast. It was a national disgrace, no other army used such a system, why therefore should the British soldier alone 'be liable to this ignominious torture?' It is important to understand why this practice was not only tolerated in the post-Waterloo Army, but was regarded as absolutely necessary. In his masterly biography of Lord Palmerston, Jasper Ridley† not only explains this point, but gives us such an insight into the nation's view of its Army, that the passage which follows deserves quotation in full:

> Flogging was part of the price which Britain paid for its military system. It was a matter of pride to Englishmen that, instead of the slavery of conscription which Napoleonic tyranny imposed on France, the British Army was raised by voluntary methods. But only

* Flogging was introduced by William III immediately after 1688, principally to discipline his own Dutchmen, and was soon applied to the whole British Army. It was not until 1868 that Cardwell abolished it during peace-time, although it remained in force for active service until 1880.
† *Lord Palmerston*, Jasper Ridley, Constable, 1970.

men from the lowest class volunteered for the Army. The ordinary Englishman, staunch patriot though he was, was not eager to join an army where he would never, except in the most extraordinary cases, be able to win promotion from the ranks; where he would be subjected to military law and deprived of his legal rights as an Englishman under the law; where he would be sent to die on the battlefields of the Peninsula, to have his limbs amputated without an anaesthetic, and to face the far greater risk of disease in camps and hospitals where the organization was even worse than Florence Nightingale was afterwards to encounter in the Crimea; and where, if he survived, he would be discharged from the service at Dover, and left to walk, begging his way, to his home village, and if permanently maimed, left without any pension whatever – until 1811 – to face destitution and the penalties of the Vagrancy Laws. Patriotism was not enough to drive men into such an army, especially as there was no moral pressure upon anyone to join up. It was thought no more discreditable for a man of the middle classes to continue managing his business, or for an artisan to continue at his daily labour, than it was for Lord Palmerston and other young nobles, in perfect physical health, to spend the war at Almack's, or shooting on their country estates. It was an Englishman's privilege that his country could fight, and win, its wars without calling on him for military service, unless he was one of the young aristocrats who chose to purchase a commission and run all risks for glory, or a poacher, convict, vagrant or dare-devil who joined the ranks to escape from the village constable or from the irate father of a pregnant girl. The majority of Army leaders and politicians were firmly convinced that fear of the lash was the only way of preserving discipline in an army composed of criminals.

Certainly this was the view of the Duke of Wellington, so we may understand why Palmerston held it too. On the day following this debate in the House of Commons, news of the victory at Waterloo was confirmed, and in his meticulous way Palmerston noted that since July 1793 the British Army had been engaged in over 180 actions, in which nearly 1,000 officers and more than 15,000 soldiers had been killed. In his book, Ridley notes that although the Duke of Wellington was granted £400,000, no such attention was paid to the ordinary redcoat. Yet at the beginning of July 1815 Palmerston himself proposed to the Commander-in-Chief (reinstated in 1811, the Duke of York remained in the post until his death in 1827 when he was succeeded by Wellington) that all Waterloo veterans should be entitled to reckon two extra years' service towards pay and pension increases. This was agreed, as was also Palmerston's idea that these same men should be shown on their regimental rolls as 'Waterloo men' which 'would constantly keep alive in the minds of the Soldiers of the Army the memory of this unexampled victory'.

The victory, together with her naval supremacy, enabled Britain further to pursue her traditional foreign policy of European balance of power, so that no one nation could dominate the Continent. There was, of course, after the prolonged upheaval caused by Napoleon a deep longing for peace. The influences most likely to upset the peace were Liberalism ('the greatest good of the greatest number' which meant constitutional government) and Nationalism (the right of each nation to control its own destinies). The Four Powers, who were the arbiters of Europe – Russia, Austria, Prussia and Great Britain – took somewhat different views of these influences. Alexander I of Russia was liberal and benevolent in theory, harshly autocratic in practice. Metternich was above all dedicated to maintaining the *status quo* and was thus implacably hostile to liberalism, in his eye another word for revolution. Prussia's Frederick William III began by sympathizing with liberalism, but soon turned away from it, partially because of Metternich's influence, and became an Absolutist. Castlereagh, who directed British foreign policy from 1815 until his death in 1822, opposed constitutional principles (even though his country's government was based on them), believed in diplomacy by conferring with the other Powers – hence the endless series of Congresses – and refused to acknowledge the inevitable consequences of the differing attitudes of constitutional and autocratic countries. On the other hand he was far more realistic in his treatment of France. Seeing the importance of France in maintaining the balance of Europe, and strongly supported by Wellington, he rejected the vindictiveness of the other three great Powers. Fortunately the Allied army of occupation was commanded by Wellington (who made sure, simply by posting a British sentry on it, that the Prussians did not blow up the Bridge of Jena) who soon saw that this army of 150,000 was far too large and recommended its reduction.

The British Army itself set an example of discipline and good behaviour. Their naturalness was characterized even by their drill movements. 'The Russians', says Arthur Bryant,

> kicked out their toes like rampant bears, the Prussians goose-stepped by like turkeys, the white-coated Austrians like supers at a German opera, the French royal guards pirouetted with the little steps of turnspits in the performance of their duty. All moved stiffly, with high, rigid collars and limbs that seemed mechanically jointed. Only the British, taught in the school of John Moore, used the free and natural gait of man.

When it came to putting on a military display, they did it with the minimum of orders, fuss or preparation. Their day-to-day conduct was not like that of the Prussians, Russians and Austrians who arrogantly took all they wanted without paying for anything, who seemed to take pleasure in destroying and ravaging houses, farms and furniture, who played the conquerors with their bullying, stealing and wanton destruction. The British redcoat was much milder, respecting property, paying for what he consumed, helping the Parisians, avoiding injury to people and property. They even enjoyed the jokes made about them. After three years British troops were withdrawn from French territory, and Wellington was free to become a member of the Cabinet as Master-General of the Ordnance.

It cannot be said that he used his position to improve the lot of the ordinary soldier greatly. Of course, almost all considerations of the Army's future after Waterloo were governed by money, and from a peak of prestige and competence in 1815, there followed a period of stagnation, economy and decline. The system of administering the Army was an absurd hotchpotch of divided responsibility. Palmerston was Secretary for War, whose precise duties were unclear, not that this prevented his constantly disagreeing with the Commander-in-Chief, the Duke of York, who controlled appointments, promotions and discipline; the Master-General of the Ordnance dealt with the artillery, engineers, firearms, ammunition and greatcoats; the Home Office administered the Militia, Volunteers and Yeomanry; the Treasury supplied transport, stores and provisions; there were separate departments for medical, pay, audit and clothing matters. All attempts to centralize control of these various functions were opposed by Wellington. As if this were not bad enough, he also set his face against improving the conditions under which the soldiers lived. That these conditions were appalling is best illustrated by the fact that they were worse than those of convicts in prison: the space allowed them was less, there was no pure water, clothing was too tight and not warm enough, married quarters – if they existed at all – had no privacy, the very tubs for washing in the mornings were in the barrack rooms at night for the soldiers to relieve themselves in. It was small wonder that the right sort of young men had no desire to join the Army, or that for those who did, death rates from tuberculosis and other diseases were so high.

Moreover, the pay was bad, the food was inadequate, there were no facilities for entertainment and even the canteens made profits from the soldier by charging high prices for poor drink. Although a private soldier's pay was set at seven shillings a week, all except 2¾d (1p) a day was taken from him in charges for messing, laundry and maintenance. There were only two meals a day, breakfast and dinner, each man had 1 lb of bread and ¾ lb of meat (always boiled beef), there was no supper provided until the 1850s and even then the men had to pay for it themselves. It was hardly surprising that morale was low, quarrelling frequent and discipline harsh. Foreign service – and for every five years at home, the soldier was abroad for ten – was even

King George III Reviews the Dragoon Guards, 1800 (*after painting by W. Beechey*)

Frederick, Duke of York and Albany, 1829
(*G. Swendale after Sir Thomas Lawrence*)

William Pitt the Younger (*John Hoppner RA*)

The Storming of Seringapatam, 1799 (*Sir William Allan*)

The Rear Guard — Rifle Brigade

Sir Thomas Picton's 3rd Division storming the Moorish Castle at Badajoz, 1812 (*Merke after Henry Smith*)

The Death of Sir John Moore, 1809 (*W. Heath, engraved by T. Sutherland*)

Waterloo 1815: Wellington Surveys his Troops in action (*Sir William Allan*)

and Napoleon Views the Field from La Belle Alliance (*Sir Wiiliam Allan*)

The Storming of Ghazni, 1839 (*lithograph by H. T. Wright*)

The Last Stand of the 44th at Gandamack, 1842 (*W. B. Wollen*)

The Charge of the 3rd Dragoon Guards 'Upon the Rioters in Queen Square, Bristol', 1831 (*lithograph after W. J. Mullen and T. L. S. Rowbotham*)

The Charge of the Light Brigade at Balaklava, 1854

The Defence of Rorke's Drift, 1879
(*Lady Elizabeth Butler*)

The Battle of Ulundi, 1879 (*oleograph after Newick*)

The Attack on the Abu Klea Wells, 1885 (*W. B. Wollen*)

General Gordon Leaves Charing Cross Station for The Sudan: *left to right*, Duke of Cambridge, Lord Wolseley, General Gordon, Colonel Stewart

worse. Leaving aside casualties in action, the unhealthy climates of the West Indies and India took heavy toll of the rank and file. The overriding need for economy also led to constant change in the establishment of the Army, with the emphasis after 1815 on gradual reduction, until a few years later a strength of what was thought of as normal for peacetime had been reached, that is just over 100,000 infantry and cavalry, 5,000 in the artillery and 1,000 engineers. Even this modest total was resented by the British taxpayer, although it was quite insufficient to arrange for regular relief of battalions serving overseas. Despite peace in Europe (although not at home, as various risings showed – at one of which near Manchester, the Yeomanry charged the crowd, killing eleven and injuring 400, the celebrated 'massacre of Peterloo'), there was no shortage of military activity for these overseas battalions, which were engaged in a series of campaigns in Asia and Africa.

Many of the wars which the beggars in red fought during the Great Peace in Europe were waged to protect or enhance the British position in India. Even before Napoleon made his final exit from the military stage, the British were engaged in what Fortescue called the first and most arduous of hill campaigns, against a hardy and brave warrior people, who subsequently formed (and still form) one of the most valued, renowned Brigades of the British Army – the Gurkhas of Nepal, from the Himalayas on the northern frontier of Bengal. India's governor-general, Hastings, was determined to put an end to the Gurkhas' marauding, and in November 1814 declared war. It turned out to be no easy campaign, for not only were the Gurkhas skilled and bold fighters, but the British, whose former battles against native troops had been conducted in the plains where the enemy either stood to be defeated or ran away when attacked, could not at first find the answers to the Gurkhas' mountain tactics. Sometimes they were too elusive to be found, sometimes disturbingly nimble and violent in their attacks with the kukri. The two most successful British commanders were Major-General Rollo Gillespie and Major-General Sir David Ochterlony. Gillespie was killed while leading an assault on the mountain fort of Kalanga in October 1814 in which a squadron of the 8th Light Dragoons were dismounted (in the hill country of Nepal mounted troops could not be effectively used in their proper role) and being so much more lightly burdened than the infantry with their knapsacks, found themselves engaging the Gurkhas well ahead of the other assaulting troops. The dragoons found their sabres singularly ineffective against the combination of their enemies' kukri in the right hand, shield on the left arm. They furiously attacked the British cavalrymen, slashing with the kukri, parrying sabres with their shields. One of the 8th Light Dragoons' soldiers described this shield as a 'damn pot lid' which like bad luck was everywhere. 'There was no getting over, nor under, nor round it.' The fort was not taken and more than half the squadron were casualties. Meanwhile although Ochter-lony had defeated the Gurkhas at Malaon, they rejected the British terms for peace, and it was not until March 1816 that Ochterlony succeeded by his patient, methodical operations in advancing almost as far as the Nepalese capital, Katmandu, in bringing the Gurkhas to terms and ending the war. They surrendered territory to the west and south of Nepal, including the provinces of Kumaon and Garwhal. It was not long before hill stations were established in these provinces for both the government and the army of India, among them Simla, which was to become the summer refuge of many a future Viceroy and Commander-in-Chief.

Simla was to become what James Morris described as

one of the most extraordinary places in the world. It was small, and set delectably in a bowl of the hills, in tiers on the south side of a ridge like an English watering-place, except for the grand mass of the Himalaya behind. From a distance it looked archetypically Anglo-Indian ... exactly what one would expect of a British hill station – quiet, sedate, and logically laid out. This was not its style at all. Simla was a very brilliant, savage, ugly little town. The air was electric, thin enough to make you pant upstairs at first, sharp enough off the snows to keep you unnaturally alert and vivacious, almost feverish. No carriages were allowed in the centre of the town, except those of the Viceroy, the Commander-in-Chief and the Lieutenant-Governor of the Punjab ... somehow the place did not feel quite solid. It was like a stage set, quivering, full of character actors, walking fast and talking hard. There were the British themselves, of course ... There were the hill Indians of the north, whom the British loved, warlike and confident people, with beards and gay colours on them, no nonsense about political rights and a steady hand with a rifle. And here and there in the streets, giving Simla a tantalizing hint of unknown places beyond the mountains, there strode groups of swarthy Tibetans ... There was an Italianate fizz to the piazzas of Simla after dark, as the evening crowds swung here and there ... In the morning Simla seemed different again, for in the brilliance of the mountain sun one could see with an awful clarity the monuments of its power.

All this was in the future, of course, and was made possible only by the continued policy of Hastings and his successors as governor-general to consolidate British power in India. Having been taken by the sword, India was to be kept by the sword, and the extent to which this process dominated the activities of the British Army during the period from Waterloo to the middle of the nineteenth century is well illustrated by a glance at the chapter headings of that matchless

History of the British Cavalry* by the Marquess of Anglesey. In his first volume covering the years 1816 to 1850 every single campaign he describes, whether against the Gurkhas, Marathas or Sikhs, whether in Afghanistan, Sind or Gwalior, is concerned with India. Hastings' next campaign (1817 to 1819) was designed to eliminate the Pindaris, the robber bands numbering some 25,000, excellently mounted, capable of moving great distances at astonishing speed, operating from the Maratha states not under British control. It would mean that the British forces would have to attack the Pindaris *in Maratha country* and so risk bringing in the Maratha princes against them. The entire security of central India was at stake. Hastings was gambling indeed for he would need both to round up the Pindaris and take on the Maratha armies. Together the enemy might muster well over 200,000 troops, more than half of whom were cavalry. Hastings had but half that number, of whom only 10,000 were British soldiers, the rest Indian regulars and irregulars. In this last category there were two regiments raised by the founders themselves of the *silladar* cavalry, two of the most extravagantly adventurous and colourful leaders of irregular horse ever to emerge from the rich, gaudy and violent story of the British Raj – William Gardner and James Skinner. After many exciting years in the service of Maratha princes, Gardner raised his own regiment of Hindustani Mahomedans for the British, composed of some 600 superb horsemen and swordsmen, dressed in long green coats and red *pyjamas*, organized into six troops, each led by a native officer, with the only British being the Commanding Officer himself and two others. The regiment was renowned for its dashing exploits throughout Hindustan. James Skinner was perhaps even more famous. Son of an East India Company officer and a Rajputani girl, Skinner too fought in the Maratha service until, like Gardner, he was persuaded by General Lake (Commander-in-Chief during Wellesley's governor-generalship, and apart from his brilliance as a soldier, remembered for his laconic: 'Damn your writing; mind your fighting') to throw in his lot with the British. He was chosen by his own former comrades-in-arms (when serving Scindiah of Gwalior) who had also expressed their willingness to serve the British and who hailed him as 'Sikander Sahib' (Alexander the Great in Hindustani). Writing of this astonishing regiment, Anglesey tells us that Skinner 'infused into his men a corporate spirit and regimental pride seldom equalled anywhere. Benevolent and just, he was nevertheless a strict disciplinarian.'

* Leo Cooper, 1973. Although, of course, the cavalry was only part of the British Army, that it was an important part was made clear by Wellington when he observed that nothing could be more useful in battle than a body of disciplined cavalry – adding, however, that nothing was more expensive or useless than cavalry that was ill-disciplined. On another occasion he classified the cavalry as the most 'delicate' of arms, because so few officers knew how to use it properly. The Marquess of Anglesey's great ancestor was a striking exception. In any event there were few campaigns at the time we are now dealing with when the cavalry did not play a major role.

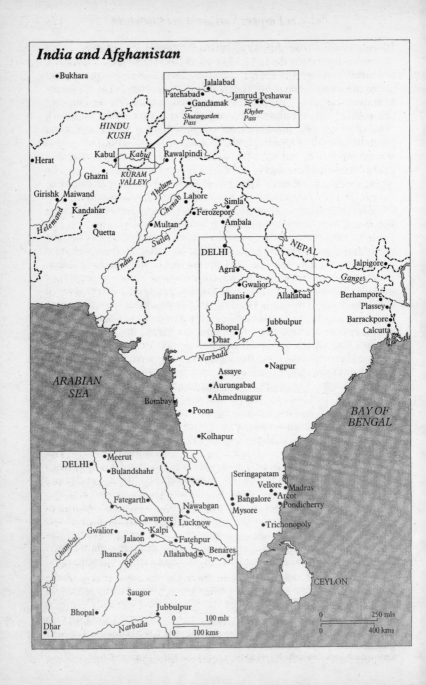

India and Afghanistan

•Bukhara

HINDU KUSH

Fatehabad• •Jalalabad
 •Gandamak Jamrud •Peshawar
 Shutargarden   _Khyber_
 Pass   _Pass_

•Herat   Kabul• _Kabul_ •Rawalpindi
   KURAM
 •Ghazni VALLEY

Girishk• •Maiwand _Jhelum_ •Lahore
  •Kandahar _Chenab_ •Ferozepore •Simla
 Helemand   •Ambala
  •Multan
 •Quetta
   Sutlej DELHI
   •Agra
 Indus •Gwalior NEPAL •Jalpigore
   •Jhansi •Allahabad _Ganges_
     •Berhampore
   •Bhopal •Jubbulpur •Plassey
  •Dhar   •Barrackpore
     •Calcutta
 Narbada

**ARABIAN
SEA**   •Assaye •Nagpur
   •Aurungabad
   •Ahmednuggur
 Bombay• **BAY OF
 BENGAL**
  •Poona

  •Kolhapur

 DELHI• •Meerut
  •Bulandshahr
   •Seringapatam
    •Vellore
 Fategarth• Bangalore• •Madras
  Nawabgan• •Arcot
  Cawnpore• •Lucknow Mysore• •Pondicherry
 Gwalior• •Kalpi
 •Jalaon _Berwa_ •Trichonopoly
 •Jhansi •Fatehpur
 Chambal Allahabad• •Benares

  •Saugor
    CEYLON
 •Bhopal •Jubbulpur
 •Dhar _Narbada_ 0   100 mls
  0   100 kms 0   250 mls
    0   400 kms

He ruled his soldiers with an iron hand. Grant them indulgence and they would go to the devil. He dressed his men in striking uniform – red turbans and cummerbunds, white *pyjamas* and long yellow coats, hence their nickname 'The Yellow Boys'. So well did they do in the Maratha wars that a second and third regiment were raised, and Skinner's Horse still plays its honoured part in the Indian Army.

In 1817 three of the Maratha princes – Holkar of Indore, Appa Sahib Bhonsle of Nagpur and the Peshwa of Poona – elected to turn against the British and soon had cause to regret it. By the end of that year all had been defeated in the field, although operations to mop up resistance continued until April 1819. From the British point of view the campaign was entirely successful. The Pindaris were eliminated, Holkar and Nagpur both lost territory and the Peshwa of Poona was pensioned off. Of the various engagements, the main one was the battle of Mehidpur, when General Hislop, commanding the Deccan army, decisively defeated Holkar on 21 December 1817. Let us briefly accompany Hislop and his subordinate, John Malcolm who commanded the 3rd Division, as the British force of some 5,000 soldiers confronted perhaps six times that number supported by sixty or so heavy guns, strongly posted on the northern banks of the river Sipra with only one ford to cross directly in front of the enemy's guns and infantry. Hislop's bold, but simple plan was to launch an infantry attack, supported by horse artillery and to follow up with his cavalry. Malcolm was in charge of the leading infantry, which included the Royal Scots, Madras European regiments and native infantry, and was so determined to set an example by leading from the front that at one point he had to be restrained by one of his own lieutenant-colonels. But the troops under his command pushed valiantly forward in the face of heavy fire from enemy guns, and after these guns had been captured, the enemy's resistance quickly crumbled. Holkar himself, his infantry and cavalry, all melted away to be pursued by the 22nd Light Dragoons and both Madras regular cavalry and Mysore Silladar Horse. It was this last regiment which succeeded in capturing Holkar's family treasure to the tune of about one million pounds, which by the current regulations as to prize money for irregular cavalry they were authorized to keep. In his report after the battle Malcolm paid tribute to the bravery of the enemy gunners, the only part of Holkar's army really to put up a fight, lamenting the casualties they caused. Of his own contribution of inspiring his troops forward by infectious courage, he says little, merely commenting that the rapid charge on the enemy's guns executed by those under his command was successful.

Hastings, by his bold and decisive actions, had not only brought security to central India. The North-West Frontier was secure for two decades. Before completing his time as governor-general (he was succeeded by Lord Amherst in 1821) Hastings had also lent his support to Stamford Raffles in acquiring Singapore. These stirring events in the rapidly expanding overseas possessions (Ceylon had been added during Hastings' time in Bengal) were hardly matched by what Palmerston was up to at home. In 1820 one of his principal concerns was that of using the Army to contain disorder in Britain. In particular he wanted to ensure that soldiers should be housed in barracks, away from people whose revolutionary ideas might spill over to the military. For similar reasons Palmerston was in favour of abolishing the Volunteers, who came mostly from town-dwelling shopkeepers, and increasing the strength of the Yeomanry, whose landowning and farming members were politically reliable. Another measure taken by the Government in 1820 to ensure public order was to increase the size of the army at home. It was in this year too that George IV, having been Prince Regent for nearly ten years, finally succeeded to the throne, an event marred by his ludicrous attempt to divorce Queen Caroline, her exclusion from his coronation ceremony, her death soon afterwards and then, during the funeral procession, a clash between the following crowds and the Household Cavalry. Stones were thrown at the troops, shots were fired over the heads of the people, the Life Guards cavorted about, and the whole ugly incident was only brought to a close by the intervention of General Sir Robert Wilson, a Peninsular veteran, diplomat and radical Member of Parliament, who persuaded the troops to retire out of range of the angry crowd, and was for his pains dismissed from the Army by the Duke of York. George's accession did not alter the continuance in office of Liverpool's Tory government, nor did Castlereagh's suicide in 1822. Canning became Foreign Secretary and leader in the Commons.

During George IV's brief reign – and the process continued modestly during the even briefer reign of his brother, enormously in the unprecedentedly long one of his niece – the apparently unstoppable expansion of territory under British control went on. The mere presence of British administrators and troops garrisoning the country's colonial possessions, no matter how reluctant the Government was to accept further responsibilities, led paradoxically to more and more acquisitions. One of the characteristic illustrations of this process was the case of Burma. The Burmese chose to interfere with the government of India, and as a result the Indian Government found itself obliged to conquer Burma. It was a slow and costly business, for Burma was a country little-known, mountainous, unhealthy and almost impossible for an army to traverse on land. As the main cities of Burma (including Ava, whose King had invaded Indian territory) were on the Irrawaddy river, the British expedition was mounted by water, and in May 1824 some 11,000 soldiers, commanded by General Archibald Campbell, took Rangoon, where they stayed for about six months – as the rains prevented movement up-river – with inadequate supplies, no means of moving by land and subject to disease. Despite appalling losses from disease – almost all the British soldiers, and there were more than 3,000 of them, died during the campaign – Campbell pushed on early in 1825, by now having mules and proper food supplies for hot weather, reaching Prome in April, when he was again obliged to suspend operations because of the monsoon. Further fighting in November and December resulted in a heavy defeat for the Burmese, who accepted British terms when Campbell's army was about fifty miles from Ava itself. The Burmese king agreed to cease interfering in Assam and the British acquired coastal territory in Burma from the Irrawaddy to Chittagong.

The Burmese war had consequences of great meaning to the Army. In the first place the need to reinforce India brought home to Palmerston the absurdity of the system whereby regimental establishments were too low to enable reliefs from long service overseas to be managed properly. This meant that for an infantry battalion consisting of eight companies, only one company remained on the home establishment when the battalion was ordered abroad. By increasing the establishment to ten companies, four of which would remain at home, Palmerston not only made possible the means of organizing reliefs sensibly. He anticipated the 'two battalions for each regiment' system introduced by Cardwell in the 1870s, which enabled every county regiment to have one battalion at home, recruiting and training, and one overseas on operational or garrison duty.

There was also unrest in Maratha country in 1826, which required Combermere to storm the fortress of Bhurtpore. His capture of it did much to persuade other potential trouble-makers to leave John Company alone for the time being. There is a remarkable story about the taking of Bhurtpore which illustrates vividly the way in which the priceless regimental system of the British Army found very special sympathy among the ranks of Indian soldiers. The story is told by Philip Woodruff* in *The Men Who Ruled India*:

> When Lord Lake in 1805 was twice repulsed before Bhurtpore, a battalion of Rajputs had their colours shot to pieces in a particularly bloody assault. The colours could no longer be used; after the campaign, they spent a last night in the guardroom before the day when they were to be ceremonially destroyed and new colours dedicated. In the morning the old colours had disappeared. Not a shred was to be found; no questioning threw any light on what had happened. Thirty [*sic* – in fact twenty-one] years later, the same battalion was at the taking of Bhurtpore. They led the assault. They stormed the breach. In the hour of victory, the old colours reappeared; they had been taken from the guardroom thirty years before, the fragments saved, each carefully preserved as a religious amulet and secretly handed down from father to son. Now the

* *The Founders*, Cape, 1953; *The Guardians*, Cape, 1954. Philip Mason published many books under this pseudonym.

disgrace was wiped out; the fragments re-appeared and the strips were united and tied to the new colours on the spot where the repulse had occurred. Of all this, the officers had known nothing; the men of the regiment formed a close hereditary corporation, knit together by blood, religion and a deep emotional feeling for the colours.

In another and equally spellbinding book about the Indian Army* Philip Mason elaborates on this story, tells us that the regiment concerned was the 31st Bengal Native Infantry, who in the repulse of 1805 lost 180 men killed and wounded out of a total of 400, all in the space of two hours, and goes on to explain that Bhurtpore had become a kind of symbol, a defiance of both the Company and its Army, and that therefore the reputation of both had somehow to be restored by a successful return to avenge former failure. But Mason's final sentence on these events puts the emphasis where it truly belongs:

> The men of that regiment, who had seen their comrades die, who taught their sons to cherish those pieces of silk, were concerned about something much more intimate than the good name of the Company – the honour of one regiment, which was theirs; it belonged to them and to their families more closely than it belonged to their officers, and it was their honour that was sullied until their colours went back to the breach from which they had been recalled.

It is only one story, about only one regiment, yet it illustrates the spirit that pervaded a whole army. If we are able to comprehend and applaud – indeed honour – this point about the Sepoy Army, then the entire thread and theme of this story about the beggars in red, who achieved such remarkable fame and fortune during the next six decades of the nineteenth century, will become plain for all to see.

In 1827 the Duke of Wellington became Commander-in-Chief of the British Army. On the death of the Duke of York at the beginning of that year, there was really no other choice. Characteristically his first General Order to the Army was a model of brevity, simply demanding and pledging duty and service. He did not remain in the post long, as in 1828 he became Prime Minister, and was obliged to sanction further economies in the Army, including the reduction of the Royal Waggon Train, so vital in war. He continued to oppose reform and set his face against the abolition of flogging as he believed that most of Britain's fighting would be done in defence of her overseas empire in unpleasant conditions where only those who required harsh discipline to control them would be willing to serve. In 1829 we find him observing that 'the man who enlists into the British Army is, in general, the most drunken, and probably the worst man of the trade or profession to which he belongs, or of the village or town in which he lives.'

* *A Matter of Honour*, Cape, 1974.

Wellington was still Prime Minister when George IV died on 26 June 1830, and was succeeded by his brother, the Duke of Clarence, now William IV. The Sailor King was not renowned for discretion, calling out to the generals and admirals at his brother's funeral to keep in step, congratulating Wellington on his victories over the French at a dinner with the French Ambassador as one of the honoured guests, and at another military dinner emphasizing his classless approach to social affairs by reminding one guest, Lord Fitzroy Somerset*, that he was descended from the Plantagenets and a second guest, Sir James Kempt, one of the Peninsular generals, that he was descended from the very dregs of the people. William would have liked to retain Wellington as Prime Minister, but the issue of parliamentary reform was too much for both of them and Wellington left office in November 1830.

We may perhaps pass over the seven years of William's reign, for although there was the excitement of reform† at home and revolutions in Europe, the British Army had a relatively quiet time, saved from further reduction, as it was said, by Wellington's having hidden it away in the Colonies, with India for once not seething with military activity, and only the Kaffir wars in South Africa rumbling on from time to time. But with the arrival of Queen Victoria on the throne in 1837, all this was changed, and now we enter the gaudy, grasping era of Imperial adventure with small groups of redcoats taking on Asian and African enemies in deserts, mountains and veldts, sometimes rapidly triumphant, at others suffering disastrous setbacks, to be later revenged – with one bizarre expedition to administer correction to a European giant thrown in to highlight the Army's shortcomings – all these events illustrating in the end that there were few able to withstand the British Tommy in a stand-up fight, except perhaps Dutch farmers, fanatical Zulus and ignorant Fuzzy-Wuzzys.

Victoria's first Prime Minister was Melbourne, Lord M., of whom David Cecil so elegantly wrote that 'he saw every question from so many sides, most problems seemed to him so hopeless of solution, that he was generally for doing nothing at all . . . he did not think it worth while stirring a finger to mould circumstances to his will. Smiling, indolent, and inscrutable he lay, a pawn in the hands of fortune.'‡ The same could hardly be said of Melbourne's Foreign Secretary, Palmer-

---

* Who had been with the Duke at Waterloo and whom we will meet again as Lord Raglan in the Crimea.

† Although things may have been quiet in India and elsewhere in the early 1830s, they were certainly not so in England during the agitation which preceded the passing of the Reform Bill in 1832. One of the worst riots took place in Bristol in October 1831 when mobs burned most of the city's commercial district, and were rewarded for this breach of the peace by the intervention of three troops of cavalry (3rd Dragoon Guards and 14th Light Dragoons) who repeatedly charged the rioting crowds, killing a dozen of them, wounding more than a hundred and effectively putting an end to the disturbance.

‡ *Lord M.*, Constable, 1954.

ston, whose industry, self-confidence, bluntness and patriotism made
him a favourite among the people, and who, like Churchill in a later
century, came at last to personify his country. With Palmerston, whose
idea of diplomacy was often limited to the dispatch of gunboats, as
Foreign Secretary and later Prime Minister, there would be no
shortage of opportunity for the Royal Navy and the British Army to
earn their keep. 'War came naturally enough to the British,' wrote
James Morris in *Heaven's Command*,* 'after so much experience of it,
and empire offered them a more or less perpetual battle-field.' He goes
on to describe the two armies which were available for the waging of
Queen Victoria's wars.

At the time of her accession the British Army was still about
100,000 strong made up principally of infantry of the line, together
with the three Guards regiments, the cavalry, artillery and some
engineers. More than half its numbers were usually overseas, garrisoning various parts of the Empire, and indeed in 1840, when Victoria's
wars really got under way, of the hundred or so infantry battalions in
the Army, nearly sixty were in the colonies, about twenty more in
India, Burma and China, and only twenty at home. So stretched was
the army at this time that Macaulay, who was Secretary for War in
Melbourne's administration,† was obliged to propose a modest
increase in its strength – from 110,000 to 120,000 – when he
introduced the Army Estimates in 1840. Apart from these periodic
fluctuations in its strength, there was not much difference in the life of
a soldier then from that during Wellington's time of active service. For
the officers, who had bought their commissions, there was little to do
in the way of duty, if they were serving at home. Field sports, looking
after their horses and shooting, the social whirl in town, occasional
demands for their attendance at some review or manoeuvre – it was all
very agreeable and undemanding. For the soldiers things were rather
different. Most of them came from rural areas, with a good many
Irishmen thrown in; some were unemployable delinquents, others
concealed their real identities in pseudonyms or were unable to find
any other means of obtaining shelter, food and above all, drink, yet all
somehow, in the magical way that the British Army's regimental
system transformed the most hardened riff-raff into dedicated redcoats, imbued with the spirit of courage and comradeship engendered
by the dangers and disciplines of active service. 'The Army lived
ritualistically,' wrote James Morris. 'Flags, guns and traditions were
holy to it, and loyalty to one's regiment was the emotional keynote of
the service . . . Ceremony and display was immensely important to the
British military ethos, and this taste for splendour was carried over to

---

* Faber & Faber, 1973.
† 'I wish I was as cocksure about anything,' observed Melbourne, 'as Macaulay is
about everything.' But he, like almost everyone else, listened to Macaulay, perhaps the
most dazzling, yet dogmatic talker of the age.

the Empire, and became an imperial technique too.'

There was no lack of splendour in Victoria's other army, which for two centuries had been maintained by and had served, the East India Company. More than twice the size of the British Army itself, the forces of John Company were divided among the three Presidencies of Bengal, Madras and Bombay, and apart from a few regiments of Europeans, was composed of the martial peoples of India – Marathas and Sikhs, Dogras, Rajputs, Muslims and Gurkhas – to whom soldiering was an honourable profession. There was never a shortage of eager volunteers, anxious to pursue the hereditary military vocation of their caste, who fitted readily into the tight loyalties and proud traditions of the British regimental system. Their British officers were carefully selected and trained for their duties, and between them and the sepoys there existed a very special relationship, as Philip Mason has reminded us in *The Men Who Ruled India*:

> It was a mercenary army, officered by foreigners. That must not be lost sight of. They were not only foreigners but of another faith, and the personal habits of officers and men were so widely different that each regarded those of the other as disgusting. Perhaps the Brahman's disgust at his officer's use of beef and brandy was as great as either felt at the toilet and sanitary arrangements of the other. All the same, between those foreign officers and their Indian soldiers there sprang up – much more often than not – a confidence and affection of which both English and Indian may well feel proud. It was something that could survive long marches, through burning deserts and icy mountains, sieges on starvation diet, torture and the threat of instant death. Indeed it throve on such fare as this.

There was to be plenty of opportunity for demonstrating the qualities of both these Victorian armies in one of the most unnecessary, ill-handled and catastrophic campaigns in which the British ever indulged during their long history of Imperial expansion: the first Afghan War. It was all tied up with the playing – or rather in this case the misplaying – of the Great Game, the move and counter-move by the Russians and the British in the not quite no-man's-land between the Czar's dominions and British India, the chessboard formed by Central Asia, Persia, the Punjab and Afghanistan. Hardly surprisingly Palmerston's policy was to keep any conflict between the various contestants for power and territory as far away from the frontiers of India as possible. Therefore he would lend his support to Persia against Russia; to Afghanistan if threatened by Persia; to the Punjab if endangered from Afghanistan. In so far as Palmerston's support for the Afghans against Persia's designs on Herat was decisive in persuading the Shah to accept the Czar's advice to abandon the idea, Britain's policy had prevailed. But his direct interference in Afghanistan itself was to have dire consequences. Given the obsession of both

Lord Auckland, governor-general, and Palmerston with preserving Afghanistan's independence and warding off any Russian notions of extending her influence there, it was not hard to find some pretext for interfering. They also had their suspicions that Dost Mahommed, ruler of Afghanistan, was not only plotting some association with the Russians, but – and here it was more than suspicion – planning to take back from Ranjit Singh, powerful ruler of the Punjab, firm ally of the British, Peshawar which he had seized from Afghanistan thirty years earlier. The only Englishman who really understood Afghanistan was Alexander Burnes, who knew the country well and had been sent as British envoy to the court of Dost Mahommed. Burnes's opinion was that, despite his flirtation with the Russians, Dost Mahommed would prove a trustworthy friend. But to support him would be to antagonize Ranjit Singh, whose aim was to overthrow Dost Mahommed and replace him with his predecessor, Shah Shuja, flabby, vicious, despised by Afghans, whose only recommendation was that he was a pensioner of the British in India and might therefore, if restored to the throne, pursue a pro-British policy. Auckland rejected Burnes's advice and recommended to the British Government that Dost Mahommed should be turned off the throne, that the rightful ruler should be restored, supported against any interference, external or internal, by a British Army, and that once he was secure in power with Afghanistan's integrity and independence assured, the British Army should be withdrawn. At home Palmerston and Melbourne discussed the matter in great secrecy with other members of the Cabinet (Palmerston suppressing Burnes's favourable view of Dost Mahommed) and it was agreed to endorse Auckland's proposals. In fact he had already acted on his own authority. From the first, the expedition was doomed. It was based on the wholly false idea that Dost Mahommed was untrustworthy, that he was unpopular with his people and that the British candidate, Shah Shuja, would be welcomed back by his country and would prove an effective ruler and ally. It also totally ignored the nature of the Afghan tribes – savage, chauvinistic, treacherous, fiercely independent, murderous and unpredictable, they were unlikely to accept an unwanted ruler imposed by the British, or for that matter the presence of a British army.

From a purely military point of view things went quite well at first. The so-called Army of the Indus, with nearly 10,000 troops of British and East India Company regiments and some 6,000 of Shah Shuja's own soldiers, assembled near Lahore towards the end of 1838, indulged in somewhat ill-organized and disreputable entertainments given by Ranjit Singh who as was customary with him drank too much and then, after suitably impressive military reviews, began to make its ponderous way across the Indus towards Quetta, accompanied by nearly 40,000 camp followers and 30,000 camels, with a view to approaching Kabul via Kandahar and Ghazni. Kandahar was reached in April 1839 and the only real battle that took place at all was at Ghazni. Before we reach Kabul itself, we may get an impression of what going to war was like in those days of the Raj by a glimpse of James Morris's matchless portrait:

> Every regiment had 600 stretcher-bearers. Every platoon of every regiment had its water-carriers, its saddlers, its blacksmiths, its cobblers, its tailors, its laundry-men, and there were the men who polished brasses, and the men who put up tents, and the cooks, the orderlies, the stable-boys – together with all their wives, and all their children, and often aunts, uncles or grandparents – and fortune-tellers, metal-workers, wood-gatherers – with herdsmen to look after the cattle, sheep and goats, and butchers to slaughter them – and there were carts and wagons by the thousand, palanquins, drays, chargers, ponies, dogs – and so all this great multitude stumbled away to war, each corps with its band playing, a regiment of Queen's cavalry, two of Company cavalry, nine regiments of infantry, engineers, gunners, Shah Shuja's hopeful sepoys and those splendid prancing banditti, the Yellow Boys.

The wonder of it was not so much that on arrival at Kabul everything began to go wrong, but that most of them got to Kabul at all. There was little resistance to the invading army other than from marauding bands of horsemen, although the utmost vigilance was necessary at every halt to ensure that these marauders were kept at bay. Before the assault on the fortress of Ghazni, however, a more determined attack by a horde of Ghazi horsemen on Shah Shuja's camp had to be repelled by the combined efforts of Shuja's cavalry, the 16th Lancers and the Bengal Light Cavalry. During the attack on Ghazni itself, one British infantry regiment, the 13th (Somerset Light Infantry) and the 36th Bengal Native Infantry were so impressed by each other's gallantry – they appeared to be equally valorous – that after the battle the men of the 13th went round the ranks of the 36th to shake them all by the hand. At this stage of the campaign it seemed that the British had the upper hand in morale and skill. It was not to be so for very long. In August 1839 Shah Shuja re-entered his capital, Kabul, by courtesy of the British Army, watched with sullen resentment by the people, who took little notice of him. General Keane, in command of the joint army, reported to Auckland by dispatch, expressing the hope that he had accomplished what had been intended. Yet it was he who confided his real opinion to Lieutenant (later Major-General Sir Henry) Durand, who accompanied Keane on his return to India in the autumn of 1839, that before long there would be – and his words have come to epitomize the entire expedition – 'some signal catastrophe'.*

* The best recent account of the campaign is Patrick Macrory's *Signal Catastrophe*, Hodder & Stoughton, 1966.

Dost Mahommed had fled, there were no Russians in Kabul, Sir William Macnaghten, a learned, distinguished Indian civil servant, was Envoy and Minister in Kabul, assisted by Sir Alexander Burnes, British Resident; much of the army had returned to India, leaving behind at Kabul about two brigades of infantry, a regiment of cavalry and one battery of horse artillery. The garrison settled down to the sort of life they had previously enjoyed in India, with a minimum of work and a maximum of entertainment and sport. Riding, cricket, racing, band concerts – all had their place. There were also, as in Kipling's poem, The Ladies: 'the things you will learn from the Yellow an' Brown, They'll 'elp you a lot with the White!' The Kabul women were tall, handsome, lithe and athletic creatures, and, as many Afghan men had more of a taste for painted youths, they were hungry and eager too. They may have been enveloped in that curious, cylindrical white garment, the *burkha*, but underneath they were clearly sisters to the Colonel's Lady an' Judy O'Grady. This may have been all very well for the British officers. It hardly endeared them to the Afghans. Nevertheless the British felt secure, and in 1840 took the incalculably unwise step of moving their garrison from the Balla Hissar, the citadel within Kabul, which dominated it and could be made more or less impregnable, to an almost inconceivably unsuitable cantonment on a low, swampy piece of ground about a mile to the north-east of Kabul, virtually indefensible, overlooked by hills and forts from all sides, with, between it and the city, orchards and canals which would totally inhibit rapid deployment of horses and guns, with a perimeter far too lengthy to be manned, and crowning it all, as Patrick Macrory put it: 'Finally, by a truly stupendous piece of folly, the commissariat stores were carefully sited a quarter of a mile *outside* the cantonment.'

There were just two more conditions required to turn a dangerous situation into an irretrievable one. First was to lose any sort of control over the mountain passes which led back to India; the second was to appoint a military commander in Kabul who would be totally lacking in energy, judgement, leadership and determination. The British now hastened to fulfil these two requirements. Although Dost Mahommed* surrendered in November 1840 and was escorted back to India by regiments which could ill be spared from Kabul, Auckland economized still further by cutting subsidies to the Ghilzai tribe controlling the passes; the Ghilzais not surprisingly began to break their promises of guaranteeing safe conduct. While many soldiers serving in Afganistan, whether in Kabul or Jalalabad, began to sense the isolation, the unease and the stirring of rebellion among the tribes,

---

* Dost Mahommed had escaped from Bokhara and returned to Afghanistan. Also captive in Bokhara was Colonel Charles Stoddart who with the man sent to rescue him, Captain Arthur Conolly (it was he who coined the phrase 'the Great Game') was executed by the Emir in June 1842, showing once more what a hazardous game it was to play.

in April 1841 Auckland appointed an elderly, sick, unwilling and – as far as India and Afghanistan went – utterly inexperienced general to command, Major-General Elphinstone, of whom one writer had this to say: 'I still state unhesitatingly, that for pure, vacillating stupidity, for superb incompetence to command, for ignorance combined with bad judgement – in short, for the true talent for catastrophe – Elphy Bey stood alone . . . Elphy outshines them all as the greatest military idiot of our own or any other day.'*

Elphinstone could do nothing to stem the rising tide of discontent in Kabul and among the tribes, indeed he did nothing at all. At length events overwhelmed him. In November 1841 the Kabul mob surged round and attacked the British Residency and Burnes, after a brave attempt to calm the Afghans, tried to escape, was seized by the mob and cut to pieces. If ever there was a time when instant, decisive and ruthlessly punitive action was needed, it was then. If Elphinstone and his army had stormed Kabul, retaken the Balla Hissar citadel, blown a few dozen rebels from guns, established an iron grip on Kabul and then dispatched some fast-moving columns to sort out the Ghazis and Ghilzais, it is just possible that some kind of accommodation might have been reached, permitting reinforcements to move from India to strengthen the garrison at Jalalabad and organize a secure withdrawal of the army through the mountain passes. But apart from two or three pathetically inadequate sorties from the cantonment, which resulted in rapid defeat and ignominious retreat, nothing was done. The Afghan rebels grew stronger and bolder day by day. They seized the commissariat, blocked the roads and virtually besieged the British in their wholly indefensible cantonment. It would be difficult to conceive a more hopeless position for a British army than the one in which it now found itself – inadequate food supplies, the winter almost upon them, troops with low morale, a commander destitute of ideas, of will and of energy, no hope of reinforcement, thousands of terror-stricken camp-followers, and an Envoy, Macnaghten, who saw his policy in ruins and now decided to do the one thing that could only make matters worse – negotiate from a position of weakness.

He negotiated with Dost Mahommed's son, Akhbar Khan, who had recently arrived back at Kabul with a formidable band of Uzbeg horsemen. The broad agreement they reached on 11 December 1841 was that the British would evacuate Afghanistan and restore Dost Mahommed, provided the Afghans would ensure their safe conduct and supply sufficient provisions. Even at this late stage, something might have been rescued from the appalling mess into which Macnaghten had got himself, but he chose then to respond to a secret proposal from Akhbar Khan (delivered by 'Gentleman Jim' Skinner, a descendant of the founder of Skinner's Horse who was killed during

* George MacDonald Fraser puts these words into the mouth of his eponymous hero in *Flashman*, Herbert Jenkins, 1969.

the retreat) that Akhbar would become the Vizier to Shah Shuja, and be handsomely rewarded by the British, while the British themselves would remain in Afghanistan for a further eight months and then withdraw voluntarily, having achieved all they set out to do. Such a secret clause involved betrayal of the other Afghan leaders – an unlikely policy for Akhbar – yet Macnaghten accepted the terms, only to find when he met Akhbar again on 23 December that it was he who had been betrayed. When Macnaghten confirmed that he was willing to accept the secret agreement, Akhbar ordered his Ghazis to seize him, and he was bundled away, shot and cut to pieces by the Ghazis, who subsequently paraded his severed head through the streets of Kabul. Once more Elphinstone had cause to exact vengeance for treachery and murder. Once more he did nothing except renew negotiations with Akhbar and submit to the terms imposed by the Afghans. The British army was to withdraw forthwith, forfeiting most of its guns and money. Hostages would remain to guarantee the safe return of Dost Mahommed, and the Afghans would escort the army with its followers through the mountain passes to the frontier with India. Everything was now set for final disaster.

'Possibly there has been a greater shambles in the history of warfare than our withdrawal from Kabul,' recorded Flashman, 'probably there has not. Even now, after a lifetime of consideration, I am at a loss for words to describe the superhuman stupidity, the truly monumental incompetence, and the bland blindness to reason of Elphy Bey and his advisers. If you had taken the greatest military geniuses of the ages, placed them in command of our army, and asked them to ruin it utterly as speedily as possible, they could not – I mean it seriously – have done it as surely and swiftly as he did. And he believed he was doing his duty. The meanest sweeper in our train would have been a fitter commander.' On 6 January 1842 about 4,500 soldiers, with 600 of the 44th Foot (Essex Regiment) and a troop of Horse Artillery – the rest were East India Company troops, including 1,000 cavalry – set off from Kabul accompanied by some 12,000 camp-followers and families. Among the British wives, who mainly travelled in camel panniers, were Lady Macnaghten, widow of the murdered Envoy, and the redoubtable Lady Sale (wife of General Sale, commanding at Jalalabad) who kept so informative a diary and of whom it was said that if only she had been in command, instead of Elphinstone, things might have gone better.

This heterogeneous column of redcoats, sepoys, camp-followers and animals – apart from the horses, there were thousands of camels, mules and bullocks – faced a march of about a hundred miles to Jalalabad over mountain passes as high as 5,000 feet, in icy winter weather, with snow everywhere, inadequately clad, hungry, with no assured supplies and no protection from the hazardous passages through a series of defiles made for ambush. Had most of them reached Jalalabad in any sort of order, without interference by, even with the aid of, the Afghans, it would have been an astonishing achievement, even a near miracle. But given that they would be subjected to constant attack, ambush, harassment and treachery – and this is what happened from the moment they left Kabul – it was hardly surprising that the whole unfortunate multitude (except for one man who did reach Jalalabad) was either killed, dispersed, starved, captured or horribly wounded and left to die. What is most memorable is that despite all this, despite the merciless cruelty of the weather, the utter lack of order or organization, the unceasing savagery, deception and murderous attacks of the Ghazis and Ghilzai horsemen, despite Elphinstone's departure to parley with Akhbar, despite the almost total collapse of discipline, there were individual acts of heroism and sacrifice which even today must excite our wonder. The march took terrible toll of numbers. After four days, when the British women and children were handed over to the Afghans for safe-keeping, the fighting strength of the army was down to about 300 British soldiers, mostly of the 44th Foot, some 500 sepoys and 170 of the 5th Light Cavalry. Two days later as the still further diminished column was approaching the worst defile of all, the Jugdulluk, there were no sepoys left at all, only men of the 44th and the Light Cavalry, plus camp-followers. But the Afghans had built barriers of holm-oak with its holly-like leaves across the track, and as the soldiers struggled to tear a way through, the Ghilzai horsemen fell upon them, slashing with their swords and knives, so that when the survivors reached the tiny village of Gandamack, there were but twenty officers and forty-five British soldiers left alive, surrounded by Afghans, who then called for a parley. Among the British officers was Captain Souter of the 44th Regiment, who had wrapped the colours round his waist for their preservation. It was simply another example of Afghan treachery. The tribesmen slaughtered all the surviving soldiers except for a handful who were made prisoner, among them Captain Souter, whose colourful appearance made him in their eyes a ransomable article. Now only a few horsemen who had by-passed Gandamack were left, among them the surgeon, Dr Brydon, who had been given a pony by a dying Indian soldier, and who alone reached Jalalabad, thus fulfilling the prophecy of Colonel Dennie, 13th Foot, who had predicted a year earlier that one man would reach Jalalabad from Kabul to tell them that the rest of the army had perished. The signal catastrophe forecast by General Keane had come to pass.

It was all reversed and revenged by Generals Pollock and Nott later in 1842. By this time Ellenborough had succeeded Auckland as governor-general, and authorized an expedition under Pollock, who marched his force through the Khyber pass to find that the Jalalabad garrison had successfully withstood its besiegers. In addition, Nott was secure at Kandahar and, when instructed by Ellenborough to withdraw, he did so by way of Ghazni, where he destroyed the fortress; he then proceeded to Kabul and blew up the bazaar there, joined up with Pollock's force, and with him subdued the Afghans, releasing all British prisoners and generally restoring the military prestige of the Raj. The British armies then returned to India. The irony of it all was that Shah Shuja was murdered, and Dost Mahommed restored to his throne. It had all been for nothing really, yet there was to be another Afghan war, as we shall see, in 1878, and in between the British could get on with the business of playing the Great Game once more, a game which as far as India's security was concerned was soon to go disastrously wrong.

Palmerston was not content to confine his interference in Eastern affairs to Afghanistan. He had a go at China too. The so-called Opium War of 1840 to 1842 was caused by the Chinese determination to suppress opium smuggling, their seizure of British-owned opium in Canton and their refusal to deal with British representatives as anything but those of a tributary power. Macaulay, who was Secretary for War, was at his eloquent best when appealing to the House of Commons that an appropriate response should be made to such an insult to the British flag. Having disposed first of the Opposition's criticism of the initiative taken by men on the spot – how all of us who have ever commanded British forces in far-off places would endorse Macaulay's contention that men who built (or, as we might now add, helped to liquidate) the British Empire had the sense and spirit to treat all orders that came from home as waste paper – he went on to contend that the rightful quarrel should be pursued to a successful conclusion and that 'the brave men, to whom is entrusted the task of demanding that reparation which the circumstances of the case require, may fulfil their duties with moderation, but with success, that the name, not only of English valour, but of English mercy, may be established'. There was, however, not much moderation shown by the 4,000 British and Indian troops who, having been assembled off Macao in the company of five East India Company steamers and fifteen British men-of-war, went ashore on the island of Chusan, after the fleet had bombarded Tinghai. Not only did the troops plunder the houses of Tinghai, but under the influence of the Chinese spirit, *samsu*, they became uncontrollable. In spite of the spirit being little used by the Chinese themselves, who preferred opium, there were many distilleries of *samsu*, so that it was impossible to prevent the soldiers getting at it, and as one of the officers reported 'its effect on them was of the most dreadful nature and very different from that of the spirits we are used to in England. A man no sooner took a small quantity than he was in a most dreadful state and committing the most horrible atrocities.'

The attack on Chusan did not end the war, and next year in 1841, the British mounted an assault on Canton itself, with Major-General Sir Hugh Gough in command of some 2,500 troops, including the

26th Regiment (Cameronians) and 37th Madras Native Infantry. The Chinese fought bravely, but Gough took Canton, even though there was a subsequent set back to the north-east of the city at a village called Sanyuan-li, where a detachment of British soldiers, separated from their main body, was defeated. The war took on a different character when a new British plenipotentiary, Sir Henry Pottinger, formerly Governor of Madras, arrived, together with reinforcements amounting to nearly 3,000 troops to join Gough's army. Between August and October 1841 the British captured Amoy, Tinghai, Chinchai and Ningpo: they were all the kind of amphibious operations at which the Royal Navy and the British Army had become so expert. But there was still some hard fighting to do. The Chinese attempt to retake Ningpo was notable both for their reckless bravery and their appalling casualties, caught as they were in the narrow confines of the town by British infantry fire from either flank and the devastating blast of heavy artillery to their front. Lieutenant Ouchter-lony reported that the effect was terrific and that the enemy to the rear, not realizing what was happening in front, pushed boldly forward, only to be shot down themselves as they clambered over the dead bodies of their comrades. 'The infantry resumed their firing and such a storm of balls was kept up upon the enemy, that in a short time the street was choked up, and when, for want of a living mark, the men were ordered to advance, their steps fell upon a closely packed mass of dead and dying.' Lieutenant Murray had a similar story to tell about dead bodies piled five or six deep, and how when the Chinese withdrew, pursued by him and his men, they continued to suffer many killed, in spite of their overwhelming numbers compared with those of the few British. But, he went on:

> The most extraordinary part of the scene was the coolness with which the country people looked on, crowding the bridges and every spot from which they could see well, in amazing manner. We were obliged to call and make signals to get out of the line of fire, to prevent their being shot, and I can safely say not an unarmed person was touched. The circumstance of their thus assembling showed what confidence they had that we would not injure them; but the little interest they took in their countrymen did not raise them in my estimation. They seemed rather to enjoy their defeat, regarding what was passing as an amusement.

It was not always to be so easy for the British. Although the 18th (Royal Irish) Regiment had found the going good at Ningpo – one soldier having disdained to use anything more lethal than the butt end of his musket to dispose of the attacking Chinese – when the same regiment came to assault Chapu, they found the defending Tartar troops not only fanatically brave in resisting their repeated attempts to take a defended temple, but when the British artillery had made further resistance pointless, preferring to hang, drown or poison themselves rather than submit to defeat. It cannot be said that the behaviour of British troops – the Barbarians or Foreign Devils as the Chinese called them – brought much credit on them, for plunder and rape seemed to be the order of the day. It was all finally brought to an end by the capture of Chinkiang in mid-1842, and the Treaty of Nanking imposed humiliating terms on China – Shanghai, Canton and other ports would be open for trade as 'treaty ports', Hong Kong was ceded to Britain and a huge indemnity was to be paid. Such conditions were unlikely to keep the peace for long, given the greed of European merchants and the contemptuous aloofness together with an absolute certainty of superiority of Imperial China. In less than twenty years the redcoats would be back to inflict more cruelties and humiliations. We may perhaps leave the last word for the present to Colonel Wyndham Baker, who observed at first-hand that the Chinese 'would make such perfect soldiers if taken properly in hand'.

In the same month as the signing of the Treaty of Nanking, August 1842, another event of importance to the British Army was the re-appointment of the Duke of Wellington as Commander-in-Chief. In his customary way he refused to solicit favours for people of whom he knew nothing, yet continued to be generous to old soldiers who had served with him. The Chartist movement, unrest in Ireland because of famine and O'Connell's agitation for Home Rule, demanding more troops there, the repeal of the Corn Laws, the inadequacy of the defences at home against a possible French threat, squashing Prince Albert's ideas about new military caps for officers – these were the things that concerned him more than introducing any real reform for the Army. He did, however, agree that the new Minié rifle should be supplied, yet absurdly in an *unrifled* model so that the huge supply of musket balls should not be wasted. He even objected to the word rifle itself, and would not permit the soldiers equipped with them to call them rifles: 'We must not allow them to fancy they are all riflemen, or they will become conceited, and be wanting next to be dressed in green, or some other *jack-a-dandy* uniform.' On the broader issue of the army's strength he had sounder views. So concerned was he in 1847 and 1848 (this last year saw revolutions all over Europe) about both the possible danger from France and mounting discontent in Ireland that he recommended privately to Palmerston, still Foreign Secretary, Anglesey, Master General of the Ordnance, and Burgoyne, Inspector General of Fortifications, that the Regular Army at home should be increased from 50,000 to 80,000 or, if this could not be accepted, an expansion of the Militia to 150,000.

Yet, given the strict policy of economy, neither of these measures was likely to be approved. Much more necessary for the Army's general efficiency was to overhaul the administrative system, to ensure that the Royal Waggon Train was not totally disbanded, to supply those deficiencies in tents, medical support and other equipment and services essential to the deployment of troops in the field. But here Wellington took no action. He disliked innovation, indeed he looked on the Army, in the words of Elizabeth Longford, as an anomaly, to be kept away from the public eye, best hidden overseas in the colonies to protect the country's interests there. In his attitude to the Army he was ultra-conservative, unwilling to risk any change, any new ideas, if he thought the old would serve. The fact is that he became Commander-in-Chief for the second time when he was already too old and he stayed in the job far too long. The Duke cannot escape the charge that much of the incompetence shown by the Army in the Crimean War was the result of his unwillingness to introduce new equipment, organization and method. It is this indictment which sticks – not Sir John Fortescue's accusation that Wellington did not care for the Army. He cared too much to risk changes which he did not understand. On the other hand, his arrangements to cope with the Chartist crisis of 1848, when huge crowds threatened to march on Westminster, by judiciously posting his troops out of sight, and having a large number of special constables enrolled, showed how sure was his touch when it came to defusing potentially ugly situations. There was happily no fighting for his Army to do at home. But there was plenty of action overseas.

The main business of the British redcoats together with the Company's sepoy army was tightening their grip on India, and some exceptionally able men directed them in doing so. Charles Napier, of Peninsular fame, conquered Sind and suppressed *suttee*, widow-burning, in the simplest and most effective way – 'when men burn women alive, we hang them'. Napier was in every way a remarkable man. Fearless in action, full of common sense, in no doubt about the benefits of British rule, totally honest about the real purpose of taking Sind (that is, to the Company's advantage), but genuinely believing that his rule would be infinitely better than that of the Amirs, he defined the Imperial mission of conquest as a process of administering a good thrashing, followed by kindness. It almost echoes Hamlet's 'I must be cruel only to be kind'. In describing Napier, James Morris instantly excites our sympathy and admiration for him by saying that 'he felt only a vehement contempt for most politicians, most civil servants, most bigwigs of the East India Company and all the Amirs of Sind'. There must be good, we might comment, in a man with feelings like this. Morris goes on to tell us how Napier's brother, William, whom we last met in Chapter 7 giving us a picture of Peninsular battles, gave this account of how what is now The Cheshire Regiment conducted themselves in the decisive battle of Miani in 1843: 'Guarding their heads with large dark shields [the Sind troops] shook their sharp swords, gleaming in the sun, and their shouts rolled like peals of thunder as with frantic might and gestures they dashed against the front of the 22nd. But, with shrieks as wild and fierce, and hearts as big and strong, the British soldiers met them with the queen of weapons, and laid their foremost warriors wallowing in blood.' So Sind was annexed, and Ellenborough, who was concerned that the Sikh army in the Punjab might combine with the army of Gwalior, first defeated this latter force, turning Gwalior into a protected state, so that he might then turn his attention to the Punjab.

His action in Gwalior, however, caused his recall and replacement by Sir Henry Hardinge, who soon found that the Sikh army was indeed bent on making trouble. In December 1845 they crossed the Sutlej and were met at Mudki by Sir Hugh Gough with a mixed force of British and Indian troops. He defeated them there and again at Ferozshah, but it was not until early in 1846 that two more battles – one at Aliwal, where our old friend, Sir Harry Smith, commanded (he called the charger which he took to South Africa 'Aliwal' and even gave a South African town the same name) and another even more decisive one at Sobraon – broke the Sikh power for the time being. Early in 1848, however, when the Resident, Henry Lawrence, was on leave in England, the Sikh army rebelled once more. These further troubles coincided with the arrival of Dalhousie as governor-general, who knew nothing about war in India, and was faced with the proclamation of a holy war by Mulraj, governor of Multan province. Once more Gough led a mixed army of British and Company troops, and fought two actions against the Sikhs who were splendid soldiers. The first of these battles, Chilianwala, has gone down in history as a disgrace for the British cavalry. It was fought on 13 January 1849 and we may perhaps accompany some of those who took part in it.

Chilianwala was primarily an infantry battle, preceded as was customary by an artillery bombardment. Gough had decided to attack the Sikh army, perhaps 30,000 strong, with his own mixed force of British and Company regiments of about 14,000 men, including two cavalry brigades. While the infantry battle was in progress, the Sikhs attempted to outflank both British wings with their cavalry. On the British left a spirited charge by the 3rd Light Dragoons 'Grey' squadron, during which they lost, killed or wounded, nearly half their total of about a hundred, so dismayed the Sikhs that they retired from the field. On the British right, however, it was a different story. There, the brigade commanded by Alexander Pope, who had no experience of leading anything larger than a squadron in the field and who was so unwell that he had to be lifted on to his horse, contained two British regiments, the 9th Lancers and 14th Light Dragoons, and two Bengal Native Cavalry regiments. Having initially deployed his brigade in a long thin line, which not only got in front of the supporting guns and infantry, but was tactically absurd in close country, his order to change deployment, at the very moment when a small body of Sikh cavalry attacked, was so completely misunderstood (what was probably an order to form threes to the *right* was taken by the Native

Cavalry to mean turn *about*) that the disgraceful sight of an entire brigade galloping off to the rear – the British cavalry getting mixed up with their Bengal comrades – was enough to encourage the Sikhs to follow up and attack the horse artillery. Captain Thompson of the 14th Light Dragoons has left this account of it:

> Having previously drawn swords, the brigade was now ordered to advance at a trot, without a skirmisher or scout in front, or a man in support or reserve in rear, through broken, jungly ground, where some of the enemy's horsemen were seen to loiter, watching our movements. Brigadier Pope himself led the line in front of the native cavalry, forming the centre by which we had been ordered to dress and regulate our pace, when insensibly its trot dwindled to a walk, and then came to a dead halt at the sight of a few Sikh horsemen peering over the bushes . . . I then saw Colonel King, commanding the 14th Light Dragoons, gallop to the Brigadier in front, energetically pointing with his sword towards the enemy position and evidently urging an attack, which the other seemed unable to make up his mind to order. The Sikhs seeing the hesitation, a handful of their horsemen, some forty or fifty in a lump, charged boldly into the thick of the native cavalry, who instantly turned with the cry 'threes about', and disappeared for the rest of the day.

The Commanding Officer of the 9th Lancers, Hope Grant, had a similar story to tell, adding that when the native cavalry turned about, his own squadrons did the same, without any orders from him, and despite all his efforts to stop them and turn them back again to face the enemy, they galloped away mixed up with the native cavalry. 'They appeared,' he wrote, 'to have got panic-struck'. Pope was mortally wounded during the action, and Colonel King subsequently committed suicide. Because of the cavalry's retirement, Gough's right-hand infantry brigade had a hard fight, but succeeded in holding on; when night fell the battle concluded without decision. About a month later, however, at Gujrat, and although Charles Napier had been dispatched from England to take over command, Gough met the Sikh army again. This time, with great superiority of guns, he fought a conventionally sound battle, hammering the enemy with his artillery, following this with a sustained infantry assault which broke the Sikh army, and then delivering the final *coup de grâce* with a prolonged cavalry pursuit. The Scinde Horse, observed General Thackwell commanding the cavalry, rushed upon the enemy with fiery speed, driving all before them, sabres flashing and circling. Captain Delmar, 9th Lancers, reported some terrible scenes:

> I never saw such butchery and murder! It was almost too horrible to commit to paper – there were our own men sticking their lances into them [the Sikhs] like so much *butter*, but the way in which this

sticking business took place, was truly shocking – fancy a man piercing you thro' the head and body, and, after all this, shooting you by way of a finish . . . But besides all this *ground* shooting, there was an immense deal of *tree* shooting . . . Every tree that was standing was well searched, and two or three Sikhs were found concealing in almost every tree we passed – this afforded great *sport* for our men, who were firing up at them as at so many rooks . . . Down they would come like a bird, head downward, and bleeding most profusely.

Gujrat effectively ended the war; the Sikhs surrendered and Dalhousie annexed the Punjab, which was then superbly administered by men like the two Lawrence brothers, Henry and John, and John Nicholson, of whom it was said that no Punjabi could hear his name spoken without shivering in his pyjamas.

All the great battles which the British fought for the final subjugation of India are brought freshly to our memory when we visit garrison towns like Colchester or Tidworth – Assaye, Aliwal, Bhurtpore, Gwalior, Sobraon – they are all there still and many others enshrined in the names of Barracks. Dalhousie had not finished his business of extending British rule in annexing the Punjab. The states of Satara, Sambalpur, Nagpur and Jhansi (we shall meet the legendary Rani of Jhansi before long) were added to British rule between 1848 and 1854. He annexed Oudh in 1856, and four years earlier had sent an expedition to Burma to punish the king of Ava for attacking the British at Rangoon, defeating the Burmese army and then annexing the province of Pegu. Dalhousie transformed India's rail and canal communications, set up schools, revolutionized local administration and generally brought great benefits to all the territories he had conquered and annexed. But all this did not prevent his being blamed for the great Indian Mutiny which broke out within a year of his returning home.

In 1852 the victor of Assaye, the sepoy general, the Fabian soldier, the Iron Duke, without whose presence in command the battle of Waterloo might have been lost, the Commander-in-Chief of the British Army for the previous ten years, died. 'He was honest, brave, loyal and generous. He was universally loved and respected. He walked with kings and kept the common touch. He was a great and good man, whose example was an inspiration to his contemporaries, and when he died the whole nation mourned him.'* Two years later one of Wellington's pupils, Fitzroy Somerset, Lord Raglan, was to show that in all the years he had been understudying his renowned master, he had learned practically nothing.

* *Wellingtonian Studies*, ed. Michael Howard, Gale & Polden, 1958.

CHAPTER TEN

The Crimea

I am convinced from what I see that Lord Raglan is utterly incompetent to lead an army through any arduous task. He is a brave good soldier, I am sure, and a polished gentleman, but he is no more fit than I am to cope with any leader of strategic skill . . . For a long time I was close to Lord Raglan on the 5th. He was wrong in two palpable respects: he exposed himself uselessly to fire, and he gave no directions whatever; he was a mere cool and callous spectator. But the most serious disadvantage under which he labours is that he does not go among the troops. He does not visit the camp, he does not cheer them or speak to them, and his person is in consequence almost unknown to them.

WILLIAM HOWARD RUSSELL*

The Crimean War was caused by the arrogant bullying of Turkey by Czar Nicholas I in his championing of the Greek Church; by the refusal of Turkey to give in to such bullying; by Great Britain's determination both to maintain Turkey's integrity and to put a stop to the extension of Russian power in the East; and by Napoleon III's ardent desire to cut a figure in the world and attract more military glory to France. Crisis was precipitated by Napoleon's demand in 1851 that custody of the Holy Places,† which had been granted to France by the Sultan of Turkey in both the sixteenth and eighteenth centuries, should be restored. Early in 1852 the Sultan agreed. Nicholas I took violent exception, ostensibly as champion of the Greek Church, but really because he believed the time had come to expel the Turks from Europe and divide up the property of 'the sick man'. To achieve a settlement of the so-called Eastern Question, he

---

* Russell, the foremost journalist of his day, was war correspondent for *The Times* reporting on the Crimean War, the Indian Mutiny, the American Civil War and the Franco-Prussian War. His influence was great, and his reports gave Russia too much information.

† The Holy Places included the Bethlehem Church enclosing the Sanctuary of the Nativity, the tomb of the Virgin Mary at Gethsemane, and the Jerusalem Church of the Holy Sepulchre. The dispute about their custody was between Greek and Latin Christians, or put another way, between Russia and France.

was prepared to go to war. Thus a trivial argument was employed to justify what was in fact a struggle for supremacy in the East.

In March 1853 the Czar sent Prince Menschikoff, who was both tactless and insolent, to Constantinople to demand that the Sultan should recognize both the Greek Church's claims to custody of the Holy Places and – much more significantly – Russia's right to protect the Sultan's Greek Orthodox subjects. At this point there re-enters the Constantinople stage Lord Stratford de Redcliffe, who had been British Ambassador at the Sublime Porte for ten years from 1842, who had been acclaimed the 'Great Eltchi' (Ambassador) by the Turks because of his encouragement of reform, and who was strongly prejudiced against Nicholas I. In distinguishing between the two Russian demands, Stratford induced the Sultan to satisfy the Greek Church with regard to the Holy Places, but at the same time lent his support to the Sultan in Turkey's rejection of Russia's claim to be the protector of the Sultan's Greek Christians. In June 1853 Russia invaded the principalities of Moldavia and Wallachia, and after much diplomatic manoeuvring during which the Great Powers attempted to produce a compromise acceptable to both Russia and Turkey, but failed to reach agreement, Turkey declared war in October 1853. Thereafter events led rapidly to an extension of the war: Omar Pasha defeated a Russian army at Oltenitza, the French and British fleets passed the Dardanelles, the Russian fleet destroyed a Turkish squadron at Sinope off the southern coast of the Black Sea, and in January 1854 the Allied fleets entered the Black Sea. In March France and Britain declared war on Russia.

The difficulty facing the Allies, who wanted to ensure that Russian armies both evacuated the Principalities and did not reach Constantinople, was what military strategy should be adopted to achieve these aims. The French and British armies had arrived at Gallipoli and Scutari by the end of May 1854, and it quickly became clear how ill-prepared the British Army was, with no tents, no land transport corps (the War Office had turned down Raglan's request), and totally inadequate medical arrangements. The Allied armies made their way to Varna in order to deal with the Russians in the Principalities, although by the time they got to Varna in August, the Russians had withdrawn. At this point both malaria and cholera struck the Allied soldiers. It was then decided by the Allied governments to attack Sebastopol with a view to taking and destroying this centre of Russian power in the Black Sea and so removing the threat to Turkey. Opposition to the plan from Allied commanders on the spot was overruled, and in September the French and British armies landed in the bay of Eupatoria to the north of Sebastopol, and began their advance. The French army under General St Arnaud (who was gravely ill and soon to die) numbered some 30,000 with 70 guns, the British about 26,000 men and 66 guns. Lord Raglan (whose long years

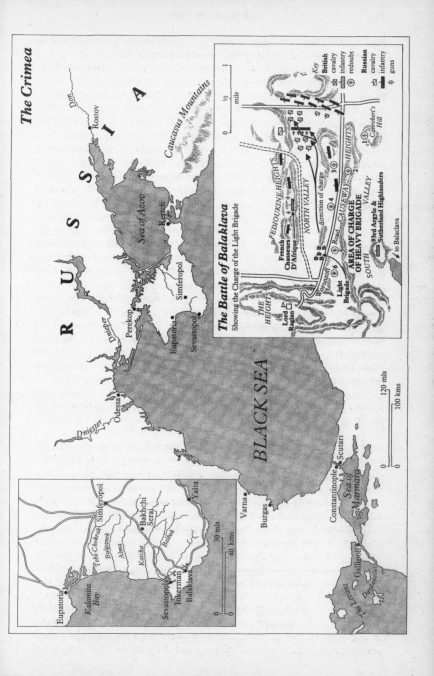

The Crimea

RUSSIA

Don

Rostov

Sea of Azov

Caucasus Mountains

Kerch

Dnieper

Perekop

Simferopol

Dniester

Eupatoria

Sevastopol

Odessa

BLACK SEA

120 mils

100 kms

Varna

Burgas

Constantinople

Scutari

Sea of Marmara

Gallipoli

Dardanelles

The Battle of Balaklava
Showing the Charge of the Light Brigade

Key

British
⊠ cavalry
▨ infantry
⊞ redoubt

Russian
⊯ cavalry
⊟ infantry
╫ guns

FEDIOUKINE HEIGHTS

French
Chasseurs
D'Afrique

NORTH VALLEY

direction of charge

HEIGHTS

CAUSEWAY

Woronzoff Road

⊞6 ⊞5 ⊞4 ⊞3 ⊞2 ⊞1

SOUTH VALLEY

Cantrobert's Hill

93rd Argyle &
Sutherland Highlanders

to Balaclava

AREA OF CHARGE
OF HEAVY BRIGADE

THE HEIGHTS

Lord
Raglan

Light
Brigade

0   ½   1
mile

Eupatoria

Kalamita Bay

Sevastopol

Inkerman

Balaclava

Tchernaya

Simferopol

Tchi Chokruk

Bulganek

Alma

Katcha

Belbek

Bakhchi Serai

Yalta

30 mils

40 kms

fighting the French had made such an impression on him that even as his allies in the Crimea he still referred to them as the enemy) was not best served by his subordinate commanders – Lucan commanded the cavalry, with his brother-in-law, Cardigan, in charge of the Light Brigade – and as Captain Portal of the 4th Light Dragoons observed, 'two bigger fools could not be picked out of the British Army'. The infantry divisional generals, who included the Duke of Cambridge and Sir George Cathcart, could hardly fail to be an improvement, but could not be compared with the brilliant infantry leaders who had served under Wellington. Airey was Raglan's Chief of Staff. Opposing the Allied advance towards Sebastopol was a force of some 40,000 Russian soldiers under the command of Prince Menschikoff, who had established his men and about a hundred guns on the high ground overlooking the river Alma, fifteen miles north of Sebastopol. It was here that the first of the four battles of the Crimean War (with Balaklava, Inkerman and the siege of Sebastopol itself still to come) took place. The battle of Alma was fought on 20 September and was characteristic of most Crimean encounters as far as the Allies were concerned – no proper reconnaissance, no clear plan, poor co-ordination, those who were supposed to be directing the troops in the wrong place, exercising very little control, and the outcome determined by the sheer courage and endurance of the British infantry. One of the most extraordinary features of the battle was that a key Russian strongpoint, the Great Redoubt, had to be taken *twice*, first by the Light Division and 2nd Division, and then again – because the reserve divisions were not moved forward quickly enough to consolidate its capture – after the Russians had reoccupied it, by the Guards and Highlanders. We may perhaps look at each in turn, after Raglan had given the order to advance:

The first line of the British army, the Light Infantry Division and the 2nd Division, rose to its feet with a cheer, and, dressing in a line two miles wide, though only two men deep, marched forward towards the river. Under terrific fire – forty guns were trained on the river, and rifle bullets whipped the surface of the water into a bloody foam – the first British troops began to struggle across the Alma, the men so parched with thirst that even at this moment they stopped to drink . . . During the terrible crossing of the river formation was lost, and it was a horde which surged up the bank and, formed by shouting, cursing officers into some ragged semblance of a line, pressed on up the deadly natural glacis towards the Great Redoubt. It seemed impossible that the slender, straggling line could survive . . . Again and again large gaps were torn in the line, the slopes became littered with bodies and sloppy with blood, but the survivors closed up and pressed on, their officers urging, swearing, yelling like demons.

The men's blood was up. The Light Infantry Division, heroes of a dozen stubborn and bloody battles in the Peninsula, advanced through the smoke, swearing most horribly as their comrades fell ... suddenly, unbelievably the guns ceased to fire ... the British troops gave a great shout, and in a last frantic rush a mob of mixed battalions tumbled into the earthwork. The Great Redoubt had been stormed.*

But, alas, the Duke of Cambridge's division with a brigade of Guards and the Highland Brigade, which should have been following up, had not moved forward from its position above, that is to the north of the river. The result was that after an artillery bombardment large numbers of Russian infantry moved forward to reoccupy the Great Redoubt, pushing the British troops who had just captured it down the hill again. So, the Guards and Highlanders, fired at now by Russian guns from the Lesser Redoubt and from the slopes of the hill, advanced in their turn to retake the Great Redoubt. Despite terrible fire from cannon and rifles, they advanced with as steady a line as if they were taking part in a Hyde Park review. When an officer, seeing the casualties being inflicted on the Grenadier and Coldstream Guards, suggested to Sir Colin Campbell that they should retire or risk the destruction of the Brigade of Guards, he received the magnificent reply that it would be better for every man of Her Majesty's Guards to lie dead on the field than for them to turn their backs on the enemy. Not only did the Guards and Highlanders retake the Great Redoubt, they successfully repelled a further Russian infantry attack, and as they then charged forward, the enemy fled, leaving the Allies in triumphant possession of the battlefield. Lord Raglan wanted to follow up this success with an instant advance to seize Sebastopol, a move that would probably have succeeded, but the French would not hear of it. Instead, a methodical move to the east and then the south of Sebastopol was made, giving the Russians time both to strengthen the city's defences and to reinforce the Crimea, leading in the following month, October, to one of the most memorable episodes, featuring at once crass stupidity on the part of general officers and glorious courage on that of ordinary soldiers, in the British Army's history. It took place near the port of Balaklava.

'You have lost the Light Brigade!' It was thus that Lord Raglan bitterly reproached Lord Lucan on the evening of 25 October 1854. As a simple statement of fact the words were not unfounded. Before the charge, according to Captain Portal who rode in it, the Light Cavalry Brigade had mustered on parade some 700 men; after it they numbered a mere 180.† But had *Lucan* lost it? Controversy as to who

---

* *The Reason Why*, Cecil Woodham-Smith, McGraw-Hill, 1954.
† In act 607 charged; 198 were at roll-call afterwards.

was to blame features in many a dissertation. The truth is, of course, that many people were to blame, Lucan among them. It was a coalescence of personal ill-feeling, general mismanagement and peculiarly bad orders which led to so great, yet glorious, a blunder. Given the circumstances which prevailed, however – a Commander-in-Chief who had no very clear idea of how to conduct operations and, unlike his teacher, The Duke, accustomed to expressing himself with as little precision and as much ambiguity as the putting together of words would allow; a Lieutenant-General of cavalry wholly at odds with his Commander-in-Chief's direction of the campaign and with the way in which the Light Brigade was being handled by his brother-in-law, Lord Cardigan; and an aide-de-camp who at the critical moment of delivering the fatal order was almost insane with impatience and injured pride, so much so that he actually appeared to point to the wrong objective – given these circumstances, we may perhaps accept General Airey's laconic judgement that it was 'nothing to Chilianwala'.* For when all is said and done, it was a feat of arms principally recalled not for foolhardiness and wanton sacrifice, but for courage, discipline and devotion to duty.

Two important actions, both part of the battle of Balaklava, preceded and led to the Light Brigade's charge. One was the gallant thin red line stand of Sir Colin Campbell's 93rd Highlanders†; the other was the charge of the Heavy Brigade. The battle was brought about by a Russian attempt to capture Balaklava, the British Army's only port through which all the sinews of war must come. And on the morning of 25 October the British Army was singularly ill-deployed to meet and defeat this Russian attack. Apart from the 93rd Highlanders and about 1,000 Turks, the only troops between the port and General Liprandi's advancing force of 25,000 horse, foot and guns were the two brigades of the Cavalry Division, positioned some two miles north of Balaklava at the foot of the Fedioukine Heights.

Lord Lucan received four orders from Lord Raglan during the action of 25 October. None of them was precise. Each of them was either too late to be executed as intended, violently resented by Lucan, misunderstood by him to the point of being ignored, or so mis-interpreted that the result was calamitous. There is nothing either new or old about this. Even today with excellent communications, as orders are transmitted from one level to another, they change in emphasis and purpose, for each commander has his own view of a battle, broad or narrow. Each has his own general and particular intention. No wonder they seldom coincide. But the misinterpretation of Raglan's fourth order which led to Cardigan's restrained, yet momentous declaration: 'The Brigade will advance' was as absolute as it could have been, and we must understand the other three to see how

---

* An odd comment, for although, as we have seen, Chilianwala was a fiasco, there were very few cavalry casualties.
† The Argyll and Sutherland Highlanders.

it came about. The first order was: 'Cavalry to take ground to left of second line of Redoubts occupied by the Turks.' To execute the order, although he did so, was not merely distasteful to Lucan, as it seemed to condemn his command to a static (in the cavalry a word synonymous with useless) role. Much more important, much worse in Lucan's eyes, for his tactical sense was sound enough, the order was dangerous, even absurd, since by moving to the redoubts on the Causeway Heights, the cavalry would isolate still further Sir Colin Campbell's tiny force of 500 Highlanders, the final defence of Balaklava itself. Thus at the very beginning of the action, the General of Cavalry found himself unable to understand his Commander-in-Chief's tactical purpose and in furious disagreement with his tactical methods. The main reason for this almost total discord was, of course, that being in very different positions on the ground, the two men had very different ideas of what the enemy and their own troops were up to. This perilous disparity of view was underlined by what now transpired.

To those coolly sitting their horses with Lord Raglan on the Sapouné Heights, the incident must at first have appeared to be an example of that insolent indifference to danger which characterized many a British military event in the nineteenth century; later it must have seemed more like culpable inactivity, and indeed it became comprehensible only when the contours of the ground upon which they were looking were themselves appreciated. A large body of Russian cavalry on its way to attack the Highlanders had appeared to pass within a few hundred yards of the British cavalry now stationed where Lord Raglan had directed – on the left of the second line of Redoubts. But although one of these cavalry formations passed so close to the other, the two could not see each other, were not even aware of each other's proximity, simply because of the high ground between them. Yet for Raglan and his staff looking down upon them, this unawareness was not apparent. The Russian cavalry then proceeded to attack the 93rd Highlanders, but 'the slender red line' was more than a match for half a dozen squadrons of enemy cavalry. Three times the Russians came at them; three times they were met with disciplined steadiness – although Sir Colin Campbell was once obliged to damn his men's eagerness to charge – and precise fire-power. It was enough. The enemy retired.

These Russian squadrons were, however, only the vanguard of a much larger force of cavalry which had crossed the Causeway Heights after them. But even before the 93rd's gallant little action had been fought, the mere threat of it had given rise to Raglan's second order to Lucan: 'Eight squadrons of Heavy Dragoons to be detached towards Balaklava to support the Turks who are wavering.' This was the order which led to the Heavy Brigade's resolute, controlled and astonishingly successful charge against what seemed to be overwhelmingly superior numbers of enemy horsemen. 'How can such a handful resist, much less make headway through such a legion?' wondered Lord George Paget, commanding the 4th Light Dragoons, as he watched. Yet such was the timing as each of the three lines charged, and such was the spirit of the dragoons, that they did. The Russians broke, disintegrated and fled. 'It is over', Paget went on. 'They give way! The heaving mass rolls to the left. They fly! Never shall I forget that moment.'

It was *then* that the Light Brigade *should* have charged. Fortescue judged that had they done so, 'the host of the Russian horse might have suffered a discomfiture with few parallels in the annals of war'. But Cardigan was not the man to act without specific orders. Initiative, except in designing bizarre uniforms or ogling pretty women, was foreign to his nature. The moment passed, and the Russian cavalry, unmolested further and complete with their artillery were allowed to establish themselves at the eastern end of the North Valley, guns unlimbered and ready for action. They would not have long to wait. There is a certain inevitability about each bad order of Raglan's leading relentlessly to the next one. The uncovering of Balaklava by his first order to Lucan was followed by the Russian cavalry advance, and this in turn prompted his second order which resulted in the Heavy Brigade's charge. Then came the deployment of the Russians in such a way that Raglan issued his third and fourth orders. It was makeshift of the worst sort. Not only was the purpose of Raglan's orders misunderstood by Lucan; there was such a long time between Raglan's making up his mind as to what he should do and its actually being done, a circumstance largely brought about by the remoteness of his position, on commanding ground though it was, from the scene of the fighting, that the conditions which had led to his giving the orders were wholly altered. Raglan had never intended that the Heavy Brigade should take on the bulk of the Russian horse; he wanted them to *protect* the Highlanders and the Turks.

Now came his third order, which was at once misunderstood by Lucan. When, as a result of the Heavy Brigade's action, the Russians recrossed the Causeway Heights and were north of them, Raglan determined to recapture the Redoubts, the Causeway Heights and the Woronzoff Road. To take and hold ground would demand infantry, and although the 1st Division was available, the 4th Division, under command of the disgruntled and almost insubordinate Sir George Cathcart, was taking its time. But Raglan did not wish to lose his moment and conceived the idea of recovering the Heights with cavalry, so facilitating their subsequent reoccupation by infantry divisions. Not only was Raglan's third order a masterpiece of ambiguity, but the version of it retained by Raglan differed slightly in words but significantly in possible meaning from that which reached Lucan. Raglan's version read: 'Cavalry to advance and take advantage of any opportunity to recover the Heights. They will be supported by

the infantry, which have been ordered to advance on two fronts.'
What Raglan meant by this was that the cavalry was to advance *at
once*, recapture the Redoubts and control the Heights, while the
infantry, who had already been told what to do, would follow. Had
the words 'at once' been inserted after 'advance' in the first sentence,
and the word 'later' after 'supported' in the second, all ambiguity
would have been removed. As it was, however, we must concede in
fairness to Lucan that there was room for misinterpretation; moreover
his version was different in that after the first sentence, came two
more: 'They will be supported by the infantry which have been
ordered. Advance on two fronts'. Lucan's reading of the order was
that he was not to advance until supported by the infantry, in other
words the exact opposite of what Raglan intended. Lucan thereupon
took some action, but not what his Commander-in-Chief wanted and
expected. The Cavalry Division was mounted, and while the Light
Brigade positioned itself at the western end of North Valley, the Heavy
Brigade was drawn up behind them on Woronzoff Road. So disposed,
Lucan waited for the infantry.

With mounting impatience Lord Raglan gazed down at these
manoeuvres. He was sure that a movement by the cavalry across the
Causeway Heights would force the enemy to withdraw from the
Redoubts, and he was sure that the time to move was now. Yet still
Lucan made no move. When it became clear that parties of Russian
artillerymen were preparing to take their guns away from the
Redoubts, Raglan's agitation knew no bounds, and it was then that he
sent out the fatally misunderstood fourth and last order to Lucan. It
had been written out by General Airey from Raglan's instruction, and
read:

> Lord Raglan wishes the Cavalry to advance rapidly to the front –
> follow the enemy and try to prevent the enemy carrying away the
> guns. Troop Horse Artillery may accompany. French cavalry is on
> your left. Immediate.

We see again that a precise word or two substituted for an imprecise
phrase would have removed all ambiguity. What 'to the front' means
to one man is very different from what it means to another. Had
Raglan so phrased the order that it clearly complemented his previous
one, the one relating specifically to the Causeway Heights, as he meant
it to, how differently Lucan would have read it. Had it said: Cavalry to
advance to the Causeway Heights to prevent enemy carrying away the
guns from the Redoubts, Lucan would have been in no doubt as to
what his Commander-in-Chief wanted. But he read the two orders as
separate, unrelated ones. And to make confusion worse confounded, it
was Captain Nolan of the 15th Hussars who carried the order to
Lucan, Nolan, the passionate advocate of light cavalry, who had
endured agonies of humiliation and frustration at the Light Brigade's

inexplicable inactivity when so splendid and classic an opportunity –
after the Heavy Brigade's charge – had presented itself. Furthermore
Raglan had aggravated both the imprecision of his order and the
furious impetuosity of Captain Nolan by calling out to him as he rode
off: 'Tell Lord Lucan the cavalry is to attack at once.'

To Lord Lucan the written order was not merely obscure. It was
crazy. The only guns that he could see were those at the eastern end of
North Valley – *to his front*. For cavalry to attack batteries of guns
frontally and alone was to contravene every tactical principle and to
invite destruction. As Lucan read and re-read the order with growing
consternation, Nolan, almost beside himself at Lucan's apparent
reluctance to take immediate and decisive action, repeated in tones of
arrogant contempt the Commander-in-Chief's urgent postscript that
the Cavalry should attack at once. Small wonder that Lucan should
have burst out angrily: 'Attack, sir? Attack what? What guns, sir?
Where and what to do?' It was then that Nolan with his gesture of
fury, but not of direction, and with his words, full of insolence but
empty of precision – 'There, my lord, is your enemy, there are your
guns' – pointed, or appeared to point, at the very guns that Lucan
could see, those at the end of North Valley. This then was the objective
which Lucan passed on as the Commander-in-Chief's order to Lord
Cardigan. Even Cardigan felt obliged to point out that the valley was
commanded by guns not only to the front, but right and left as well.
Lucan acknowledged his objection, but insisted that it was Lord
Raglan's wish and that there was no choice but to obey.

The position then before Lord Cardigan gave his order to advance
was this. The Russians occupied the Fedioukine Heights with horse,
foot and guns, and the Causeway Heights including the 1st, 2nd and
3rd Redoubts with infantry and guns. At the head, that is the eastern
end, of North Valley were twelve guns facing west and behind them
the main body of Russian cavalry. About a mile and a half away, at the
western end of the valley, was the Light Brigade. Colonel Lord George
Paget of the 4th Light Dragoons was enjoying a 'remarkably good'
cigar when Nolan and Lucan had their angry conference. Meanwhile
the 1st Division had occupied the ground held by the 93rd Highlanders and the 4th Division had marched to the area of No. 4
Redoubt. They were about to witness something that had not been
seen since the days of Murat. After receiving his orders from Lucan,
Cardigan rode over to Paget. As he did so, Colonel Shewell of the 8th
Hussars reprimanded some of his men because they were still enjoying
their pipes. They were, Shewell complained, 'disgracing the Regiment
by smoking in the presence of the enemy'. We may readily conceive
Paget's dilemma. Was he disgracing his own Regiment by smoking the
cigar? 'Am I to set this bad example?' he asked himself. Reflecting that
a good cigar was no 'common article in those days', he determined to
keep it. The 4th Light Dragoons were not called 'Paget's Irregular

Horse' for nothing. The cigar lasted until the charge was over.

Lord Cardigan deployed the brigade in two lines. He placed three regiments in the front line, from right to left the 13th Light Dragoons, the 17th Lancers and the 11th Hussars, the latter being slightly in rear of the other two. The second line, under Paget's command, had the 8th Hussars on the right and the 4th Light Dragoons on the left. Even at this stage Lucan could not resist interfering, and he instructed Colonel Douglas, commanding the 11th Hussars, Cardigan's own regiment, to drop back to a position supporting the front line. Paget, still smoking his cigar, placed himself at the head of his regiment ready to give Cardigan his 'best support'. It was because of Cardigan's repeated request for Paget's best support that well before the brigade had reached the guns, the 4th Light Dragoons had come up to the left of the 11th Hussars to form the second line, with the 8th Hussars in the right rear.

'Walk march. Trot.' Cardigan gave the order and his trumpeter sounded 'March'. The charge was on. But the story of the charge is best told by those who rode in it. Here is Captain Portal, 4th Light Dragoons:

> We went at a steady pace at first, and when we saw all the Russian cavalry retiring, all the men cheered and went on to a gallop. When we had ridden a quarter of a mile from our starting-point, a most fearful fire opened on us from the hills on both sides of us, grape, shells and minie ball fell like hail round us, to say nothing of 18-lb shot which whistled through our ranks dealing death and destruc-tion all around. However, on we still kept going, knowing not whither, till at last we had got so far that we had crossed through this cross-fire and found ourselves in the middle of all the gunners, and would, had we had plenty of support instead of none, have brought all the guns back with us ... we retired in perfect order towards our original position; of course, at full gallop. To do this, we had again to pass through this murderous cross-fire I have told you of; if anything, the fire was more severe than before, and neither I nor anyone else who saw what we had to do, thought that the few left of us would ever get back.

Lieutenant Calthorpe of the 8th Hussars did not take part in the charge as he was serving on the staff as an aide-de-camp, but he observed it, and this is what he had to say in his *Letters from Head Quarters*:

> The pace of our cavalry increased every moment, until they went thundering along the valley, making the ground tremble beneath them. The awful slaughter that was going on ... did not check them. On they went headlong to death, disregarding aught but the object of their attack. At length they arrived at the guns, their

numbers sadly thinner, but the few that remained made fearful havoc amongst the enemy's artillery . . . This was the moment when a general was most required, but unfortunately Ld Cardigan was not present . . . his horse took fright – swerved round – and galloped off to the rear, passing on the way by the 4th Light Dragoons and the 8th Hussars before those regiments got up to the battery.

Calthorpe was wrong about Cardigan's horse. It had not taken fright. Nor had Cardigan. His indifference both to the hazards of the charge and the fate of his brigade once it had charged was remarkable. Having evaded some Cossacks by galloping back through the enemy guns, he judged his duty done and calmly rode back down the valley. Calthorpe goes on:

The Russians sent a large body of Cossacks of the Don to cut off our retreat. This was first observed by one of the troop-officers of the 8th Hussars, who immediately rode up and informed Colonel Shewell . . . Colonel Shewell at once ordered his regiment to wheel about, which being done, he gave the order to charge, and was himself the first to enter the herd of Cossacks. These unfortunates, completely surprised by the manoeuvre, offered but feeble resistance, and this single squadron of the 8th passed through the Russians of four times their strength, cutting down all in their way, while the rest dispersed to the right and left. A way was thus cleared for the remainder of our cavalry to return, unopposed – but not unmolested, as the enemy opened upon them with grape from their guns on both flanks, besides throwing out swarms of skirmishers, which combined fire made fearful havoc of the gallant remains of the Light Brigade.

Perhaps it was Lord George Paget who had the most vivid memories of it all. As the Brigade charged home, the leading lines of the 13th Light Dragoons and the 17th Lancers suffered terrible casualties as the guns in front of them opened fire. The remnants, about fifty, galloped through the guns, sabres and lances at work, and on to rout some Russian Hussars until checked by numerous Cossacks. Next came the 11th Hussars, again right through the guns to pursue a regiment of fleeing enemy Lancers. Then Paget led the 4th Light Dragoons at full gallop on to the enemy gunners, while on the right the 8th Hussars in exact formation under the iron discipline of Colonel Shewell galloped through the battery and halted on the far side. Those who had survived now faced a double danger – in front they were threatened by huge bodies of enemy cavalry; behind them were six squadrons of Russian Lancers who had ridden down from the Fedioukine Heights. Lord Cardigan was nowhere to be seen, and it was Paget who rallied the 4th Light Dragoons and the 11th Hussars, and by charging towards the enemy Lancers, succeeded in brushing past them. Meanwhile Shewell had taken similar action with his seventy troopers, and then began the retreat, worse, far worse than the charge itself. When Mrs Duberley, wife of the 8th Hussar paymaster, saw the pitiful groups of men making their way back, she thought at first that they were skirmishers. 'Good God!' she exclaimed when she realized the truth. 'It is the Light Brigade.' Paget's comments on the bearing of riderless horses during the charge show the terror they felt without the reassuring presence of their riders:

> They made dashes at me, some advancing with me a considerable distance, at one time as many as five on my right and two on my left, cringing in on me, and positively squeezing me, as the round shot came bounding by them, tearing up the earth under their noses, my overalls being a mass of blood from their gory flanks (they nearly upset me several times, and I had to use my sword to rid myself of them). I remarked their eyes, betokening as keen a sense of the perils around them as we human beings experienced (and that is saying a good deal). The bearing of the horse I was riding, in contrast to these, was remarkable. He had been struck, but showed no signs of fear ... And so, on we went through this scene of carnage, wondering each moment which would be our last.

Paget was well-placed to witness the return as he rode at the rear of the 4th Light Dragoons and the 11th Hussars, noting the last mile strewn with dead and dying, all of them friends, some of them limping or crawling back, horses in agony, struggling to rise, only to flounder again on their mutilated riders. It had been, in Cardigan's words, 'a mad-brained trick', but all the regiments of the Light Brigade had covered themselves with glory. Even in 'the jaws of death' discipline had been superb in completing the business of 'sabring the gunners there'. Some of those that rode back even told Cardigan that they were ready to go again.

For the time being the British position had been saved, but soon – on 5 November 1854 – the Russians tried again, launching an attack with some 70,000 troops against the Allied lines which were extended both to cover the defences of Sebastopol and protect their ports. The main weight of the Russian offensive fell on the British right and front in a dawn mist. It was not a battle of manoeuvre but of close-in fighting between infantry, at which the sheer steadiness of the British redcoats, inspired by the leadership of General Pennefather, temporarily in command of the 2nd Division, and aided by their Minié rifles, prevailed against heavy odds. At one stage of the battle of Inkerman between 3,000 and 4,000 British soldiers successfully checked the advance of more than four times their numbers. It was dogged gallantry of the first order, and showed by the large number of casualties* in senior officers that in those days divisional and brigade commanders, to say nothing of officers commanding battalions, led from the front. Many regiments proudly bear the battle honour 'Inkerman' on their Colours, including the Brigade of Guards, Highlanders, today's battalions of The Queen's Regiment, Royal Anglians, King's Regiment, Light Infantry and many others. Inkerman is often referred to as 'a soldiers' battle'. Sir Llewellyn Woodward, in his superb history of England 1815–1870,† points out that 'every battle is a soldiers' battle', but goes on to concede that there might be special reason for so describing Inkerman, because of the dearth of major tactical moves and because the outcome was decided by soldier versus soldier in the fiercest and closest sort of combat. It was, as the result showed, the sort of fighting at which the beggars in red excelled.

The poor beggars were to suffer still worse miseries from the climate, shortage of supplies and disease. Their uniforms were quite inadequate for a Crimean winter, and in mid-November appalling snow storms blew away tents, and destroyed the hospitals. Cholera, dysentery and malaria were rife, and the medical services were a disgrace, although soon to be improved by the work of Florence Nightingale and her colleagues. Yet early in 1855 some 14,000 British soldiers were in hospital. This new year saw many other changes. Palmerston succeeded Aberdeen as Prime Minister; Pélissier took over command of the French army from Canrobert; and after the Allied assault on Sebastopol of mid-June had failed, Raglan gave up the ghost and was succeeded by General Sir James Simpson, a veteran of the Peninsula, Waterloo and the Sind wars, who although sound and exact was hardly thought of as being the man for supreme command. He was good enough, however, to supervise together with Pélissier the fall of Sebastopol in September – the French doing rather better in taking the dominant Malakoff Redoubt than the British in not taking the Redan – which effectively ended the fighting, although the peace treaty of Paris was not signed until March 1856. Russia (Nicholas I had died in March 1855 and was succeeded by Alexander II) agreed to the Allied proposals concerning the Principalities, to be guaranteed by the European Powers, and the waiving of Russian protective rights over Turkey's Christians. For the time being Turkey's integrity had been upheld and Russia's ambitions in the Near East restrained, but the Eastern Question was by no means resolved.

As for the British Army, one of the most interesting observations was made by de Tocqueville, who wrote about it in 1855 that: 'The heroic courage of your soldiers was everywhere and unreservedly praised, but I found also a general belief that the importance of England as a military power had been greatly exaggerated, that she is utterly devoid of military talent, which is shown as much in

* The British lost about 2,500 killed and wounded in all, the Russians 12,000.
† *The Age of Reform*, Oxford University Press, 1962.

administration as in fighting, and that even in the most pressing circumstances she cannot raise a large army.' This was a far cry from the high prestige of the British Army forty years earlier after Waterloo. Yet the accusation of poor administration was wholly deserved. Some attempt was made to put it right. A series of Select Committees looked into conditions in the Army and some improvements were made. Better camps were established, including those at Shorncliffe, Colchester and, what is still thought of as the home of the British Army, Aldershot. A number of special schools were set up and trained soldiers in musketry and gunnery. Medical schools and hospitals began to take seriously the special problems of wounds and diseases resulting from battle and active service overseas. The reporting of war correspondents, like Russell, and the influence of Florence Nightingale had done much to bring the army before the public eye, and Queen Victoria herself took a hand in affairs by her insistence – despite the opposition of the new Commander-in-Chief, her own cousin, the Duke of Cambridge,* appointed in 1856 – on the institution of a new decoration which was open to officers and men, the Victoria Cross, the first winners of which were actually awarded it in 1857 for acts of valour performed in the Crimean War and the Indian Mutiny. Two other measures affecting government were the assumption by the Secretary of State for War of the duties performed by the Secretary *at* War, and the taking over of responsibility for the commissariat by the War Office. These measures were all very well, but it was not until some ten years later, when Cardwell took over direction of the affairs of the Army, that real reform got under way. Indeed as Trevelyan in his *English Social History*† observed:

> One thing that the Crimean War did not produce was Army Reform. It was indeed recognized that though the veteran soldiers had fought well, maintaining the regimental traditions inherited from the Peninsula, they had been ill supplied with recruits, ill led, ill fed and ill organized as an army . . . the reformers of the age were not interested in the Army. They regarded it as a hopelessly aristocratic institution, not really needed by a civilized State. They were concerned not to gain security by improving it, but to save money by cutting it down.

Two of the young officers who showed their coolness under fire and saw much of what was wrong with the army during the Crimean War, and who in their separate ways were to achieve considerable fame as soldiers were Charles Gordon and Garnet Wolseley. Gordon told people later in life that he had gone to the Crimea to be killed, and he certainly showed an enviable disregard for danger, yet he greatly distinguished himself and was awarded the Legion of Honour by the

* Of whom more later.
† Longmans, Green & Co., 1942.

French. Wolseley was contemptuous of the Army's generals and its staff officers who 'were uneducated as soldiers . . . whom I would not have entrusted with a subaltern's picket in the field. Had they been private soldiers, I don't think any colonel would have made them corporals.' Wolseley also commented in later life that it was very merciful of 'the Great Ruler of all worlds' to end the Crimean War before allowing the Indian Mutiny to start. Otherwise, he added, the Army's resources might have been badly strained. They were strained enough as it was and it is to this shattering event to which we must now turn our attention.

CHAPTER ELEVEN

The Sepoy War

Where have we failed when we acted vigorously? Where have we succeeded when guided by timid counsels?

JOHN LAWRENCE

Victorians called it the Sepoy War, a better name perhaps than the Indian Mutiny which implies that the Indian Army mutinied as a whole or that there was a national uprising against the British. It was not like that at all. To start with only a portion of the army of Bengal mutinied (the Bombay and Madras armies did not), the fighting was confined to an area roughly bounded by Meerut, Delhi, Agra, Allahabad, Cawnpore and Lucknow, many of the native regiments remained loyal and fought with the British in restoring their rule, and the whole thing was over in seven months. But it left ineradicable scars. There had for long been reason to suspect that native troops might rebel. It would not be for the first time. There had been the so-called massacre of Vellore in 1806 when three battalions of Madras Native Infantry mutinied because of an order to change their turban for a round hat partly made of leather and also to remove painted marks on their faces which had profound religious significance. Not only were these proposed changes deeply offensive, but they raised once more the suspicion that the British were trying to impose Christianity on the native soldiers, a suspicion exploited by the descendants of Tipu (whom Wellington had defeated in 1799) hoping for a return to the great days under the Tiger of Mysore. On the night of 10 July, the native battalions shot down British sentries of the 69th Foot (Welch Regiment) who were guarding the fort, murdered troops in the hospital and attacked the 69th's barracks and officers' quarters, killing some fourteen officers and over a hundred men. Next day, however, Colonel Rollo Gillespie with the 19th Dragoons, some Madras cavalry and horse artillery, attacked the mutineers in the fort and rapidly defeated them, killing between three and four hundred. Afterwards about twenty mutineers were executed, either being blown away from guns, hanged or shot. The three battalions involved were disbanded.

Despite such warnings the British persisted in making the mistake of *appearing* to attack the caste and religion of sepoys. In 1824 during the first Burma War the 47th Bengal Native Infantry mutinied because of a dispute concerning bullocks to carry their private possessions, and because bullocks could not be found, the threat of the battalion's being transported to Burma by sea – the sepoys believing that to go by sea would be to lose caste. Their refusal to parade, seizure of the regimental colours and threats of violence led at length to their being confronted by a joint force of British infantry, guns, a troop of cavalry and a battalion of native infantry. When the 47th still refused to obey orders, two guns opened fire on them by command of General Sir Edward Paget. Many were wounded, a few killed and the rest fled, some being taken prisoner. The subsequent court martial sentenced about forty mutineers to death, although not all were executed, and the regiment was disbanded. Causes of discontent leading eventually to mutiny were nearly always the same – a feeling among the sepoys that they were not valued as they had been, the introduction of changes, suspicion that the British wished to undermine their religious beliefs and convert them all to Christianity, and in many cases the departure to the staff or political duties of the officers they knew and trusted. Philip Mason emphasized this point in his superlative study of *The Men Who Ruled India*, when after describing the remarkable and admirable trust and liking that grew up between British officers and their Indian soldiers, he added:

> But forget that the army was a living organism, treat it as a dry skeleton, sit at a desk and look at returns of strength, tables of ranks, and rations, send away the officers he knew to other regiments – and the sepoy's confidence would wither. And once his affection was gone, once his confidence had withered, his fidelity to that far extravagance, that shadow of a name, that abstract nothing the Company, was liable to shatter to brittle fragments, at a whisper, at a hint from the bazaar of some imagined peril.

It was not, of course, only the desks and ration returns that were taking the British officers away from their close, affectionate relationship with the soldiers. There was also, as James Morris put it, 'the arrival of that archetypal snob, the memsahib. Colder and colder, the rulers were withdrawing into their cantonments and clubs, to clamp themselves within a round of amateur theatricals, pig-sticking, gossip and professional ambition which shut them off from Indian life outside, and made them more and more contemptuous of it.' Nothing could have been more fatal, nor more likely to stimulate the resentment and discontent felt by the Indian rulers who had been dispossessed during Dalhousie's policy of annexation, among them Nana Sahib of Cawnpore, adopted son of the last Mahratta ruler, and the Rani of Jhansi, both of whom we shall meet later as they throw their lot in with the sepoy mutineers.

To all Indians harbouring grievances, the vulnerability of the British position – all their power and military prestige notwithstanding – was plain to see. Numbers alone told their tale. Dalhousie himself, despite his confidence in the sepoy army, had warned the British Government at home that there were too few British soldiers in India. He had returned to England in 1856 and was succeeded by Lord Canning, son of George Canning. Early in 1857 when Canning had been governor-general for about a year, there were a mere 34,000 European soldiers in India compared to nearly 260,000 native soldiers. Moreover the myth of the Company's invincibility had been badly dented by the retreat from Kabul and reverses in the Crimea. It was at Barrackpore again, this time in January 1857 that events leading up to the explosion of the Mutiny took place, precipitated by the rumour that the fat of cows and swine had been used for making cartridge grease for the new Enfield rifle. As the end of each cartridge had to be bitten before it was inserted into the rifle, both Hindus and Moslems using the rifle would be polluted. None of the measures taken by the British, which included orders that factory-greased cartridges would be used by British soldiers only, while sepoys would grease their own with beeswax and vegetable oil, was effective. First the 19th Native Infantry refused cartridges which, even though they were for different rifles, were thought to be tainted and would therefore defile them. Then in March a soldier of the 34th Native Infantry named Mangal Pande (Mungul Pandy*) who, like Clive's adversaries at Arcot, was intoxicated with _bhang_, ran amok and fired on his British officers without being restrained by the guard commander, while other sepoys actively encouraged Pande, who at length unsuccessfully tried to commit suicide with his musket. He was subsequently tried and hanged. Both the 19th and 34th were disbanded, and the British authorities hoped that the trouble would blow over. Yet the commanding officer of another regiment, the 43rd Native Infantry, received an anonymous letter which made it clear that there was a widespread belief among the sepoys that the British were pursuing a deliberate policy of destroying their religion, and that although the Lord Sahibs might be masters of the country, they, the sepoys themselves, served 'for honour and religion' and 'we will not give up our religion'.

The next incident at Meerut was far more serious and emphasized the weakness of the British position on the line of communication between Calcutta and the Punjab. Although at Meerut itself there was a cavalry regiment (The Carabiniers), an infantry battalion (60th

---

* For the British soldier the word 'Pandy' became synonymous with mutineer while the Mutiny itself lasted. Later it was used to refer to an Indian soldier generally, which to say the least of it was unfortunate.

Rifles) and strong artillery detachments, elsewhere there were few British troops — at Agra and Lucknow weak infantry battalions, at Cawnpore a depot and some artillerymen, at Delhi and Allahabad no British units at all. Again the trouble sprang from a refusal to handle cartridges, but this time there were several features which made it worse than before. To start with, the regiment concerned was the 3rd Cavalry, the first occasion that cavalrymen, many of whom were Muslims, had given trouble; further, the cartridges concerned were not the new ones at all, but had been used by the 3rd Cavalry for years — but rumour and seditious tales were stronger than reason; and then Meerut itself was a military station of some consequence. On 24 April 1857, eighty-five seasoned troopers disobeyed orders to accept the cartridges and were court-martialled. On 9 May a punishment parade was held, designed by the British authorities to impress the rest and deter further disobedience. It was a degrading ritual during which the prisoners were stripped of their uniforms and then put in chains by smiths, while the garrison looked on. At length they were led away to prison. The effect on the sepoys watching it all had been to induce intense feelings of shock and gloom. One of the regiment's young officers, who had only recently joined, was Hugh Gough, whose great-uncle we met fighting the Sikhs at Chilianwala and Gujrat, and who was himself to become a general. Visiting the men in prison that evening he shared in their despair at being dishonourably discharged from military service, recording that he had not witnessed so touching a scene as the bemedalled old soldiers bitterly weeping and imploring help to save them from such disgrace. Later that day one of his own native officers warned Gough that on the following day all the native troops in Meerut would mutiny, and although he passed on this warning both to his own Colonel and the Brigade Commander, they both pooh- poohed the idea. Next morning, Sunday 10 May, seemed quiet enough, but in the evening the garrison exploded.

While preparing for his duties Gough was again visited by the same native officer — who was clearly risking his own life — to be told that the rising had actually started. Going at once to the Native Infantry lines he found 'a scene of the most wild and awful confusion . . . huts on fire . . . sepoys dancing and leaping frantically about, calling and yelling at each other and blazing away in the air . . . a maddened crowd of fiends and devils'. Things were no better when Gough went next to see his own troop: total disorder with troopers galloping about, setting fire to the buildings, pocketing the very cartridges which they had con-demned as defiling. He had lost all power of discipline over his men, and still in the company of the loyal native officer made his way through the bazaar to the European lines. They had to fight their way through hundreds of fanatical, armed men, for it seemed that the entire population of Meerut had joined the rebellion. Yet the behaviour of that one native officer, whom Gough did not even know very well, risking his life, saluting Gough as he turned to go, having aided his escape through the tumult, tells us something of the other face of the Sepoy War – 'a braver or more loyal man', Gough concluded, 'I have never met'.

Meanwhile the mutineers themselves were out of control, led, it appeared, by the 3rd Cavalry who released their imprisoned comrades from the gaol, and were soon joined by two regiments of Native Infantry, 11th and 20th. Together they indulged in an orgy of burning, murder and looting, the main targets being the bungalows of officers and civil officials. But it was all uncoordinated and haphazard. There was clearly no master plan, no single Indian directing what happened; it was not a response to some long-laid plot for a general rising, but rather a single spark caused by fear, resentment and rumour, which then ignited the whole native garrison of Meerut. All the murder, arson and pillage raging about was being perpetrated by groups of sepoys, without organization or method, with no one in command, and this general lack of direction was further manifested by the mutineers' next move. Leaving the blazing cantonment behind them, having murdered all the Europeans they could find and any sepoys unwise enough to try to protect them, the 3rd Cavalry made their way southwards towards Delhi in small groups, to be followed by the Native Infantry. Perhaps the most astonishing aspect of it all was the almost total inactivity of the British regiments. This was partially explained by the age and disposition of those in command – General Hewitt was a Falstaff-like figure, elderly, large and relaxed, who would certainly have endorsed the fat knight's declaration that the better part of valour was discretion, yet who totally lacked his nimbleness of mind and wit. He was certainly quite incapable of vigorous action in a crisis. The Brigade Commander, Archdale Wilson, was in Philip Mason's words 'correct, cautious, the kind of man who knows the regulations and sees objections to every course proposed'. We have all come across such men, and not only in a military environment. Even the regimental commanding officers seemed to be at a loss as to what should be done. It has always been the pride of cavalrymen to be quick off the mark, although those of us who belong to the light cavalry might suggest that few heavy dragoons have been noted for their intellect. As it was, the commanding officer of the 6th Dragoon Guards (Carabiniers) did get his regiment on parade, and then proceeded *to call the roll*! When they eventually moved off, the mutineers were well on the way to Delhi, only forty miles to the south-west. The 60th Rifles, whose reputation for fast marching and straight shooting was second to none, made sure that the Treasury and bungalows still intact were secured, and marched about in an attempt to find a rebel force to deal with. But as the rebels were in small groups, there was no such force, so the regiment settled down to wait until morning. Had there been an instant pursuit and had a British force been able to catch up with the mutineers before they reached Delhi, dealing with them there and then, who can say what the outcome might have been? But the fact that nothing was done could only give encouragement to those sepoys who had mutinied already and to those who had a mind to do so. And so, the scene now moves to Delhi itself.

At Delhi in the once beautiful palace, which was a fortress too, of the Moghul Emperors, lived the last of that line, Bahadur Shah Zafar, an old, frail, scholarly and dignified monarch, long since pensioned off by the British; he wanted only to be left alone to write poetry, and wander about, leaning on his staff, among his innumerable wives and children. He was the very last figure to take a lead in master-minding and inspiring a mutiny by Indian sepoys against the Raj. Yet it was to him that the rebels of Meerut came with precisely this in mind. Once the mutineers were in Delhi, it was not long before they had killed all the British officers they could find, together with other Europeans. The six battalions of native infantry joined the mutineers, and as the sounds of rioting, shooting and fire came from the city, and the palace was filled with the sepoy leaders prostrating themselves at his feet, Bahadur Shah was once more proclaimed Mogul Emperor of India and found himself a most reluctant leader of the Indian Mutiny. It was, of course, especially important that Delhi should be retaken by the British as soon as possible because of its significance to the people as the ancient capital of India. The longer it stayed in rebel hands, the more the people would doubt the British determination and ability to prevent their being driven from the country. After Delhi in order of importance and significance came Lucknow and Agra, both of which were being besieged by sepoys to whom mutiny had spread.

Yet the British were being remarkably slow in taking the counter-offensive. Canning had arranged for reinforcements by speeding up the return of troops from Persia, diverting others en route for China and sending for regiments in Burma. At Allahabad the small garrison which had moved there could not leave the fort; at Cawnpore General Wheeler was fortifying a position in the cantonment; while Henry Lawrence was preparing the Lucknow residency for the siege which he saw was forthcoming. The Commander-in-Chief, General Anson, who was being pressed by Canning to march on Delhi, gave orders for the assembly of what troops he could muster at Ambala, about 120 miles north of Delhi, where they would be joined by the British regiments from Meerut. Anson, however, died of cholera on 27 May and Sir Henry Barnard, who had recently arrived in India with the bonus of successful command in the Crimea, took over. He wasted no time and marched on Delhi with a mixed force consisting of the 9th Lancers, two squadrons of the Carabiniers, the 75th Foot (Gordon Highlanders), most of the 60th Rifles, two battalions of the Company's Bengal Fusiliers (European), a field battery and three troops of horse artillery, a siege train, and some 500 of the Sirmoor Gurkhas (2nd Gurkha Rifles). In all he had just over 4,000 men and with them Barnard attacked some 30,000 rebels who had taken up a position on the Ridge north-west of Delhi. Although the sepoys fought bravely 'with the courage of desperation', they were no match for the manoeuvring by the British horse artillery or the bayonets of British infantry. The British took the Ridge, and the rebels retired into the city of Delhi.

We may perhaps follow the action at Delhi before moving to Cawnpore and Lucknow. Although Barnard and his force had taken the Ridge and had been reinforced by troops from the Punjab, far from being able to press home the 'siege of Delhi', they were themselves besieged as more and more mutineers joined those controlling the city. Barnard himself died of cholera on 5 July, and was succeeded first by Reed, then by Archdale Wilson, whom we last met being indecisive at Meerut. The mutineers made frequent attacks on the British position and on their communications with the Punjab. In one of these latter engagements, a newly raised irregular regiment, Hodson's Horse, went into action for the first time. William Hodson was an extraordinary man, depicted by James Morris as 'Hotspur brought to life' who 'enjoyed war for war's sake, fought it with superb panache, and was one of the greatest British leaders of irregular troops'. In this action at Rohtak, some forty miles from Delhi, Hodson had less than 400 cavalrymen and took on a force of mutineers about five times that number. With his own regiment and a hundred or so of Guides Cavalry, Hodson played the old trick of pretending to withdraw before a body of the enemy who then came at him in the open. Hodson's own account of it illustrates the sheer relish with which he sent them about their business:

> The enemy thought we were bolting and came on in crowds, firing and yelling, and the sowars brandishing their swords as if we were already in their hands, when suddenly I gave the order, 'Threes about and at them'. The men obeyed with a cheer; the effect was electrical; never was such a scatter. I launched five parties at them, each under an officer, and in they went, cutting and firing, into the very thick of them . . . We cut down upwards of fifty in as many seconds. The remainder flew back to the town, as if not the Guides and Hodson's Horse but death and the devil were at their heels . . . In three days we have frightened away and demoralized a force of artillery, cavalry and infantry some 2,000 strong, beat those who stood or returned to fight us twice, in spite of numbers, and got fed and furnished forth by the rascally town itself.

One of the British cavalry regiments which distinguished itself throughout the period of the Mutiny was the 9th Lancers. In his classic

History of the British Cavalry the Marquess of Anglesey* tells us that it was the only regiment that fought at Delhi and the two battles at Lucknow, its siege and its relief, and that it covered more than 3,000 miles throughout the campaign, losing five officers and 143 men out of its total strength of less than 500, and winning fourteen Victoria Crosses, a number not equalled by any single unit of the British Army for more than fifty years afterwards. It was at Delhi that the first of these Victoria Crosses was won and where the regiment acquired from the mutineers themselves the nickname of the 'Delhi Spearmen' (still the title of the Regimental Journal – now 9th/12th Royal Lancers). In one of the desperate fights they had when the mutineers almost penetrated the British camp on the Ridge, Hope Grant, who had been commanding the regiment until a more senior officer arrived a week earlier to take over, actually found himself unhorsed after one charge to save some guns, and surrounded by rebels. He was only saved by the loyalty and courage of a 4th Bengal Irregular Cavalry soldier – most of whose regiment had mutinied – who first offered Hope Grant his horse, and then, when this offer was declined, dragged him out to safety holding on to the horse's tail. In another charge, where again the regiment was trying to save guns from capture by the enemy, the new commanding officer, Yule, was himself killed.

In mid-August 1857 there arrived at the British camp a man likely to strike terror into the hearts of anyone challenging British rule in India and as certain to inspire confidence in the inevitability of victory among the British soldiers – John Nicholson, of whom all men spoke with boundless admiration. The future idol of the British Army, Lord Roberts, affectionately known by the soldiers as 'Bobs', called him the beau-ideal of a soldier and a gentleman; Lord Gough, whom we have seen in action several times, thought the same. Dalhousie said that Nicholson cowed whole provinces with his name, and John Lawrence, who had dispatched him now from the Punjab with his Movable Column to assist in the taking of Delhi, declared that the memory of his deeds would never perish as long as the Raj itself endured. They are still remembered today. It is hardly surprising therefore that when such a man as Nicholson found himself at the Ridge, even though he was not in command, rapid and decisive steps were taken to recapture Delhi. First he defeated an attempt by the mutineers to intercept the siege train which had been making its way from Ferozepore, and at the beginning of September all 34 heavy guns were in the camp. These guns were, of course, necessary for storming the city, and within a week of their arrival after careful, concealed deployment, they opened fire on 11 September. Three days later the British force, now numbering less than 8,000 began its assault on the city in four columns, the first led by Nicholson himself. The battle lasted a week

* Vol. 2: 1851–1871, Leo Cooper, 1975.

and involved the fiercest and bloodiest kind of street fighting, which the British soldiers – always at their best and bravest in the open – did not care for. Indeed at one point two British infantry battalions, the 8th and 75th Foot (King's Regiment and Gordon Highlanders) declined to continue the advance. But Colonel Baird Smith of the Royal Engineers, who had so successfully established the heavy batteries in their forward positions, more than made up for the hesitancy of the nominal commander, Archdale Wilson, by pressing, indeed insisting, that the advance continue. Continue it did, and after the Lahore Bastion had been taken on 19 September, on the following day the city and the Red Fort were found to be almost abandoned. The cost had been heavy. Some sixty British officers and more than 1,000 soldiers had been killed or wounded in the initial assault alone. Nicholson, leading from the front as usual, had been mortally wounded, dying on the 23rd, having threatened to shoot Archdale Wilson if he talked any more of retiring. Once inside the city and fort, the British spilled a great deal more blood, for every sepoy found was killed. It was assumed that all of them were guilty of the very worst of crimes, and as Sir John Kaye wrote in his history of the Mutiny 'many who had never struck a blow against us . . . and who had been plundered and buffeted by their own armed countrymen, were pierced by our bayonets or cloven by our sabres or brained by our muskets. Seldom, if ever, since the War began had there been so much to exacerbate and infuriate an army as then inflamed the brains and fevered the blood of the men who found themselves inside the blood-stained city.'

One particular and almost personal act of vengeance has been hauntingly described by James Morris. It was when William Hodson, whom we saw earlier dispersing mutineers at Rohtak, was given the task of arresting Bahadur Shah who had taken refuge at the tomb of Humayan some miles away from the palace. At this time Hodson was suffering from a severe sense of grievance because of his belief that he had been unjustly judged to be unsuitable for a political appointment – always the zenith of an officer's service to the Raj. He was to have a free hand in dealing with the King of Delhi's family, but was ordered to take the King himself back to the Red Fort. So Morris tells us:

Off to the tomb of Humayan Hodson rode, with fifty of his own wild troopers, slashed about with cummerbunds and sabres, bearded, turbanned, booted, like a savage praetorian guard of the Raj – galloping heedless through the crowd of refugees who poured out of Delhi with their carts and bullock-wagons, and who cringed into the gutters as this terrible squadron swept by. The force halted in the open square outside the gate of the shrine, and sending an emissary inside to demand Bahadur's surrender, Hodson awaited the supreme moment of his life. One can almost see him now in the great dusty square, half an Englishman, half a Sikh, dusty, lithe, ardent, dressed in the haphazard flamboyance dear to irregular cavalrymen down the centuries, the son of the Archdeacon of Lichfield awaiting the submission of the last of the Moghuls.

Bahadur did submit, was taken back to the Red Fort and there imprisoned. Yet Hodson's vengeance was not fully appeased. Next day he returned to the tomb, took prisoner two of the King's sons and, on the way back, giving as an unlikely pretext that the mob were about to rescue the princes, shot them himself. It was an unedifying conclusion to the taking of Delhi. Now that this had been done, it might have been thought that it would herald the end of the Mutiny itself. Far from it – too much had been happening elsewhere.

Some of the most appalling atrocities of the Sepoy War were committed at Cawnpore, where Nana Sahib and his lieutenant, Tantia Topi, together with 3,000 mutineers had besieged a small force of 300 British troops and 100 loyal sepoys under General Wheeler in a fortified hospital barracks. With the troops were 100 civilians and about 400 women and children. Nana Sahib was the last of the Mahratta princes, and he harboured a grudge against the British who had exiled him to the small town of Bithur and denied him both the comfort of a pension and the ceremony of position. Nevertheless Wheeler trusted in his loyalty, and when news of the Meerut rising reached Cawnpore in the middle of May 1857, he accepted Nana Sahib's offer to position some of his soldiers at Cawnpore to help maintain order. At the beginning of June, however, when the sepoys rose in revolt – there were four native regiments – and ransacked both the Treasury and the magazine, setting off in triumph towards Delhi, Nana Sahib and his troops did nothing to prevent it. On the contrary he took command of the mutinous sepoys, sent a message to Wheeler that he intended to attack the British position, and on 6th June the siege began. The defenders, who included members of the 42nd Regiment (Black Watch), conducted themselves with the utmost heroism. Short of water and later on of food too, but well-supplied with ammunition, they were subjected to almost continuous fire from artillery pieces and muskets, in frightful heat and almost no shade, with casualties mounting day by day and, in spite of urgent messages sent by Wheeler to Lucknow, no apparent prospect of aid. The thing went on for nearly three weeks, by which time the remaining defenders were confined to one building, the other having been burned to the ground when its thatched roof caught fire. There were innumerable sick and wounded women and children and Wheeler's own son had been killed by a roundshot, yet still they held on, beating off further sepoy attacks, until at last, his patience running short, Nana Sahib offered terms on 25 June. The offer was that if the garrison laid down its arms, both troops and civilians would be granted safe conduct to

Allahabad by boats. Wheeler accepted, insisting only that his soldiers kept side-arms and ammunition. On 27 June the survivors, wounded being carried in palanquins and bullock-carts, made their way down to the Ganges, and there began to wade into the stream to embark on the river boats awaiting them.

Once they were all aboard, however, the boatmen jumped into the river to wade ashore, and then all the boats were subjected to devastating fire from guns and muskets from positions concealed by the river bank. It was nothing short of massacre, corpses floating about, those who struggled ashore instantly shot or cut down, rebel horsemen riding into the shallows to sabre anyone still alive. Except for two officers and two soldiers, whose boat did succeed in slipping away and who after hair-raising adventures lived to tell the tale, all the men were killed, including General Wheeler, while those women and children who had not already been drowned or murdered were shut away in a building called the Bibighar, which meant the House of Women because it had been put up by a British officer for his native concubine years before. But even these survivors were not to live for long. When Nana Sahib heard on 15 July that General Havelock with a relieving force of about 2,000 soldiers and civilian volunteers was only twenty or so miles from Cawnpore, he gave orders to kill them all, and although the mutineer sepoys refused to do so, the deed was done by professional and villainous butchers. The bodies were thrown into a well. All in all the massacre of Cawnpore had accounted for more than 460 officers and men together with over a hundred wives and children. Two days after the women and children had been butchered, Havelock and his troops entered Cawnpore, where the shocking sights induced in the British a kind of passion for revenge, savage and indiscriminate, which allowed them to indulge in cruelties as terrible as those of the mutineers. It gave rise to feelings of bitterness and hatred on both sides, and also in the British a sense of shame that in many cases those Indians who suffered their vengeance could not have been responsible for the crimes which were being avenged.

In July, therefore, the position was that Havelock with his relatively small force was far from secure, even though the mutineers from Cawnpore had gone to reinforce other rebels who were besieging the Residency at Lucknow. At Lucknow itself Henry Lawrence had been mortally wounded during a battle outside the Residency, and died on 2 July. He was succeeded in command by General Inglis. The garrison at Lucknow consisted of less than 1,000 British troops, some 700 loyal sepoys and 150 civilians. In spite of disease and short rations, this small force succeeded in resisting attacks of the rebel army totalling 60,000. Then in September Havelock and Outram with something like 1,000 British soldiers, including Highlanders, fought their way into the Residency. The siege had already lasted for almost three months, and so small a reinforcement simply meant that the siege continued. But both Havelock and Outram were in themselves considerable; Outram a veteran of wars in India, Afghanistan and Persia, an old hand at suppressing insurrections and a colleague of Charles Napier in Sind; Havelock, who believed that 'war was righteous and carnage beautiful', a down- to-earth fighting soldier, who had been battling in India for most of his life, and who now, although strictly speaking subordinate to Outram (Lawrence's successor as Chief Commissioner for Oudh) practised his first really independent command with furious relish. Even though Lucknow was still besieged – it was now late September – Delhi had been taken by the British and Sir Colin Campbell, in advance of reinforcements from England, was in Calcutta putting together another relief force.

During October and November 1857 the British set about restoring order. First Campbell moved from Calcutta in late October, reinforced by a naval brigade and some infantry which had been on its way to China. Collecting further troops from Delhi at Cawnpore, he raised the siege of Lucknow in mid-November. There was a splendid scene, described by James Morris, when Havelock and Outram met Campbell and his relieving force in Lucknow, with the soldiers cheering and Havelock calling out that he was happy to see them – 'a formidable lot they must have looked – Sikh cavalry in tangled draperies, English infantry in slate-grey, turbanned Punjabis, plumed and tartaned Highlanders, and the 9th Lancers, one of the smartest cavalry regiments in Europe, with white turbans twisted round their forage-caps'. But then regiments of the British Army have always somehow prided themselves on eccentricities of dress, many of which sprang from an extraordinary feat in action, or ignorance of a regulation changing something, or a *faux pas* by visiting royalty. Havelock died a few days later, and while Campbell went off to deal with Tantia Topi, whose rebel army he defeated at Cawnpore, Outram with some 5,000 troops, mostly British but with 1,000 loyal sepoys, fortified himself in the Alam Bagh outside Lucknow, and successfully held out against 120,000 rebels, who launched a series of attacks in February 1858. A month later Lucknow itself was retaken, and it was in this battle that William Hodson, Hotspur brought to life, was killed. During all these operations, it was clear that the discipline, spirit and professional skill of the British soldiers were invariably more than a match for the rebel sepoys, no matter how large their numbers. Sir Llewellyn Woodward summed it up admirably when he wrote 'a handful of British soldiers could keep a large army at bay for many weeks, while an army of mutineers, in an immensely strong position, could not resist a British assault'.

Yet there were still rebel armies to be dealt with, notably that of Tantia Topi who had escaped from the action at Cawnpore and of the Rani of Jhansi, who commanded her own army in the field, dressed like a man, was as expert with a sabre as with a horse, and was now defying the British in her fortress at Jhansi. Dispatched in March 1858 to eliminate these two rebel leaders was one of the ablest of British generals, Sir Hugh Rose* (subsequently Commander-in-Chief, India) who with about 5,000 men, half of whom were British, won an astonishing series of victories. While preparing to assault the fortress of Jhansi, his position was threatened by Tantia Topi's 20,000-strong force, which he defeated with a tenth of that number, then turned back to take Jhansi itself with trifling losses. He completed his triumphs by defeating another rebel army at Kalpi and then in a final battle with the Rani of Jhansi and Tantia Topi at Gwalior inflicting yet another defeat on them. During the battle the Rani was killed by a trooper of the 8th Hussars, whose squadron charged hundreds of enemy cavalry, winning four Victoria Crosses in the process. Tantia Topi escaped to continue his guerrilla operations, but was eventually caught and hanged a year later. His former master, the Nana Sahib, was never captured, but disappeared into the jungles of Nepal. Clearing-up operations in Oudh lasted for most of 1858, and one private soldier, Henry Metcalfe of the 32nd Foot (Duke of Cornwall's Light Infantry) who had been at Lucknow had a vivid memory of an action fought at Doudpore in November of that year:

> Well, we skirmished through this jungle. Sometimes we could not see our right or left files, and indeed our front rank men – I was in the rear rank. Well, we got out of this at last and formed up on what appeared at first to be a beautiful plain, but when we got into it and the action commenced, I thought we got into a pretty puddle, for the beautiful plains, as we thought, turned out to be a large field of rice, where the natives had been inundating with water from wells, and when we got into it and the enemy commenced peppering us with grape and round shot I thought a great many of us would bite the dust before we got out of it. Every step we took we would sink ankle deep and more sometimes. Meantime the cavalry and horse artillery – splendid arm of the service – got up on our flanks and it took them a long time to come up for they could not get through the jungle the same as the Infantry, and when they came up and commenced operations the enemy fire was drawn from the Infantry. Well, we got out of the mud after a while and went in with the bayonet, headed by our gallant Colonel Carmichael. It was a grand sight to see him. Like a giant he was, about 6ft. 2½, and built in proportion. We, I mean the Infantry, turned the enemy's flank and they soon shewed the back seams of their jackets, and the cavalry and the RHA completed the game. The Infantry were called off and highly complimented by the General, and they well deserved it, for their advance through the morass and the enemy peppering them all the time, their steadiness and coolness deserved all praise. The cavalry and artillery also deserved great praise which they got on their return.

Only one small action among hundreds, but it showed what the British

---

* Rose dressed his men in khaki. They were among the first of the 'Gentlemen in khaki' whom Kipling so admired and immortalized in verse.

horse, foot and guns could do. It was by such means that the Sepoy War was ended. Afterwards the rule of the East India Company came to an end. The Crown took over the government of India. In future there would be a viceroy, not a governor-general. The Company's European troops were themselves transferred to the Crown and became the 101st to 106th Foot. A question which aroused much controversy after the Mutiny was how large an army would be needed for India and what should be the proportion of British to Indian troops. That there must be an *Indian* army, no one doubted, for it would have been politically and militarily impossible to try and control India with British troops alone. By 1863 there were 62,000 British troops and 125,000 Indian, but all gunners, except for mountain batteries, were to be European. One benefit from it all was that there was no longer an attempt by British officials gradually to win over Indians from their own beliefs and culture. The attitude was more one of business efficiency, but some of the close, affectionate links had gone for ever.

One last story of the Mutiny told by Philip Mason in *A Matter of Honour* is well worth recounting. The regiment concerned was Skinner's Horse, whom we have met before, and the incident occurred at Multan, where there was great uncertainty as to the reliability of the Native Infantry regiments and artillery. Captain Chamberlain, in command of Skinner's Horse (in 1857 they were called the 1st Bengal Irregular Cavalry) had to rely on his own men while waiting for reinforcements to arrive so that he could disarm the regiments whose loyalty was doubtful. One of his squadrons was composed of Ranghars, Muslims claiming Rajput origin, and the native officer commanding this squadron had come to Chamberlain because his Ranghars had the idea in their heads that they were not as fully trusted as the other squadrons. 'Chamberlain heard him out', writes Mason,

> then sent his orderly to the bank, with a note requesting the banker to send him a sword he had deposited for safe custody. It was a jewelled sword, valuable to anyone, but doubly so to Chamberlain because, as everyone in the regiment knew, it had been given to him by a close friend who had captured it in battle in Sind. He handed this sword to Shaidad Khan, the ressaidar of the Ranghar squadron. 'Give me this back,' he said, 'when the war is over.' The ressaidar's eyes filled with tears; he knelt and touched the captain's knees. Nothing but death could sever the bond between them.

Skinner's Horse lives on, a greatly honoured regiment of the Indian Army. The British officers who served in the regiment until partition in 1947, few of them left now, visit their old regiment from time to time and are received with joy, esteem and affection. Every year these same officers lunch and dine together in London. They will continue to do so until none of them is left. Even then the bond between the British and Indian armies will live on.

CHAPTER TWELVE

Cambridge, China, Cardwell and Canada

Cardwell's place among statesmen is that of the greatest army reformer during the nineteenth century. In him economy and efficiency met.
SIR ROBERT ENSOR

One of the severest disadvantages under which the British Army laboured from 1856 onwards was that its Commander-in-Chief was the Duke of Cambridge, cousin to Queen Victoria and a veteran of the Crimean War. It might have been supposed that his experiences in that campaign, when he commanded a division and saw for himself appalling deficiencies in the Army's management and administration, would have made him one of the most ardent and outspoken advocates for reform. Not a bit of it – he was opposed to change of almost any sort. Fortunately for the Army and the nation, Cardwell became Secretary of State for War in 1868 in Gladstone's administration and remained so for the next six years. Before we see what he achieved in this time, however, let us remind ourselves what the Army's size was in 1859, three years after Cambridge became Commander-in-Chief, two years after the Indian Mutiny and the year in which Palmerston – always ready to find reasons and places for making use of the Army – became Prime Minister for the second time.

In 1859 the Army's strength was 237,000 and it contained about 130 infantry battalions of which about fifty were in India, thirty-seven in the Colonies and forty-four at home. Of those at home, many found themselves at what has now become known as the 'Home of the British Army' – Aldershot Camp, which had been established in 1853 by the then Commander-in-Chief, Hardinge, who had succeeded Wellington. Hardinge had recommended that 10,000 acres of sandy heathland should be bought to 'enable the military authorities to concentrate a large body of troops in the best possible position'.

Whether every soldier who has served there would endorse this description of Aldershot may be doubted, although there were clear benefits from making collective training easier. It was hardly surprising to find that with a total of 25,000 soldiers stationed there in 1861, the size of the civilian population had grown almost tenfold from its former 900, and by no means all the newcomers were conducive to the moral welfare of the soldiers. The number of public houses went up from two to well over fifty, with similar growth of 'vile places' which went by the name of dance saloons, but in fact housed 'the wrens' as the women who hung about the camp were known. As usual there was someone to come to the rescue, as the Marquess of Anglesey tells us, in this case 'Mrs Louisa Daniell, a middle-aged widow, who aided by her equally fanatical daughter, used persuasion, persistence and prayer to achieve a revolution at Aldershot. Her Soldiers' Home and Institute, forerunner of the NAAFI, opened in 1865. Cups of tea, coffee and cocoa, and slabs of cake could be bought for a penny each. Cheap, wholesome meals were served in the dining-room.' This was just as well, for the soldier had little spare money. In 1865 a private in a line regiment got thirteen pence a day (6p), a shilling for pay (as it had been in the Peninsular War) and a penny for beer-money. Deductions from his pay were such that he had almost nothing to spare. Eightpence halfpenny was deducted for food, and from what was left he had to pay for laundry, washing material, some new clothing and 'barrack damages'. The food provided was, of course, awful. In 1863 a newly joined trooper of the 14th Hussars found at his first midday meal that many of his comrades took one look at what was being served and made off for the canteen. He himself could eat neither the meat nor the potatoes, both of which were bad, and had to content himself with bread. Ten years later, as a result of numerous Committees and Commissions, the food was much better.

It was not only in the men's messes that there was dissatisfaction about food during the early 1860s. In 1862 the cadets at Sandhurst actually staged a rebellion, which required the Duke of Cambridge himself to settle. He advanced on the rebel headquarters accompanied by his aide-de-camp, determined to have it out with them:

Here he made a short speech in 'his own inimitable manner'. This meant a large number of 'damns' and other swear words, all delivered in terms of the utmost solemnity. No one perhaps even in the history of the British Army has had quite such a strong sense of personal dignity as Cambridge. In his speech to the mutineers, nevertheless, he undertook to review personally all their grievances . . . He added, however, a strict homily on the disgraceful nature of the rebels' action, adding that severe punishments could only be avoided, whatever the justice of their cause, on the assumption that such an occurrence was never repeated . . . The mutiny thus came to an end. And food and general conditions of the cadets were improved without delay.

The Commander-in-Chief may have been up to the job of quelling a food riot at Sandhurst. He did nothing, however, to tackle the principal matters of maladministration which plagued the Army, such things as flogging, purchase, conditions of service, or towards such constructive acts as making service in the Army a respectable and honourable calling for those in the ranks, training at formation level, building up both a strategic reserve of regular regiments for overseas operations, and a proper, substantial reserve of those who had left the colours. All these necessary measures had to await the appointment of Cardwell as Secretary for War.

Meanwhile the Army was keeping its hand in by having another go at the Chinese. As Foreign Secretary in 1840 Palmerston had instigated one war against Imperial China in order to wring trading concessions from the Chinese government. Now, in 1857, after the Chinese had boarded a British-registered ship, *Arrow*, imprisoning some of the crew, to which the British responded by bombarding forts in the Canton river, Palmerston, now Prime Minister, sent Lord Elgin (son of the 7th Earl who had spent so much money in getting the Marbles from the Parthenon to the British Museum) to China with instructions to make all sorts of demands, among them the right to establish a British mission at Peking. It soon became clear that the use of force was the only thing the Chinese were likely to understand to the point of making concessions. After a joint French and British attack on, and capture of, the Taku forts at the mouth of the Peiho river, the Chinese agreed to Allied trade and diplomatic demands, but then refused to ratify the agreement, and it was all to be done again. The China Expeditionary Force of about 11,000 British and Indian troops left India in February and March 1860, were joined by some 7,000 French soldiers at Hong Kong, and together they sailed for Shanghai. There it was agreed by the military commanders – Hope Grant, whom we last saw during the Indian Mutiny, commanded the British force and de Montauban the French – that the first step in advancing to Peking would be to capture the Taku Forts again. They would therefore land at Pehtang to the north of the forts, then advance to Sinho and take the forts from the rear.

The British force included the 1st King's Dragoon Guards, 3rd Foot (The Buffs), 44th Foot (Essex Regiment), 67th Foot (Royal Hampshires) and the 60th Rifles, while among the Indian troops were Probyn's Horse, Fane's Horse and the Punjab Native Infantry. Their first major action was on 12 August 1860 as they advanced towards Sinho, the 1st British Division commanded by Sir John Michel moving along a firm causeway with the French, and to the north of them on a track through mud flats the 2nd British Division under Robert Napier. One of the young officers* with the 2nd Division recalled their difficulties:

> It was a fearful trudge for the unfortunate troops across that mud, numbers kept dropping out in the line of march and rested for awhile on the side of some grave-mound; others, especially the Punjaubees, finding their boots an impediment, preferred throwing them away, and tucking up their trowsers, pushed boldly on. The appearance of languor throughout the line was distressing. The gun-carriages sank so deeply in the slush that great fears began to be entertained of their ever getting on . . . It was likewise painful to see the cavalry horses (many of whom sank up to their girths in morasses) struggling on knee-deep with their heavily accoutred burdens. The morass seemed interminable; but a travel of some four miles brought us to harder ground, and in sight of a long line of Tartar cavalry drawn up to oppose our advance.

In spite of their ancient weapons – some had only spears or bows and arrows – they came on steadily enough, undeterred by the fire of a British 12-pounder battery. It was when the Tartars came up against British infantry that they, like so many before and after them, began to waver, and it was at this point that the British and Indian cavalry loosed themselves at the enemy. The Tartars on their tough little ponies could not withstand a charge by heavy cavalry. They turned and made off, soon out of reach as their horses were in far better condition than those which had long been confined on board ship, but not before many had been cut down. It was a week before a proper attempt was then made on the Taku Forts themselves, while the necessary preparations of building roads and bridges, bringing up guns, ammunition and supplies went on. Lord Elgin was severe in his condemnation of French soldiers' behaviour to the villagers near the forts, blaming them for savage misconduct and calling into question their military ardour. 'They are cautious enough when armed enemies, even Chinese, are in question – but indisputably valorous against defenceless villagers and little-footed women.' This lack of enthusiasm for his allies was shared by General Hope Grant when making his plan to attack the forts. He very sensibly proposed to assault first the nearer of the northern forts, which was the least strongly held and when taken would dominate the other northern and southern ones. De Montauban's idea was precisely the opposite, and would have involved crossing the river and exposing the attacking troops' supply communications to flank attack by Tartar cavalry. Hope Grant's

* *Narrative of the North China Campaign*, Robert Swinhoe, Smith & Elder, 1861.

arguments prevailed, however, and events proved him right, but the battle was a bloody one.

At seven o'clock on the morning of 21 August 1860, preceded by a heavy bombardment, the assault began by both French and British infantry, who had first to cross dykes and then raise ladders to climb the fort's walls. One of the Allied shells hit the Chinese powder magazine which caused a huge explosion and gave rise to hopes that the garrison had been subdued. Not at all, as the advancing soldiers discovered. As they raced forward with their pontoons, gallantly assisted by Chinese coolies, they were furiously engaged from the fort by guns, matchlock fire, cross-bows and hunks of iron and masonry, but at length one of the French soldiers – wholly belying Elgin's suggestion of their poltroonery – succeeded in mounting his ladder, despite its being shaken about, and leaping into the fort with the tricolour in his hand. Although killed, he was immediately followed by officers and men of both the 44th and 67th Foot, and soon more and more British and French soldiers entered the fort. Attacking with bayonets and swords, they soon overcame all resistance. Within two hours the other northern fort was taken, and next day the southern forts surrendered. The Chinese commander had escaped to Peking. While the enemy losses were thought to be as heavy as 1,500, the British had suffered only seventeen dead and about 150 wounded, the French slightly less. No less than six Victoria Crosses were won. Everyone thought the war was as good as won, among them Garnet Wolseley, who was a Lieutenant-Colonel on the staff. But the Army still had to get to Peking. It took them forty-four days to do it and the whole affair was rounded off by two events, the first of which is a source of some pride in the British Army, the second one of regret that Lord Elgin should punish Chinese treachery by destroying something of great beauty.

In the final battle of the campaign which was fought on 21 September at the Palikao bridge about six miles east of Peking, some 4,000 British and French troops attacked 15,000 Chinese and routed them. Hope Grant noted down the sequence of events in his *Private Journals*, recording that with his infantry on the right and artillery placed centrally, he had positioned the cavalry to the left, so that by moving against the enemy from his left, he could force the enemy right towards their centre where the full weight of Allied fire-power would be brought to bear. When a large body of Tartar cavalry began to threaten the French positions on Hope Grant's right, however, he first brought his artillery into action against them, and then the British cavalry – King's Dragoon Guards with Probyn's and Fane's Horse – charged. Garnet Wolseley saw it all, his heart beating more quickly at the inspiring sight of the King's Dragoon Guards thundering forward with shouts that must have dismayed their opponents. But these same opponents had positioned themselves just on the other side of a sunken

road with a four-foot drop on the British side and a six-foot bank
beyond. Some of the Indian irregular cavalry found this obstacle too
much for them as they rode with short, standing martingales which did
not allow them to jump freely, so that many fell in the ditch. The
Dragoon Guards, however, were not so restricted, jumping or
scrambling over the ditch and pitching in to the Tartars 'riding over
ponies and men, knocking both down together like so many nine-
pins ... In the short pursuit which then ensued the wild Pathans of
Fane's Horse showed well fighting side by side with the powerful
British dragoons. The result was most satisfactory. Riderless Tartar
horses were seen to be galloping about in all directions, and the ground
passed over in the charge was well strewn with the enemy.' Wolseley
never forgot the effectiveness of cavalry in the Chinese campaign, its
ability to reconnoitre widely, exploit the long-range power of
Armstrong artillery pieces, and inflict heavy casualties on the enemy.
He made good use of his experience in demolishing the arguments of
those who maintained that modern weapons had made the cavalry
arm obsolete.

After this spirited action by the British cavalry, the French
succeeded not only in halting and repelling the Chinese, but followed
their own artillery barrage of shells and rockets with an advance to the
bridge itself, killing about 1,000 of the enemy with very few losses to
themselves. All that remained now was the advance to Peking itself.
The French army got to the Summer Palace first and indulged in an
orgy of looting and destruction, which sickened Elgin when he saw it.
Plundering was bad enough, he noted, but to destroy beautiful silks
and smash jade ornaments and exquisite porcelain was even worse.
War was a hateful business and the more he saw of it, the more he
detested it. The British Army was just as competent at looting as the
French, indeed rather more methodical in doing it in organized groups
under non-commissioned officers, but they were late on the scene, so
that in order to placate those who had missed the opportunity, Hope
Grant gave orders that all loot taken from the Palace would be handed
in and then auctioned, the proceeds being divided among the officers
and men.

Just how hateful a business war was had been brought home further
to Elgin and his subordinates by the atrocious cruelty meted out to
Allied prisoners treacherously taken by the Chinese under a flag of
truce during the advance to Peking. Some of Fane's Sikh horsemen had
been tied hand and foot so tightly that maggots got into their wounded
flesh, and then to make things even worse, water was poured on their
bonds to tighten them still further. When they asked for food, dung
and earth were thrust into their mouths. Some of the officer prisoners
were decapitated. Others died in gaol and their bodies were fed to
animals. Worst of all perhaps, a number of Chinese coolies in the
Allied service were buried in the ground with only their heads above

the surface. Dogs then finished them off. So appalled was Lord Elgin that he was determined to exact some retribution, 'not for vengeance but for future security' and after much consideration he 'came to the conclusion that the destruction of the Imperial Palace at Yüan-ming Yüan was the least objectionable of the several courses open' to him. So it was that on 18 October the burning of the Summer Palace began. One of the officers in charge was Charles Gordon, whom we last met in the Crimea, who now went on to win great esteem in China for his direction of the 'Ever Victorious Army'*, and whom we will meet again on his great mission of defiance and martyrdom at Khartoum. By the following evening, Wolseley wrote, 'the Summer Palace had ceased to exist'. Like most British officers, Wolseley endorsed Elgin's act of retribution, although the French disassociated themselves from it absolutely. Palmerston, as might have been expected, was pleased, writing to Sidney Herbert in December: 'I am heartily glad that Elgin and Grant determined to burn down the Summer Palace,' adding that he would have been still happier if another palace in Peking had been burned as well. As a result of the war, China agreed to open ports for commerce, accepted foreign diplomats at Peking, and regulated the opium trade.

The British Army was seldom out of action during Victoria's reign and from 1860 until almost the end of the decade, war against the Maoris of New Zealand went on. It was the customarily unedifying story of white settlers wanting more and more land, while undermining tribal rights and customs in the process. The Maoris were brave and skilful fighters and earned much respect from the British soldiers fighting them. The Maoris built defensive posts called *pas*, and in September 1860 Sergeant Marjouram of the Royal Artillery recalled that although they often expected stout resistance from them, a few shells or an assault usually carried the day. Sometimes it was more difficult and when British infantry (12th Foot – Suffolk Regiment) tried to clear a *pa* sited in the bush:

> They had proceeded but a few yards, when the rebels opened a very heavy fire of musketry, which compelled them to retire with the loss of one man, who fell into the enemy's hands. The Maoris proved to be much nearer and far more numerous than we had expected; and in less than five minutes the artillery were pouring into the bush torrents of shell and cannister, which must have occasioned great loss to the rebels, some of whom were seen to fall from the trees where they had concealed themselves. Their balls flew over and around us in all directions; and had they understood the art of taking a cool and steady aim, they might have picked us off at one hundred and fifty yards' range at pleasure . . . We maintained our

* Major, later Lieutenant-Colonel, Gordon was lent to the Chinese Government to help in operations against the peasant revolts of Christian Taipings.

attack for almost two hours, and as the rebels seemed to have had quite enough of it, the order was given to return to our camp at Waitara. Our loss was very slight indeed . . . Too much cannot be said of the friendly natives, who were in the thick of the fight during the whole time, and stuck manfully to the guns.

The principal part of the fighting was over by 1864, but things dragged on when the New Zealand government continued to confiscate land. Later with a more understanding and conciliatory policy, together with Maori representation in government, the fighting came to an end.

Palmerston died in 1865 while still in office. His last years had been taken up with concern for Napoleon III's military adventures in Italy and Mexico, and for Bismarck's resolution of the Schleswig-Holstein affair as part of his master plan to create a German Empire. After Russell's brief premiership, the Tories returned to power in 1866. Derby was Prime Minister, but the man of the moment was the Chancellor of the Exchequer, soon to succeed to the Premiership, who had great pride in the idea of Empire and who in foreign affairs had no hesitation in donning Palmerston's mantle – that romantic, striking, witty and enigmatic figure, Benjamin Disraeli.

During his first short time in office, Disraeli allowed himself one indulgence in military adventure when Sir Robert Napier commanded an expedition in Abyssinia to release British and other European prisoners from Magdala. Most of the troops which took the fortress there were Indian, but the 4th Foot (King's Own Royal Regiment) were there, and Sergeant Taffs recalled that the march to Magdala was an impressive show with 14,000 camels and bullocks, 13,000 mules and ponies, 50 elephants and 800 donkeys together with innumerable native drivers. After an engagement at Arogee where King Theodore's troops were easily defeated, the British and Indian force stormed and took Magdala and burned it. King Theodore committed suicide. For once the British decided not to add to their Imperial possessions, and although the cost of the expedition was £9 million, instead of the estimated £5 million, and although, as Robert Blake* puts it, 'Disraeli's colourful rhetoric about the standard of St George being hoisted on the mountains of Rasselas caused a certain amount of laughter . . . on the whole the episode redounded to the Government's credit'. Disraeli's principal triumphs of Empire would have to wait until his next Premiership, as he was defeated in the general election of 1868 and Gladstone formed his first administration. Of supreme importance to the British Army was his appointment of Edward Cardwell as Secretary for War.

Cardwell was presented with a great opportunity both to expand and reform the Army as a result of the Franco-Prussian war in 1870. These reforms made real changes in conditions of service and in the

---

* *Disraeli*, Eyre & Spottiswoode, 1966.

systems both of enlisting soldiers and of selecting officers for promotion. The fearful prospect of a German invasion of this country, aroused by Colonel George Chesney's arresting account of just such an event in his fictional *The Battle for Dorking*, made people ask whether the British Army would be capable of resisting an enemy invasion or indeed fighting a major war anywhere. The immediate steps taken in 1870 were to vote an additional 20,000 men for the Army and in the following year a similar increase again, including 5,000 artillerymen. Even before the Franco-Prussian war Cardwell had done much. He had abolished flogging in peacetime (it was not abolished for active service until 1880) and this was a wholly necessary measure in raising the business of being a soldier from its formerly despised reputation to that of an honourable profession. In keeping with this idea he introduced new arrangements which authorized the Army to discharge men of bad character. Another important step was his policy of raising local forces in the colonies to assist with their own defence, so releasing a further 20,000 British soldiers for duty elsewhere. In particular, by concentrating more of the Army at home he was able not only to strengthen defences there and build up a kind of strategic reserve, but also to give this reserve proper formation training.

These measures were not controversial. Three others were – the War Office Act, the Army Enlistment Act and the Army Regulation Bill. In the first of these Cardwell divided the business of the War Office into military, supply and finance sections, housing them all under one roof and making them all subordinate to the Secretary of State. This meant that the Commander-in-Chief, the Duke of Cambridge, not merely underwent the indignity of subordinating himself to Cardwell (thereby greatly displeasing the Queen, who in 1871 wanted to make Cardwell Speaker of the House of Commons, so removing him from interfering with her special love, the Army, of which she maintained he knew nothing), but suffered the further inconvenience of removing his office from the Horse Guards. There was, however, a consolation for him in that henceforth the Commander-in-Chief would command all land forces, whether regular or reserve, at home and overseas. As for the Enlistment Act, Cardwell introduced a system of short service – six years with the colours, six with the reserve. 'In time of peace', he told the House of Commons, 'the army will feed the reserve and in time of war the reserve will feed the army.' The benefits of this measure were very great. Recruitment improved, as the men were not committing themselves for too long a period, regular soldiers tended to be younger and fitter, and by British standards a substantial reserve of trained soldiers – the number rose from about 3,000 in 1867 to 80,000 in 1900 – was created.

It was Cardwell's third great reform that encountered the most opposition – his proposal to abolish purchase. Arguments for and against it are familiar. In favour of purchase was nearly all the officer corps. Wellington had praised and defended it on the grounds that those entering the Army were men of fortune and character who would look after the country's interests. He had won all his battles with officers emerging from the system. So had Marlborough. Many Commissions which had examined it, including those of Melbourne, Raglan and Palmerston, supported it. Yet it allowed rich young men to hold military positions for which they were totally unfitted. It blocked the promotion of really able officers who could not afford the purchase sum. It may have officered the Army with gentlemen who excelled in the hunting field and on the grouse moors, and who in battle displayed the most reckless courage, but they knew very little about their profession. And the emergence of military science as exemplified by Prussia's overwhelming defeat of the French Army made it necessary that the British Army's officers should have some military knowledge. So hostile was the reception of Cardwell's Bill by Parliament, however, that the Government resorted to the framing of a new royal warrant under which purchase became illegal.

Apart from all this, Cardwell took steps to make the Army more efficient in weapons, organization and deployment. He re-equipped the infantry with the first proper breech-loading rifle they had had – the Martini-Henry. He changed the entire infantry regimental system to one which today is virtually the same. By dividing Great Britain and Ireland into a number of regimental districts, within which they could recruit and have their depot, he territorialized the infantry, so that they would in future be associated with a particular county, rather than simply have a number. Each county regiment was to have two regular battalions and a number of militia battalions. With two regular battalions each regiment could have one overseas and one at the home depot, where recruits could be trained. In this way battalions were able to replace each other at home or abroad without losing efficiency. The fighting record of the infantry in wars which we still have to examine – Ashanti, Afghanistan, Zululand, Egypt, the Sudan – will speak for itself. Cardwell also introduced improvements for the artillery, increasing their establishment by some 5,000 men and almost doubling the number of horse artillery guns to 336. Incredibly, however, he was unable to prevent ordnance experts from reverting to muzzle-loading artillery pieces, despite the great success of the Armstrong breech-loading guns in the Chinese war and the more recent demonstration of the effectiveness of breech-loading in the Franco-Prussian affair. He also increased the total strength of the cavalry to over 10,000, but even Cardwell could not interfere with their organization. His achievements are admirably summed up by Sir Robert Ensor*:

* *England 1870–1914*, Oxford University Press, 1936.

His reforms during the quarter of a century following left a broad mark on British history. Without them not only would prompt and crucial successes, such as the Egyptian campaign of 1882, have been unobtainable, but the power-prestige, which Lord Salisbury had behind him in his diplomacy, would scarcely have existed in the same way. Not their least exceptional feature was their economy. Cardwell left the estimates lower than he found them, and yet he had increased the strength of the army in the United Kingdom by 25 battalions, 156 field guns, and abundant stores, while the reserves available for foreign service had been raised from 3,545 to 35,905 men.

One of his great contemporary admirers and assistants was Wolseley, who later recorded his view that there was no man he could think of 'whose memory and whose great services entitle him to be remembered by all ranks of the army, in the nation, the age and the empire at large'. Wolseley had been making his own contribution and proving his entitlement to such a reputation by his masterly organization and command of the so-called Red River expedition in Canada. With a battalion of the King's Royal Rifle Corps and some Ontario militiamen, Wolseley took his force from Lake Superior through unmapped, hitherto untraversed forests, lakes and rivers in May 1870, taking ninety-six days to travel the 660 miles to Fort Garry, there to settle accounts with Louis Riel, leader of the Metis (half-breeds with Indian, French and Scottish blood in them who lived by trapping, boating and trading in what is now Manitoba) at Red River. Riel had declared his people independent and in July 1870 was acting Governor of the newly formed province of Manitoba. But during the skirmishes for possession of Fort Garry, a loyal Canadian had been killed, and so now Wolseley was coming to deal with Riel, whom he regarded as a murderer. The expedition was an unqualified success. Fort Garry was abandoned by Riel and his men before Wolseley arrived and entered on 23 August, and the Union Jack hoisted. During the expedition Wolseley formed enduring friendships with some of the officers, who later made up his famous 'Ring', which James Morris described as 'the most influential cabal of the late Victorian army', and whose members, including William Butler and Redvers Buller of the Red River affair, we shall meet again, as Wolseley went from triumph to triumph.

CHAPTER THIRTEEN

Imperial Wars

Ship me somewheres east of Suez, where the best is like the worst,
Where there aren't no Ten Commandments an' a man can raise a thirst.
                                        RUDYARD KIPLING

1874 was a good year for Imperialism. Disraeli became Prime Minister for the second time with six years of power in front of him. Wolseley enhanced his growing reputation by triumphs in the Gold Coast. And Winston Churchill was born. The later 1870s and early 1880s were a good time for soldiers too, at least for those soldiers who sought action and excitement. Ashantis, Zulus, Afghans, Burmese, Fuzzy-Wuzzys – there were plenty of natives awaiting the benefit of being subjected to disciplined fire from a square of British redcoats. Yet it was not always a one-sided affair. As Charles Carrington tells us in his introduction to Kipling's *Barrack-Room Ballads* 'in those days there was little advantage for the European soldier over the Sudanese or Afghan tribesman on rough ground ... the British military memory had several sore spots, when "savages" like the Zulus at Isandhlwana, the Sudanese at Tamai or the Afghans at Maiwand had beaten "civilized men" in "fair fight"'. There was at this time no shortage of 'barbarious wars' for the 'poor beggars' being paid by the Widow at Windsor. And there was always the North West Frontier of India. Winston Churchill, who followed his own recommendation (recorded much later in *My Early Life*) that if a young man wanted to enjoy himself, to spend a few years agreeably in a military companionship, he could hardly do better than join the British cavalry,* added 'to the youth who means to make himself a professional soldier, an expert in war, a specialist in practical tactics, who desires a hard life and adventure and a true comradeship in arms, I would recommend the choice of some regiment on the frontier, like those fine ones I have seen, the Guides and the 10th Bengal Lancers'.†

---

* Churchill joined the 4th Hussars in 1895, the Regiment to which the author had the honour to belong.
† Hodson's Horse.

'Wolseley is an egotist and a braggart,' observed Disraeli, 'So was Nelson.' Some months before Disraeli became Prime Minister in February 1874, Gladstone's administration had decided to send an expedition to the Gold Coast to deal with the Ashanti warrior king, Kofi Kari-kari, who had been making a nuisance of himself since 1872. In that year the British had taken over from the Dutch a number of coastal forts used among other purposes for the suppression of the slave trade. This activity did not suit Kofi, whose wealth depended on slavery, and who particularly wanted one of the principal forts, Elmina, for use as a headquarters for slave trade. From his capital, Kumasi, he claimed Elmina and when negotiations faltered, invaded the British-controlled area early in 1873, advancing rapidly to within a dozen miles of the British headquarters and then suffering a check at Elmina itself where in June 1873 a mixed force of Royal Marines and native troops (including Mohammedan negro Hausas from Nigeria) succeeded in holding the town and fort. Enough was enough, and in September Gladstone's Government dispatched the very man to deal with King Kofi, the model of an Imperial soldier and in W.S. Gilbert's words 'of a modern major general', who would have total confidence in himself, his soldiers and his mission, and who would take with him a band of picked colleagues – 'the Ring'* – Sir Garnet Wolseley. Following him from England were about 2,400 British soldiers, including the Black Watch and the Rifle Brigade, and Wolseley would also have companies from the Royal Welch Fusiliers and the West India Regiment. All in all he would have a force of some 4,000 men with native artillery; hospital ships were off the coast; thousands of native porters were mustered; and the British soldiers were specially equipped with light grey uniforms, insect veils, quinine and cholera belts. But it was not until January 1874 that the force was ready to move, and since the worst rains were to fall in March, Wolseley's principal problem was one of *time* – to reach Kumasi, defeat the Ashantis and return to Cape Coast all within the space of two months. His absolute conviction in the justice of his mission and certainty of success was illustrated by his announcing that no amount of deadly forest could protect King Kofi, his people or anyone else from the British Army. Their punishment was inevitable. Moreoever, in telling his soldiers to 'be cool; fire low, fire slow and charge home' he expressed his belief that their enemies, the black men, held the British in superstitious awe. This last point was far from true, but it made no difference to the result.

It took Wolseley and his men about a month to reach Kumasi, cutting a pathway through the gloomy jungle, building innumerable bridges, with constant skirmishes and one major engagement about half-way to Kumasi at a village called Ejinasi. Here the main Ashanti

* Including Evelyn Wood, Lord Methuen, Henry Brackenbury, Redvers Buller, William Butler, Frederick Maurice and George Colley.

army was positioned in a semi-circular position with its flanks either side of the British line of advance, largely concealed on a jungle ridge, firing their muskets rather ineffectually at the British soldiers in their traditional hollow square. In *Heaven's Command* James Morris shows what a colourful, almost stagey, sort of battle it was: Wolseley, supremely in command of the situation, smoking cigars while chatting to his staff, acknowledging messages, issuing orders, regretting his troops' losses, while commenting on their good fortune to be killed in battle, and surrounding him the kneeling soldiers in their grey uniforms and pith helmets, firing at their occasionally glimpsed enemies, being attended by doctors when wounded, quartermasters checking ammunition, buglers blowing commands, and above the sounds of rifle and rocket fire the eerie wail of Highland bagpipes competing with unearthly Ashanti war-cries. It was all just the sort of thing for a thrilling illustration in *Boys' Own Paper* or another battle picture by Lady Butler.* 'In the end', Morris observes, 'the Ashanti broke, faced by vastly superior fire-power, unshakeable discipline and a confidence equal to their own. On 3 February 1874, the Black Watch, sweeping aside successive Ashanti pickets and ambushes, and once interrupting the act of human sacrifice, entered the city of Kumasi.' The whole operation cost the British less than twenty killed and 400 wounded. After destroying Kofi's palace and burning the town, Wolseley marched his men back, and on the way they were overtaken by messengers from the king, who had fled his capital, with overtures for peace. By the treaty signed a month later the British got all they wanted – renunciation of Ashanti claims over British territory, free trade and passage to Kumasi, suppression of human sacrifice and an indemnity – except for one thing. Ashanti military despotism remained intact and it would not be long before the British Army would have to return to Kumasi and do the job all over again. Before we leave them this time, let us briefly accompany Rifleman Gilham as he makes his way through the jungle, having just received the order 'Chin-straps down, open out, and push on':

> We cut our way right and left into the jungle with our cutlasses, lying down in the underwood, standing behind trees for cover, pegging in where we could, and forming a semi-circle to the front; but the foliage was so dense that it was like being in a net, and the farther we went the thicker it seemed to get, so that I don't believe we advanced a hundred yards during the whole of the fight.
>
> The enemy were all armed with flintlock muskets, obtained from the old Dutch settlers, and they fired at us with rough bits of lead, old nails, pebbles and rusty iron, which at first passed over our heads and showed us that the enemy were on a slope below us,

* In fact she did not paint a picture of the Ashanti war, even though her husband, William Butler, one of Wolseley's 'Ring', was there.

whereupon we fired low and did terrible execution among them, although we could only catch sight of them here and there. Our men numbered about two thousand, while the Ashantis were believed to muster something like twenty thousand. They outflanked us on several occasions, but we changed front, first on one side and then on the other, so that we were always ready for them.

They took the village of Amoaful, camped there and next day pushed on to Kumasi. After crossing a river there was another sharp encounter with heavy fire on both sides, 'but they had to give in at last and make for the bush behind the town, King Coffee going away with the first of them'. As they approached Kumasi they were encouraged by Wolseley himself, crossing a shallow river about 300 yards wide; the General urged them forward with promises of a house, perhaps a palace, to sleep in that night. 'We pushed on with a cheer, and soon the British flag was flying over the miserable old town.'

The same flag was to fly over a good many places by courtesy of the British Army during the 1870s and 1880s, and perhaps we may pause a moment to savour both contemporary comment and some not so contemporary (before we visit further battlefields to record once more the redcoats' meetings with those two impostors, triumph and disaster) as to the nature of those 'what makes up the forces O'Missis Victorier's sons'. James Morris has pointed out that the tidy, swift, clockwork, 'All Sir Garnet', success of the Ashanti expedition was a comforting reassurance to the British that their armies and navies knew what they were about. The European nations might have huge conscript armies, and at least one of them, the Prussian Army, had shown what it could do in sweeping aside the glory of France with blood and iron efficiency, but for the British it was different. In the first place there was no conscription. Victoria's soldiers were, as soldiers are today, all volunteers. Even though Cardwell had put an end to purchase, the officers had both money and position. It was something (and still is) to hold a commission in this or that regiment. Some may have been smarter than others. But all prided themselves on their history and their traditions. All thought their own particular outfit was the best. And it was this very special *esprit de corps*, rather than devotion to Queen and country, that created between rich, privileged officers and their deprived, almost nameless private soldiers a bond which was able to withstand the very extremes of danger and hardship. 'The temper of the Army,' writes James Morris, referring to the 1870s, 'was eighteenth century, and its outlook had not been softened by the experience of empire. The drinking was terrific, the whoring insatiable, the looting endemic.' It was, of course, for the preservation and expansion of Empire that the Army seemed to exist. It was at this stage in Victoria's reign not merely a question of keeping by the sword what had been won by the sword. Commercial profit and national pride might be all very well. But there was something more in the British attitude to Imperialism now. It had become a duty, a vocation, and one which could be pursued only by constant resort to force of arms. For Kipling's 'Young British Soldier' this meant that he would often be shipped, somewheres east of Suez, and be subject to more hazards than simply those presented to him by an Afghan or Dervish enemy:

> When the 'arf-made recruity goes out to the East
> 'E acts like a babe an 'e drinks like a beast,
> An' 'e wonders because 'e is frequent deceased
> Ere 'e's fit for to serve as a soldier.

Kipling, of course, excelled at portraying British 'Tommies'. Charles Carrington maintained that, search English literature as you would, the only places where you would find a proper account of the British soldier, his thoughts and opinions, what he talked about, were in Shakespeare and in Kipling. Although in *Barrack-Room Ballads*, we see the soldier in South Africa, the Sudan and Burma, it is mainly of India that Kipling writes, where the private soldier was to many Indians not a *sahib* at all, but simply a member of a low, working caste. Yet such was the caste system there that merely because he was white and comparatively well-paid, he found himself to be 'socially superior' to the majority of the natives, many of whom worked in the cantonments as cooks, bearers and syces for the British rank and file. As Lord Anglesey has recorded: 'It was general for men not to consider themselves "pukka" soldiers until they had served in India, "eaten rump steaks for breakfast, been shaved in bed and made a two months' march".' At the same time conditions were such – long periods off duty, no proper facilities for entertainment or agreeable society, unsuitable clothing and food, lack of relief from the oppressive heat, cholera and malaria – that many men succumbed to the temptations of the brothel or the grog-shop. Drunkenness and venereal disease were rife. One soldier summed up his view of India as a fine place to serve by saying 'you're always thirsty and there's so much to drink'. Not all of them were able to take Kipling's advice 'to steer clear o' the grog-sellers' huts' which sold them 'Fixed Bay'nets that rots out your guts'. And not all of them, who had taken their fun where they found it, were successful in heeding another piece of advice: 'So be warned by my lot (which I know you will not), An' learn about women from me.' He summed it all up like this:

> The Queen she give me a shillin'
> To fight for 'er over the seas;
> But Guv'ment built me a fever-trap,
> An' Injia give me disease.

I fired a shot at a Afghan,
The beggar 'e fired again,
An' I lay on my bed with a 'ole in my 'ed,
An' missed the next campaign . . .

I served my time for a corp'ral,
An' wetted my stripes with pop,
For I went on a bend with a intimate friend,
An' finished my night in the 'shop' . . .

I've tasted the luck o' the army
In barrack an' camp an' clink,
An' I lost my tip through the bloomin' trip
Long o' the women an' drink . . .

We will meet more of Kipling's beggars in red as they fight for the
Queen in Afghanistan, Zululand and the Transvaal in the 1870s.

When Disraeli became Prime Minister in 1874 he began to make
history, and in the process arranged for numbers of British officers and
men to cover themselves with glory. Before the fighting itself started up
again, Disraeli brought off three coups, all of which were in some way
or another connected with the so-called Eastern Question, something
which had always held a special fascination for him. For him, and
indeed for the British generally, the Eastern Question meant propping
up the Turkish Empire in order to curb Russian expansion into the
Mediterranean or anywhere else that might threaten either the British
route to India or India itself. The route which really mattered was, of
course, the one that went through the Suez Canal, giving Egypt the
same strategic importance to the British as had once been enjoyed by
the Cape of Good Hope. When, therefore, it became known to Disraeli
in the autumn of 1875 that the Khedive Ismail's shares in the Suez
Canal Company were, so to speak, on the market, he made haste to
buy them on behalf of the British Government. 'In doing so,' writes
Lord Blake, 'he displayed many of his highest qualities, boldness, flair,
intuition and above all else a sense of opportunity. It is doubtful
whether any of his contemporaries would have acted with such speed
and vigour.' When it was done, he wrote triumphantly to the Queen:

> It is just settled; you have it, Madam. The French Government has
> been out-generaled. They tried too much, offering loans at an
> usurious rate, and with conditions which would have virtually
> given them the government of Egypt.
>
> The Khedive, in despair and disgust, offered your Majesty's
> Government to purchase his shares outright. He would never listen
> to such a proposition before.
>
> Four millions sterling! and almost immediately. There was only
> one firm that could do it – Rothschilds. They behaved admirably;

advanced the money at a low rate, and the entire interest of the
Khedive is now yours, Madam.

Britain's acquired stake in the Suez Canal and her concern with the
security of Egypt were to have profound consequences for both the
British Empire and the British Army. In commenting on this James
Morris points out that it was the final link in establishing Britain's
chain of command throughout the oceans of the world and all her
imperial possessions. Wherever British ships sailed they would simply
be moving from one of the Crown's strongholds to another. 'For two
decades after the acquisition of the canal shares, British military
supremacy was scarcely tested, and the Royal Navy sailed the world,
convoying its expeditionary forces, showing the Queen's flag, as
though its admirals owned the oceans. The public responded with
growing pride, and for the first time and probably the last time in their
history, the British people acquired a taste for drums, guns and glory.'
Before we see where the drums were beaten, the guns fired and the
glory won, we should record Disraeli's other two achievements
concerning the Eastern Question. One was to add 'Empress of India'
to the Queen's titles, something which he calculated was more likely to
appeal to the Indians themselves than to the British public. The other
was even more significant. When Beaconsfield (Disraeli had become
Earl of Beaconsfield in 1876) returned from the Congress of Berlin in
1878, bringing as he put it 'peace with honour', he had employed both
diplomacy and threats in order to avoid war with Russia,* had re-
mapped the Balkans, confirmed the end to Russian–Turkish hostilities, kept the Russians from Constantinople, secured the admiration of
Bismarck, and added Cyprus to Britain's chain of Mediterranean
bases. What is more, as Sir Robert Ensor has emphasized, there was no
war between the Great Powers for thirty-six years after the Berlin
Congress, a period of peace comparable with that from Waterloo to
the Crimean War. But in that same year, 1878, and almost exactly
forty years since the last time they had done so, a British colum was
marching up to the Khyber Pass to invade Afghanistan.

It was, as usual, caused by playing the Great Game. When Disraeli
appointed Lord Lytton as Viceroy of India in 1876, Lytton was
required among other things to persuade the Amir of Afghanistan,
Sher Ali, to accept a British mission at Kabul. The Amir would receive
subsidies and even military assistance if needed, but must agree to the
stationing of British agents at his frontier posts. Such an arrangement
did not suit Sher Ali, who had for years been strengthening his military
forces with Russian assistance. When in mid-1878 a Russian military
mission was established at Kabul, Lytton decided on his own initiative
that a British mission would also be sent. But it was turned back at the

* It was at this time that the music-hall song about not wanting to fight but 'by Jingo if
we do', having everything needed to do so, gave rise to a new word – 'Jingoism'.

frontier so Lytton sent an ultimatum, and after this was ignored by the Afghans, he set the invasion in train. Three columns were dispatched. The first was commanded by the legendary General Sir Samuel Browne* VC, with more than 16,000 horse, foot and guns and the customary flood of camp followers. Its cavalry brigade under Charles Gough, another VC, had squadrons from the 10th Hussars, Guides and the 11th Bengal Lancers. Browne's force quickly overcame resistance at the fort dominating the entrance to the Khyber Pass and established itself at Jalalabad by 20 December 1878. From there a number of punitive sorties were made against the Khugiani tribesmen. One of these ended in tragedy for a squadron of the 10th Hussars, whose horses and troopers, unaccustomed to the treacherous Punjab waters, were swept away by rapids at a ford in the Kabul river. Weighted down as they were with haversacks and ammunition pouches under their khaki cloaks, even the best swimmers were soon overcome by the icy, swirling water, and of the seventy officers and men in the squadron, nearly fifty were either drowned or kicked to death by their own horses struggling in the rapids. Kipling recorded the affair in his inimitable way, as a trooper grieves over the loss of his friend:

> Kabul town is sun and dust –
> Blow the trumpet, draw the sword –
> I'd ha' sooner drownded fust
> 'Stead of 'im beside the ford . . .

> You can 'ear the 'orses threshin'; you can
>   'ear the men a-splashin',
> 'Cross the ford o' Kabul river in the dark.

> Turn your 'orse from Kabul town –
> Blow the trumpet, draw the sword –'
> Im an' 'arf my troop is down,
> Down an' drownded by the ford . . .

> There's the river low an' fallin', but it ain't
>   no use a-callin'
> 'Cross the ford o' Kabul river in the dark.

There were nevertheless some furious engagements fought by Gough's brigade, notably one at Fatehabad in April 1879, when with a mixed body of cavalry, horse gunners and infantry he took on a large body of Khugianis, whose courage in standing and fighting won the admiration of the British and Indian troops. One of the British chaplains, Swinnerton, who was present at the action noted how differently the 10th Hussars and the Guides Cavalry took on the enemy. While the English squadron charged in formation and by doing so often allowed the dismounted Khugianis to slip to one side or the other, the Guides

---

* Designer of the belt still worn by officers of the British Army.

rode in loose order, hunting down each individual enemy. It was also evident that the broad, sharp sabres of the Guides were far more effective in penetrating the enemy's thick sheepskin coats and heavy turbans than the long, straight swords of the 10th, who had to resort to the thrust, rather than the cut, to kill or wound the hillmen.

The second column, known as the Kuram Valley Field Force, was smaller, just over 5,000 strong with thirteen guns, and was commanded by the man who had won a Victoria Cross as a young officer in the Mutiny, was now to do great things in Afghanistan, went on to become Commander-in-Chief, India, defeated the Boers in South Africa, became Army Commander-in-Chief at home, and devoted forty years to improving the well-being of beggars in red, whose hero he became – Major-General Frederick Roberts, known to one and all as 'Bobs'.

> There's a little red-faced man,
>   Which is Bobs,
> Rides the tallest 'orse 'e can –
>   *Our* Bobs . . .
>
> 'E's a little down on drink,
>   Chaplain Bobs;
> But it keeps us outer Clink –
>   Don't it Bobs? . . .
>
> 'E's been at it thirty years,
> An' amassin' souveneers
> In the way o' slugs an' spears –
>   Ain't yer, Bobs?
>
> What 'e does not know o' war,
>   Gen'ral Bobs,
> You can arst the shop next door –
>   Can't they, Bobs?
> Oh, 'e's little but he's wise,
> 'E's a terror for 'is size,
> An' – *'e – does – not – advertise* –
>   Do yer, Bobs? . . .
>
> This ain't no bloomin' ode,
> But you've 'elped the soldier's load,
> An' for benefits bestowed,
>   Bless yer, Bobs!

It was perhaps no surprise to the soldiers who knew him that in this first campaign where he held independent command as a general, Roberts pulled off a spectacular success. By combining a diversionary deception with a long night march with his main body he captured the mountain stronghold of Peiwar Kotal, regarded as well nigh impregnable, which had been strongly held by the Afghans and whose possession enabled Roberts to dominate the Kuram Valley. There would be much more for Roberts to do later, but when the third column, under General Stewart, occupied Kandahar early in January 1879, to be followed in February by the death of Sher Ali while attempting to escape to Turkestan, the first phase of this second Afghan War came to an end. Sher Ali's son, Yakub Khan, was willing to negotiate and on 26 May 1879 the treaty of Gandamak was signed. The British gained control of the passes and the right to have a British minister at Kabul who would be in charge of foreign policy. It seemed for the time being that Lytton's policy had worked.

Disraeli had at first been displeased by the turn of events in Afghanistan. He had not authorized the actual dispatch of the mission, and was irritated that the Amir's intransigence had forced his hand. 'When a viceroy or a commander-in-chief disobey orders', he commented, 'they ought at least to be certain of success.' It is a point we would all do well to take note of. He was, of course, mollified by the victories of Roberts and others, yet soon discovered that when sorrows come, they come not in single spies, but in battalions. 'In administering this immense Empire,' wrote André Maurois in his still immensely readable biography of Disraeli, 'the devil of the business was that at any moment serious annoyances might spring up in the furthest corners of the earth. Afghanistan was still smouldering when South Africa burst into flames.' Before switching the scene to Zululand, however, we will continue to accompany 'Bobs' as he moves from Kuram to Kabul and Kandahar in a series of remarkable marches and engagements, and finally brings the Second Afghan War to an end.

In July 1879 a British minister had taken up residence at Kabul. He was Sir Louis Cavagnari, a singularly bad choice by Lytton, as he was regarded with profound suspicion by the Afghans. Apart from a civil assistant and a surgeon, there was only one other Englishman with him, Lieutenant Walter Hamilton VC, who commanded the escort of twenty-five Guides cavalry and fifty-two Guides infantry. On 3 September the Legation was stormed by mutinous Afghan soldiers and the British all killed, Hamilton last of all after conducting a most gallant defence. It was when the Afghans called upon the surviving Guides, who had most loyally been fighting alongside the British, to surrender, that this astonishing Corps showed what it was made of, as Philip Mason has told us:

All day, the Afghans had shouted to the Guides to leave the English; they had no quarrel with them and would let them go free. The offer was now made again. Jemadar Jewand Singh was in command. There was a pause and he consulted the survivors, of whom not much more than a dozen remained. Perhaps they did not put much faith in Afghan promises. Perhaps their one thought was the honour of the Guides. They were in the heat of action and there would be no long debate. What is known is that they made up their minds quickly and came out to die. They charged for the last time. An eye-witness, an old soldier, saw them fight to the last; Jewand Singh killed eight men before he was killed. Not a man of the Guides survived. Their defence had lasted twelve hours and six hundred of the enemy lay dead around them.

There could be no greater tribute to these magnificent soldiers or to the British officers who had raised and trained them. At home there was an inevitable reaction against Beaconsfield's policy. Gladstone, in particular, made much of it all, condemning his rival for leading the British into battle all over the world with the inevitable nemesis. Before long Gladstone would himself be supervising the slaughter of savages and earning comparable disapprobation.

Of course it now became necessary to punish the Afghans for mutiny and murder, so the war began all over again. The nearest British force was the one in the Kuram Valley under Roberts and in a remarkable, rapid march, fighting two actions on the way, he reached Kabul on 13 October, little more than a month after the massacres there. The principal battle took place on 6 October at Charasia, a strong mountain position held by thousands of Afghan regular soldiers and tribesmen. Roberts' cavalry had given him excellent information as to his enemy's deployment, and he once again succeeded in deceiving them as to where his main blow would fall. Attacking with artillery and infantry, while the cavalry* waited for the pursuit, he routed the rebels and was now only six miles from Kabul. One of the young officers taking part in the battle was Ian Hamilton (nearly thirty-six years later he commanded the first phase of the disastrous Gallipoli campaign) and he remembered charging with the 5th Punjab Cavalry against the Afghans, who would lie on their backs, out of reach of cavalry swords, whirling their huge knives and attempting to slash the legs of their enemy's horses – a tactic countered by the Punjabi sowars' drill of working in pairs, one with carbine, one with sword, giving the rebels a choice of either being shot on the ground or being cut to pieces if they rose up. It was, Hamilton recalled, a tremendous thing to be galloping at sensational speed, among the red pugarees and blue swords of the 5th Punjabs, 'a hell of a scrimmage . . . dust, shouts, shots, clash of steel'. So Bobs retook Kabul, while Yakub Khan, who had embarrassed Roberts by coming to his headquarters during the march and attaching himself with a huge retinue to the British column, then abdicated. Meanwhile the British reinforced Kandahar and then there was a pause in the fighting. In

---

* As Lord Anglesey has pointed out, Roberts had little cavalry available for this purpose as most of them were guarding his camp with its huge number of camp followers and pack animals – a soft target for tribesmen waiting in the hills.

1880 the Marquess of Ripon succeeded Lytton as Viceroy and his policy, unlike Lytton's which had been to partition Afghanistan, was one of disengagement. This time a nephew of Sher Ali's, Abdur Rahman, was installed as Amir at Kabul, and Ripon intended also to withdraw the garrison at Kandahar. But in July 1880 another claimant to the throne (there was never a shortage of them in Afghanistan), Ayub Khan, marched against Kandahar. It was then that the event which Charles Carrington described as 'savages beating civilized men in fair fight' occurred – at Maiwand.

Ayub Khan was another son of the late Amir, Sher Ali, and he decided to march from Herat province, which he ruled, with an army of something like 15,000, half of whom were regular foot and horse, with thirty artillery pieces and thousands of the fanatically brave Ghazis. His purpose was to rid Afghanistan of the infidel and he intended to start off by dealing with the puppet governor of Kandahar. From Kandahar itself there marched out to deal with Ayub Khan on 4 July a relatively small force of some 2,500 under Brigadier-General Burrows, who had never fought a battle in almost forty years' service in India. His command consisted of about 1,750 infantry, two-thirds Bombay Native Infantry plus the 66th Foot (Royal Berkshire Regiment), twelve guns, six of which were horse artillery, and nearly 500 cavalry made up of 3rd Bombay Light Cavalry and 3rd Scinde Horse. Apart from his own inexperience and his numerical inferiority, Burrows suffered from inadequate intelligence as to what his enemy was doing. By virtue of the hostility to the British harboured by all local tribesmen, Ayub Khan received timely and accurate information about Burrows' movements, whereas he had little or none about Ayub Khan's. This fatal deficiency was what lay behind Burrows' slowness in moving to occupy and control an important valley north of Maiwand, through which Ayub Khan could aim for Ghazni and Kabul, if he chose to do so, and Burrows' specific orders were that he must try to prevent this very move. During the morning of 27 July 1880 it became clear that Ayub Khan had got there first and that therefore Burrows had little alternative but to bring about a battle there and then.

If the past were anything to go by, numbers alone would not have determined the outcome, but Ayub's superiority here was such that he was able to execute a continuous enveloping movement on both flanks, while deploying his artillery ever closer to the British. Thus Burrows' infantry were subject to ever-growing pressure, and inexplicably he did not withdraw his cavalry, who were not being employed at the time, out of range of the enemy's artillery. This meant that the two cavalry regiments suffered heavy casualties, so that when the time came that Burrows required them to charge the Afghans pressing ever closer, they were too weak to do so effectively. At length a general withdrawal by the British towards Kandahar ended the action, and happily for the survivors of the battle, the lure of loot from the British baggage train dissuaded the Afghans from too stern a pursuit. Subsequent investigation into the action revealed not only bad generalship on the part of Burrows and his subordinate, Nuttall, but also that unforgivable fault of trying to shift the blame on to others. The British lost nearly half their force, the Afghans rather more of their regulars – about 1,500 – and as many as 4,000 Ghazis. Anglesey calls Maiwand the worst disaster suffered by the Anglo-Indian army, one by which its reputation was greatly harmed, but he concedes that in spite of bad generalship, it is doubtful whether even Roberts himself could have succeeded against so much stronger a force, handled as it was with the boldness and perseverance of Ayub Khan. What followed next was the siege of Kandahar, and it was now for Roberts, in what was perhaps the finest achievement of his career, to make his famous, exhausting and triumphant march from Kabul, covering over 300 miles at summer's height in scarcely more than three weeks, with 10,000 men and nearly as many camp followers, over practically roadless country and mountain passes, and at the end of it utterly routing Ayub Khan's army which had positioned itself strongly in the hills outside Kandahar. It was an astonishing feat of arms, called the 'Race for the Peerage' by one of Roberts' own staff officers, a race he certainly won, becoming 1st Baron Roberts (later Earl) of Kandahar:

> Now they've made a bloomin' Lord
>   Outer Bobs,
> Which was but 'is fair reward –
>   Weren't it, Bobs?
> So 'e'll wear a coronet
> Where 'is 'elmet used to set;
> But we know you won't forget –
>   Will yer, Bobs?

Indeed he did not forget. He went on to be Commander-in-Chief, India, doing all he could to better the soldiers' conditions, not only during his command in India, but in South Africa and at home, changing, as Charles Carrington claims, 'the reckless, drunken scapegraces described in Kipling's early ballads into the literate well-behaved soldiers of 1914.' He had certainly cleared up the Afghan problem. Abdur Rahman was confirmed as Amir of all Afghanistan, and agreed to British control of his foreign policy in exchange for a subsidy and support against aggression from elsewhere. And having tried it before with results we have already seen, the British sent no resident to Kabul.

Concurrently with all this troublesome playing of the Great Game, there was much for the British redcoats to do in South Africa. The Zulu war broke out because the new high commissioner for South Africa, Sir Bartle Frere (appointed in 1877) was greatly concerned with what he regarded as the menace from the 40,000-strong army of disciplined warriors maintained by King Cetewayo*, particularly in view of the many border disputes which arose between Zululand and the Transvaal, which had been annexed to the British Crown by Shepstone, Natal's minister for native affairs, at about the same time as Frere arrived at Capetown. So concerned indeed was Frere that in October 1878, with the strong support of the Army Commander, General Thesiger (who succeeded his father as Lord Chelmsford in December) he urgently requested the home Government for more troops. Initially Beaconsfield's cabinet refused to send reinforcements (although later they did so), while issuing Frere clear instructions to pursue a peaceful policy. Far from doing so, Frere dispatched an ultimatum to the Zulus in December, demanding disbandment of their armies and worded in such a way that he knew it would not be accepted. Thus, greatly to Beaconsfield's displeasure, Frere embarked on a course which was bound to result in war in direct contravention of his instructions.

The campaign in Zululand followed a pattern familiar among Britain's savage wars of peace. It began with a blunder by the British general in charge leading to defeat and tragic loss; this first act in the drama was then redeemed by scenes of incredible endurance and heroism in another isolated battle; and finally the British pulled themselves together and staged a deliberate, inexorable advance to Ulundi, Cetewayo's capital, and there with a combination of traditional tactics and disciplined fire-power winning the battle that really mattered – the last one. We will have a look at all three acts in the play. But before doing so, let us be in no doubt as to what a formidable, fearsome opponent the Zulu warrior was. He was quite unlike any previous enemy the British Tommy had encountered. The Zulus' military system based on universal conscription and the idea that no warrior had proved himself before 'washing his spear in blood' made for a truly warlike race. They were quite indifferent to death, knowing indeed that should they should fail in battle they were doomed to be executed by their own people. As for tactics, they moved in huge impis, perhaps 20,000 strong, crossing the hills and plains of Zululand in a relentless, unstoppable jog-trot, with a great mass in front to engage their enemies in paralysing strength, while two 'horns' swept round on either flank to envelop them completely and prevent any escape. With their shields held in front of them, assegais ready to throw or slash, ostrich plumes emerging from skin head-bands, hissing their blood-curdling war-cries, and ever moving forward in their terrible tireless jog, a sea of black, blood-thirsty, fanatically brave warriors, they were, as James Morris had it, 'among the most spectacular of all the theatrical enemies the British empire felt itself obliged to fight'.

* There seem to be several ways of spelling his name, Keshwayo and Cetshwayo among them.

So in January 1879 some 16,800 troops, divided into five columns, two of which were in reserve, and containing both British battalions and native troops crossed the border. Of the three leading columns to invade Zululand, the centre one was commanded by Colonel Glyn and had nearly 5,000 men. With this column rode Lord Chelmsford in command of the whole invading force. After crossing the border at Rorke's Drift, where there was a mission house, they moved on a further ten miles and on 20 January made camp in a plain overlooked by the great mountain of Isandhlwana. They took no prudent defensive measures, such as forming a laager or digging trenches, despite specific warnings by Boers who knew the country and the Zulus, relying instead on pickets and scouts to give adequate notice of the enemy's presence. It was not enough, for a huge Zulu impi some 14,000 strong had moved silently and unnoticed to a ravine near Isandhlwana and on 21 January was established there completely concealed. At dawn next day Chelmsford with about half the column moved out of camp to find and destroy another impi which scouts had reported to be some miles away to the north-west. While he was away on what proved to be an ineffectual engagement, the other half of the column, still in camp and still ill-prepared for defence, was practically wiped out. The hidden impi, the very main body of Cetewayo's army that Chelmsford was seeking, rose up from its ravine and poured over the ridge in a surging mass to descend on the British and native troops in the plain. The fighting itself was brutal and cruel in the extreme, as James Morris has told us:

> Thousands of Zulus died in the British rifle-fire, but nothing could stop them: when they reached the lines they slashed about them indiscriminately with their assegais, while the British fought desperately back with bayonets and rifle-butts. All over the plain isolated groups of redcoats were surrounded, helplessly struggling, by masses of feathered black men. Sometimes the Zulus threw their own dead in front of them to blunt the bayonets; the British, split, shattered and disorganized, fell back in twos and threes to wagons, or tents, or hid terrified among the field kitchens, or fought to the death all alone, bayoneting and bludgeoning to the last.

It was therefore an appalling spectacle that greeted Chelmsford when he returned that evening from his fruitless attempt to bring the Zulus to battle. The camp which he had neglected to defend properly was in ruins, dead British soldiers, most of them disembowelled, lying everywhere, all the paraphernalia of tents, wagons, equipment strewn about or burnt, and over it all a ghastly brooding silence. The Zulus had dragged away most of their own dead, but the 2nd Warwickshire Regiment, or rather six companies of them, had been utterly destroyed. About 850 British soldiers and nearly 500 of the local levies had been killed. Nothing like it had happened to the British Army since

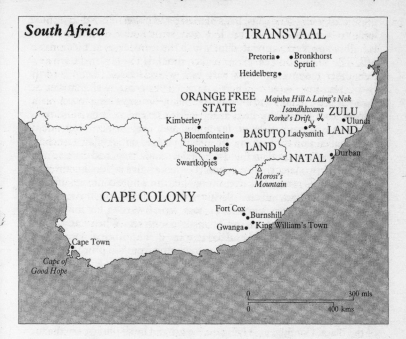

South Africa

the retreat from Kabul nearly forty years earlier. Yet, unknown to Chelmsford and all those with him, only ten miles away at Rorke's Drift and on that very same day, 22 January, another desperate struggle was in progress, where matchless courage seemed to be the norm, where overwhelming Zulu numbers pitted themselves against a small group of redcoats, a struggle in which both sides won everlasting fame, and which inspired poet and painter alike to record the event for posterity.*

The garrison at Rorke's Drift was about a hundred strong, a company of the 24th Foot† (South Wales Borderers) with a few others, including a chaplain and some local levies. The senior officer was Lieutenant Chard of the Royal Engineers. With him was Lieutenant Bromhead of the 24th Foot. Having been alerted to the danger of an attack both by hearing the noise of battle from Isandhlwana and from reports by some of the few survivors who had succeeded in escaping, the two officers organized what fortifications they could round their

---

* Including *The Defence of Rorke's Drift* by Lady Butler, reproduced in this book.
† At this time the 24th were the Warwickshire Regiment, and this company was part of the battalion overrun at Isandhlwana.

perimeter, using sandbags, bags of maize and boxes. They did not have long to wait before an impi, 4,000 strong and a 'horn' of the Isandhlwana force, appeared (at which the local levies instantly made off). The main body of 3,000 Zulus attacked the post frontally, the remainder moving by Oskarberg hill, which flanked Rorke's Drift, and assaulting the rear. Their attack went on for twelve hours, all through the evening and on into the night, in wave after wave. Zulu snipers from Oskarberg fired at the gallant defenders, a building being used as a hospital was set on fire and abandoned, the perimeter shrank ever smaller, and then slowly the assault petered out. At dawn next day the Zulus, except for their hundreds of dead and dying, had disappeared. An hour or two later they re-appeared, on the hills overlooking the post, well out of rifle range, and after sitting there for a time contemplating the redcoats who had inflicted such terrible casualties on them, jogged silently away. Eleven Victoria Crosses were awarded for this unique action, more than for any other single encounter. When Lady Butler came to do her painting, she talked to some of the 'principal heroes' who were able to assist her in depicting the battle from the private soldier's point of view. In particular she wished to include those awarded the Victoria Cross. The two officers, Chard and Bromhead, are in the centre; Private Fitch carries ammunition in his left, unwounded arm; the Commissariat Officer, Dalton, has been shot and falls with arm outflung; the Chaplain, Smith, is just behind the two lieutenants; Corporal Schiess of the Natal Contingent is lying on the ground by sandbags; the doctor, Reynolds, with white helmet, tends a wounded soldier; and two privates, Robert Jones and William Jones (most of the company were Welshmen) are seen on the extreme left.

After this and despite some further patrolling and relief operations – both Evelyn Wood and Redvers Buller greatly distinguished themselves – Chelmsford withdrew his army, determined to try again as soon as possible. During the next few months, Beaconsfield reinforced Chelmsford with horse, foot, guns and stores, but the cabinet's confidence in him had been forfeited by lack of results, and at the end of May 1879 Wolseley was appointed as High Commissioner and Commander-in-Chief in Natal, Transvaal and Zululand with complete civil and military power. Chelmsford would be required to submit his plans for Wolseley's approval. As it turned out, however, he did not wait for Wolseley's arrival, but went ahead with his own ideas for crushing the Zulu military power. Before doing so, another blunder resulted in the death of the Prince Imperial, son of Napoleon III, in a minor skirmish. Queen Victoria was devastated. Beaconsfield's bitter comment was that the Zulus were a wonderful people – 'They beat our generals, they convert our bishops, and they write *finis* to a French dynasty.' Wolseley landed at Durban at the end of June, but Chelmsford was already on his way to Ulundi.

During May and June both Evelyn Wood's Flying Column and the main column under Chelmsford had been moving forward, patrolling, reconnoitring, burying the dead at Isandhlwana, establishing bases, and this time whenever they halted taking proper measures against being surprised. Buller, who commanded the mounted element of Wood's column, would always camp at nightfall, and then move again after dark so that the Zulus were uncertain about his exact position. The horses were placed in rings, fastened together, the men at their heads in a circle, sentries outside each circle to ensure no horse broke loose. No smoking, absolute silence, vedettes and guards regularly visited, saddles not removed, only one blanket for each man. At two o'clock in the morning those sleeping were quietly wakened, and everyone fell in with their horses, ready to receive short, clear orders. So both columns moved ever nearer to the royal kraal at Ulundi, and although Cetewayo sent emissaries to Chelmsford seeking terms, Chelmsford's replies were so uncompromising that nothing came of it. Buller's reconnoitring on 3 July had discovered what he called 'an excellent position for the next day's fight' on the Ulundi plain outside the royal kraal, and on 4 July nearly 5,000 men moved forward in a hollow rectangle, the infantry forming the outer edges, colours flying, bands playing; in between them at regular intervals were artillery pieces and Gatling machine guns; on the flanks and to the front Buller's mounted men; bringing up the rear regular cavalry. Among the regiments present were the 17th Lancers* with a troop of King's Dragoon Guards; the 80th and 90th Foot (Staffordshires and Cameronians), the Frontier Horse, Transvaal Rangers and a troop of Natal Horse, all in all a magnificent spectacle. Yet to one of those present the British rectangle seemed to resemble 'a little red matchbox about to be trampled to dust by the feet of the Zulu army'.

On reaching their chosen ground, Evelyn Wood recommended the digging of trenches, but Chelmsford rejected the proposal, saying that they had been called ant-eaters long enough, and that only if they beat the Zulus in the open would 'they' be satisfied. Whether by 'they' he meant the Zulus themselves or, as James Morris has suggested, the armchair strategists at home, is not clear, but beat them in the open he did. As the 20,000-strong impi rose up from the bush and closed in on the rectangle, Buller's mounted men engaged them with carbines while slowly falling back. By about nine o'clock, all the cavalry were inside the rectangle, while artillery, machine guns and the disciplined rifle-fire of the British redcoats took terrible toll of the fanatically brave Zulu warriors attacking on all sides. For an hour and a half it went on, but not one Zulu got closer than thirty yards to the British lines. When even their last reserves in a desperate rush failed and faltered, Chelmsford ordered the 17th Lancers out and, followed by the King's Dragoon Guards troop and irregular horse, away they went to finish

* Commanded by Colonel Drury Curzon Drury-Lowe, whom we will meet again in Egypt.

off the business. A Frontier Light Horseman riding behind the lancers saw it all:

> In one movement the lances dropped to the right side of the horses' necks, a long line of poles, stretching out a distance in front of the horses, the steel heads pointing straight at the mass of retreating Zulus. As the big horses bounded forward and thundered into them, each lance point pierced the Zulu in front of it; the man fell, and as the horse passed on beyond him the lance was withdrawn, lifted and thrust forward into another Zulu in front.
>
> The movement of withdrawing the lance and again getting it into position was very rapid; I could not quite understand how it was done. It was such a mix up for us riding behind the Lancers, with our horses jumping over dead Zulus, and having to deal with those who were knocked down by the Lancer horses but not pierced, that we did not have the opportunity to study the work. I suppose we were sent out as a support in case the Zulus rounded on them; but I reckon that any body of men who were on the run, and saw that line of long spears (lances) making for them, would not think of turning but would run the harder. It was a grand sight to see them at work, but they did not appear to me to be humans and horses – just a huge machine.

It speaks much for the Zulus' courage and endurance that even during the 17th Lancers' charge, some hundreds of them who had been concealed in long grass rose up to fire at the British troopers or close with them to seize the lances and attempt to stab the horses. But they were soon dispersed by the supporting cavalry using sabre and carbine. One of the 17th Lancers' NCOs remembered it all as a 'glorious go', much better than pig-sticking, and reckoned that it made up for all the hardships of the campaign. Although he had not greatly cared for the inactivity of simply standing by the horses' heads inside the rectangle, being fired at without the chance of hitting back, for men and horses were both falling, and 'it was hardly a place for a nervous old gentleman to take a stroll', once they left the rectangle to charge the Zulus, it was different. They were soon on to the enemy, who could not escape, no quarter was given and they only stopped when the horses could go no further. But he admired the black warriors – 'all young men, splendidly-made fellows, and all stripped for fighting'. The Zulus' losses were uncertain, some thousands perhaps, while the British casualties were only twelve killed and eighty-eight wounded. The war was over. Cetewayo's capital, Ulundi, was burned, but the King himself escaped, only to be captured a few months later. He was fêted when he visited England in 1882! But his kingdom was broken up by Wolseley into a number of principalities under separate rulers. The British always admired the Zulus for their splendid fighting qualities; shortly the beggars in red would be arguing the toss with another race of South Africans who took exception to British rule and proved to be even tougher and more inflexible foes – the Boers.

By this time Gladstone was Prime Minister, having succeeded Disraeli in April 1880. Disraeli, as Robert Blake has explained, was associated by his opponents with 'jingoism'. Yet in fact by purchasing the Suez Canal shares, dispatching the Mediterranean fleet to Constantinople in 1878, and giving Victoria the title of Queen Empress of India, he was primarily concerned with pursuing British interests, and, as we have seen, when things went wrong as they did in Afghanistan and Zululand, it was usually because of the disobedience or stupidity of one of his subordinates. Sir Robert Ensor emphasizes that with all his love for England, Disraeli 'remained deeply un-English. Idealist and cynic, prophet and tactician, genius and charlatan in one, men took him for a flaunting melodramatist until they experienced him as a deadly fighter.' The last important speech he made in the House of Lords was concerned with events that we have been witnessing here, a speech in which he claimed, not originally, that 'the key of India is in London', while deprecating the Government's decision to withdraw its garrison from Kandahar.

Gladstone's refusal to reverse the annexation of the Transvaal, effected while Disraeli was still in office, brought about the first Boer war. When negotiations came to nothing, Kruger and Joubert, champions of Transvaal independence, decided to take up arms against the British in December 1880. By this time Wolseley had handed over as High Commissioner to one of his own 'Ring', Major-General Sir George Colley, who fatally underestimated the Boers' determination and skill as mounted infantry. Colley was far too gentle, chivalrous and introspective a man to deal with a situation which demanded iron will, tactical genius and ruthless efficiency. Everything he now did militarily went wrong. First the Connaught Rangers, whom we last met in the Peninsula, were ambushed while on their way from Natal to the Transvaal. It happened on 20 December 1880 as the battalion was approaching a creek. The Boers demanded their instant withdrawal, as 'foreign troops' were not permitted to enter the Republic of Transvaal. When the Rangers' commanding officer refused, so heavy a fire was opened on the battalion from the high ground all around that within a matter of minutes the battalion had some 160 casualties, half of them fatal, including all the officers. Next General Colley's attempts to enter the Transvaal to relieve the beleaguered garrisons there were easily frustrated on the Natal side of the border at Laing's Nek. The Boers' guerrilla tactics of rapid fire and movement with their mounted Commandos simply outmanoeuvred and outfought Colley's 1,500-strong force of young soldiers. This reverse notwithstanding, and now reinforced by troops from India, Colley decided to capture Majuba Hill, on the border between Natal and Transvaal, which James Morris depicts as 'unmistakable, as distinctive as Isandhlwana itself. It rose massively flat-topped above the pass, and could be seen from far across the Natal border like a sentry guarding the inner fastness of Afrikanerdom. Majuba was 6,000 feet high, but looked higher, and had a majestic if brooding presence.' There was no evident tactical purpose in taking the hill, for Colley planned to take no artillery with him, nor to make it into an entrenched defensive position. He simply seemed to believe that possession of the summit would somehow influence the outcome of his contest with the Boers. It did! But in such a way as was to lead to his own disadvantage, disgrace and death.

The thing was done on an absurdly small scale. During the night of 26 February 1881 359 men climbed up the steep southern slope of Majuba Hill. Apart from Colley himself there were soldiers of the Gordon Highlanders, 58th Foot (Northamptonshire Regiment), the 60th Rifles and even some sailors – a motley crew, one might say, 'dressed', writes James Morris, 'in all the bright panoply of the imperial wars, the scarlet jackets, the kilts, the white tropical helmets, the blue trousers, the pipe-clayed pouches'. With them too was Ian Hamilton whom we last saw charging with the 5th Punjab Cavalry against Afghan tribesmen while Roberts was making his whirlwind way to Kabul. There were to be no such triumphs here. The soldiers took no proper defensive measures, there was no real cover, no room for manoeuvre on the small plateau at the summit, and having gazed at the spectacular view and the Boers camped down below them to the north, with some men positioned round the perimeter, yet inexplicably no sensible look-outs or listening posts, the little force simply took it easy. General Colley, again for no discernible reason, had told his men that all he asked of them was that they should hold the position for three days. In the event they held it for less than half a day. Unseen and unheard the Boers on their ponies made their way up the northern flank of the hill on the morning of 27 February, dismounting before reaching the top, and then, creeping silently upwards to the crest, totally surprised the British. They poured volley after volley into them at close range, causing nothing short of panic, and resulting in about three-quarters of Colley's force being killed, wounded or captured, and the rest running ignominiously away down the hill. Colley himself was killed. James Morris suggests that rumours of Colley's killing himself might be well-founded, for 'would not a shot in the head, as the castastrophe descended, perfectly have fitted the Wagnerian drama he had directed? Majuba was a kind of abdication from the start. It was a flamboyant admission of failure – for possession of the hill without artillery could really achieve nothing – by a commander without the magic gift of victory.' We may be sure that the whole affair would not have taken the form it did if Wolseley had been there. Gladstone, who had previously opposed annexation of the Transvaal, made a peace which recognized Transvaal's independence subject to certain British controls, such as foreign policy. But Gladstone was soon to find himself caught up in another Imperial adventure, and this time with Wolseley there at the peak of his form, there would be nothing but triumph for the beggars in red.

The insurrection led by Colonel Arabi Pasha in 1881, designed to rid Egypt of all foreign interference, not only overwhelmed the Khedive Tewfik (son of Ismail who had sold the Suez Canal shares to Disraeli), but threatened the Anglo-French condominium itself. Dithering by Turkey and the failure of France and Britain to reach agreement about joint action led to Arabi Pasha's virtually taking control of the country, yet when his followers over-reached themselves, London and Paris ordered both the British and French fleets to sail to Alexandria. Further riots there resulted in many Europeans being killed. At last in July 1882 things came to a head, for Arabi's fortification of Alexandria with new batteries endangered the Allied fleets, and on 11 July, although the French steamed away, ships of the Royal Navy under Admiral Seymour neutralized the forts in a ten-hour bombardment. Arabi's subsequent threat to destroy the Suez Canal decided the British cabinet to send an army under Wolseley. The French government was invited to take part, but internal political disputes intervened. Turkey stood aloof, so Britain acted alone.

The whole expedition was managed in a characteristically 'All Sir Garnet' fashion. The speed with which some 16,000 troops were assembled at home showed how efficient Cardwell's reforms had been. There were more than 2,000 cavalrymen,* ten infantry battalions, each about 800 strong, 54 artillery pieces manned by 1,900 men; and a further 4,000 sappers, commissariat, medical, provost and other supporting staffs. Another nine infantry battalions came from Gibraltar and Malta, and from India 1,500 cavalry; five infantry regiments, three of them native, totalling nearly 6,000; plus some 4,000 others. The troops and transports from England and the Mediterranean sailed for Alexandria, those from India for Suez. Wolseley planned to deceive Arabi Pasha by making a great demonstration at Alexandria as if he intended to march on Cairo from there, while actually seizing the Canal at Suez, Port Said and Ismailia, and then taking on the Egyptian army in the desert between Ismailia and Cairo. It all worked exactly as planned. After his pretence of a landing at Aboukir Bay on the night of 19 August 1882, Wolseley landed his main force at Port Said, the Royal Navy having already seized Suez, and by 22 August he was in possession of the sweetwater canal and the

---

* Including the Household Cavalry, whose regiments had not been in action since Waterloo. In *Vanity Fair*, Thackeray suggested that they were sent to Egypt because the then Secretary of State for War, Hugh Childers, wanted to abolish them and hoped that by demonstrating their uselessness in war, he could bring it off. Needless to say, they greatly distinguished themselves.

railway between Suez and Ismailia. Thereafter with actions at Magfar, Mahsama and Kassassin, the climax of the whole campaign came at Tel el-Kebir on 13 September, where the main Egyptian force under Arabi Pasha was manning its defensive position. Wolseley's successful execution of a dawn attack after a night march, what he himself called 'the most deadly but the most difficult of military operations', took the Egyptians completely by surprise, and the initial work of infantry and artillery was finished off by the cavalry. Major-General Drury-Lowe, commanding the Cavalry Division, led the pursuit, and it was he (whom we last met at the head of his regiment, the 17th Lancers, knocking down Zulus at Ulundi) to whom Arabi gave up his sword on 14 September. It was all over. 'The occupation of Egypt,' writes Lord Anglesey in his incomparable *History of the British Cavalry*, 'which was to be such a familiar part of the British army's life for nearly three-quarters of a century had begun.' He adds that in characteristic Egyptian style, no sooner had the reluctant Egyptian soldiers shed their uniforms for the more comfortable ghalabeahs than 'they treated the cavalry more like a party of Cook's Tourists than an invading force'. Wolseley had done it all with the loss of little more than 400 soldiers. It was, as he said himself, the tidiest war in British history. It was also the climax of Wolseley's unbroken success as a commander of British armies in the field, and yet was to lead to the last of his campaigns in command, when his game began to go wrong.

CHAPTER FOURTEEN

England's Glory and Pride

We've fought with many men acrost the seas,
An' some of 'em was brave an' some was not:
The Paythan an' the Zulu an' Burmese;
But the Fuzzy was the finest o' the lot.

RUDYARD KIPLING

In the late nineteenth century there was always a savage war of peace for the British Army to enjoy somewhere, and let us now embark on one last campaign to round the story off. It is in several ways a fitting climax for its cause was avoidable, its setting theatrical, its drama stupendous and its conclusion classically tragic. For so spectacular a presentation there was a powerful cast. The stars were Charlie Gordon, Wolseley, Evelyn Baring, Gladstone and the Mahdi. Supporting players included such Imperial heroes as Hicks Pasha, Brigadier-General Sir Herbert Stewart, Redvers Buller, Kitchener and Fred Burnaby, while innumerable extras were provided by a colourful mixture of British regiments (some of whom formed in bizarre, sometimes hilarious, fashion), several Camel Corps, and on the other side to keep them all busy Dervishes and Fuzzy-Wuzzies galore.

We may readily suppose that when Gladstone uncharacteristically supported the idea of an expedition to Egypt in 1882, he had no notion that its successful conclusion would bring upon him and his Government responsibility also for what was going on in the Sudan. It would have been difficult to choose a more awkward time to assume this responsibility, for dissatisfaction with Egypt's appalling maladministration of the Sudan had boiled over in 1881, when a Dongolawi teacher, Muhammad Ahmed, had proclaimed himself the Mahdi al-Muntazar, the Expected One or Messiah, and raised his banner of holy war against Cairo's foreign misrule. Despite some setbacks in his attacks on Egyptian garrisons at el Obeid and Bara, by the end of 1882 the Mahdi's revolt, which at first swept through Kordofan, with its White Nile tribes, destroying all Egypt's outposts there, had spread throughout Sudan so that the whole country south of Khartoum had risen in his support. The so-called Dervishes were formidable opponents. As Peter Clark shows in his excellent study of the Hicks Pasha expedition,* the Mahdi's army was founded on a number of formations, called *rayas* or standards, each led by a man of some standing, whether a religious figure, a rich merchant or tribal chief. The individual armies which such men could raise varied in size from hundreds to 10,000, but they were all united in one respect. 'The divine nature of the Mahdi's Call made fighting a religious duty, thereby calling on self-discipline, loyalty and devotion to the cause.' The Mahdi's success obviously threatened Khartoum itself, and had the Khedive of Egypt's ministers been wise, they would have settled for hanging on to Khartoum and the Blue Nile province of Sennaar. But they were not wise and instead sent Hicks Pasha with a largely Egyptian army to the Sudan with the idea of seeking out the Mahdi in his own Kordofan country and attacking him there. Hicks had served in the Indian Army since the early 1850s, had seen action in the Mutiny and with Sir Robert Napier in Abyssinia, and now in March 1883 with the rank of *fariq* (lieutenant-general) was in Khartoum with an army of about 8,000 Egyptian and Sudanese soldiers, half a dozen European officers, and serious misgivings about the whole enterprise.

He was understandably concerned that his force was not large enough, that he would be marching through wholly hostile territory, that everything to be eaten must be carried and that his lines of communication would be vulnerable. There were some 14,000 animals – camels, horses, mules and donkeys. All would need water, as well as the soldiers, so water had to be carried too, although it was, of course, intended that water would be found en route. The broad plan was to move to Duwaym (or el Dueim), about 130 miles south of Khartoum on the White Nile, and then march west to el Obeid where the Mahdi and his army were thought to be. By September 1883 Hicks's force was assembled at Duwaym, and in that same month Gladstone's Government appointed Evelyn Baring (later Lord Cromer) as consul-general in Egypt. He was to remain there as virtual ruler of Egypt until 1907. On 27 September Hicks's expedition left Duwaym, not as Hicks himself wanted going west to Bara, then south to el Obeid, but because the alternative was favoured by the governor-general, Ala al-din, by a longer route which would take them through even more hostile country to Rahad, south-east of el Obeid. During the march the column was constantly dogged by a force of several thousand Mahdists 'willing to wound, and yet afraid to strike', who harassed the force, eliminating stragglers, and kept the Mahdi himself informed of their whereabouts. Thirst was already accounting for hundreds of the camels and lowering the morale of the men. It took Hicks about a month to reach Rahad, from where, after resting for five

* *The Army Quarterly and Defence Journal*, October 1978, 470–81.

days, he began his march to Alluba and Birka, where water from a lake was plentiful. Between Alluba and Birka was a seasonal lake called Fula al-Masarin – 'the pool of guts' – so named from a previous battle after which vultures fed on the entrails of the dead. It was near here that the decisive encounter took place, as the Mahdi himself predicted.

After spending two days at Alluba, Hicks marched north towards Fula al-Masarin on 3 November, and after some ten miles made camp, constructing a *zariba* – a kind of defensive perimeter usually based on trenches and enclosed by high, tough, thorny bushes. The Mahdi had already left el Obeid with an army of about 50,000. On 2 November he was at Firtingal, between el Obeid and Birka, while his principal lieutenant, the Khalifa Abdullahi, reached Birka itself. Hicks was aware of this when he made his move from Alluba. The first battle was fought on 4 November as Hicks's force left the zariba in a square formation, when they were almost at once attacked from the rear. According to Peter Clark: 'The 1st battalion in front wheeled round and attempted to drive the Mahdists back. But their square was broken. Many camels carrying water fell outside the square. So hot was the fire that they could not be recovered. Guns too were lost for the same reason. Hicks ordered the band to play. But camels, mules and men were dropping constantly, and the feeble attempt to raise morale was abandoned.' Then rather surprisingly the Mahdi called off the attack. It was probably because he suspected that many of Hicks's supposedly loyal supporters were planning to desert. In any event the following day brought the whole affair to an end. Hicks again advanced, this time in three squares, but when they were about a mile from Fula al-Masarin, the Mahdi's overwhelming numbers fell on them front and rear. Commanding the frontal attack was one of the Mahdi's *amirs*, Abd al-Rahman wad al-Nujumi (who later fought against Kitchener). So furious was their assault and so numerous the Dervishes that all but a few hundred of Hicks's army, probably some 7,000, were killed. The consequences of this campaign were profound. The Mahdi now cast his eyes towards Khartoum itself. Baring and the Egyptian government decided that the only sensible course of action would be to evacuate the Sudan south of Wadi Halfa. How to do so was the problem, for although the Egyptian garrison at Suakin, threatened by the Mahdi's lieutenant Osman Digna could easily be reinforced by sea – as it shortly had to be – all the smaller garrisons inland with Khartoum at their centre presented difficulties of control and organization requiring a masterly touch.

It was hardly to be wondered at, therefore, that after consulting Baring – who was less than enthusiastic – Gladstone picked on the man who perhaps more than any represented the archetypal Victorian soldier-hero, General Charles Gordon. Gordon knew Sudan well, having served there in 1873–6 and again in 1877–80, when he had been employed by the Khedive as governor-general and done much to suppress the slave-trade and bring a degree of order to huge areas of the country. Baring's concern was understandably based on his appreciation of Gordon's renowned valour, which might tempt him into further undesirable adventures, and therefore of the danger that his presence in the Sudan might require sending a British army to his rescue if these adventures demanded it. But most of Gladstone's immediate colleagues discounted such warnings. The Foreign Secretary, Granville, in particular supported his appointment. While deprecating Gordon's eccentricity, he was in no doubt that Gordon was 'a genius and of splendid character'. Hartington, Northbrook and Dilke all agreed with him, and so the curtain was about to go up on the drama of an Imperial martyrdom.

The first intimation that Gordon might go back to Khartoum was made, not by those in government, but by the editor of *The Pall Mall Gazette*, Mr Stead, who interviewed Gordon on 9 January 1884 about the situation in the Sudan. Gordon gave his view that there were but two courses of action – surrender to the Mahdi or hold Khartoum. He clearly favoured the latter course, for then disunity and rivalry would cause the Mahdi's forces to fall to pieces. Moreover, he argued, withdrawal from Khartoum and the other garrisons was so difficult as to be well nigh impossible. The proper thing to do would be to appoint a strong governor-general, and he even named Sir Samuel Baker as the right man for the job. But Mr Stead's newspaper in its report of this interview came down strongly in favour of Gordon himself as the man to go to Khartoum, and it was a cry taken up first by other newspapers (even though it was known that Gordon had accepted an appointment in the Belgian Congo) and then by Granville in his telegrams to Baring. Baring pointed out that Gordon would not be acceptable to the new Khedive, Nubar Pasha, whom Gordon had once challenged to a duel, but by this time Granville had the bit between his teeth. He informed Gladstone that Gordon believed he could persuade the local tribes to escort Khartoum's garrison safely to Suakin and had actually said so (this was quite untrue), and that therefore it might be prudent to convert Baring to this view. Next, Wolseley, Adjutant-General at the War Office, and an old friend of Gordon, summoned him to ask whether he would be willing to return to Sudan. Gordon agreed, but pointed out his undertaking to Belgium's King Leopold. While Gordon was actually in Brussels, Baring's telegram to Granville of 16 January arrived. In it he accepted the idea of Gordon's appointment, provided 'he would pledge himself to carry out the policy of withdrawing from the Sudan as quickly as is possible consistently with saving life'. Gordon must also take his orders from Britain's representative in Egypt, that is himself, Baring. On these conditions, yes; otherwise, not. Had Baring's conditions been followed to the letter, what a different outcome there might have been! As it was, Gordon was tasked simply to go to Suakin and report on the situation. There was at this stage no question of either evacuating the garrisons or, still less, holding Khartoum. The scene of his actual departure from Charing Cross Station on 18 January 1884 was extraordinary. The Duke of Cambridge, Commander-in-Chief of the British Army, was there to see him off and even opened the carriage door for him; Wolseley came to bid his old friend good fortune, adding slightly to it there and then by giving him some cash when it was discovered that Gordon had none with him; Lord Granville, Foreign Secretary, bought railway tickets both for Gordon and for Colonel J. D. H. Stewart, who was to accompany him. Stewart had wide, recent knowledge of the Sudan, and had remarked after the victory at Tel el-Kebir that the Egyptian army was despicable and good for nothing, so it was to be hoped that the English public would not crow too loudly over their success. Stewart was to be with Gordon in Khartoum for most of the adventure, until ordered to escape, and then to suffer a fate comparable to his chief's.

Gordon did not go to Suakin at all, for by the time he reached Cairo and conferred with the Khedive, who appointed him governor-general of the Sudan, both his purpose and the authority to whom he would be responsible were far from clear. James Morris admirably sums up the various interpretations which were put upon his mission:

> The British Government apparently wanted him to withdraw the garrisons and abandon the country to the Mahdi. The expansionists wanted him either to annex the Sudan to the British Empire, or to reorganize it as a dependency of Egypt – the puppet of a puppet. The anti-imperialists wanted him to establish a truly independent Sudan, presumably under the Mahdi. The soldiers were concerned about the security of Egypt and of the Sudanese ports on the Red Sea. The evangelicals thought Mahdism might mean a resurgence of Islamic power throughout Africa, and certainly new life for the slave trade. Some people hoped Gordon would establish his own personal regime in the Sudan.

Given all these conflicting views, and given too that before setting off for Khartoum, Gordon had telegraphed to the city from Cairo that they should stand fast, for he was coming, it was perhaps not surprising that when he arrived in Khartoum on 18 February, after a triumphal journey, to receive a rapturous welcome despite having brought neither money nor troops, belief in the Gordon magic to deliver the population from the Mahdi's threat should have been strongly reinforced.

In fact, however, what had been happening militarily to the north-east of Khartoum while Gordon had been making his way there was far from encouraging. On 4 February General Valentine Baker Pasha, with a mixed force of Egyptian gendarmerie and cavalry, had attempted to raise the siege of Sinkat and Tokar, which had been

surrounded and threatened by the army of Osman Digna. Most of the
Egyptian troops, apart from being unwilling and indeed not required
to serve in the Sudan, were almost wholly untrained. With Baker was
one of the most colourful cavalrymen in the British Army, Colonel
Fred Burnaby of The Blues. Six foot four in height, politically active, a
balloonist, fluent in eight languages, famous for his adventures like
riding across the Russian steppes and commanding a Turkish brigade,
correspondent for *The Times* during the 1874 Spanish civil war, best-
selling author, his personal courage was a legend. But even he could do
nothing to save Baker's force when they were attacked by Osman
Digna's men. Burnaby later recalled that the sight of some 4,000 men
running pell-mell for their lives with a few hundred Arabs chasing
them and spearing all within reach was something not easily forgotten.
Baker managed to extricate about one-third of his army and get them
back to Suakin by sea. Even this was only achieved because the enemy
was more interested in loot than finishing off their pusillanimous
opponents. But this setback, known as the first battle of El Teb,
resulted in rapid reinforcement. By the end of February 4,000 British
troops were at Trinkitat under Major-General Sir Gerald Graham VC,
who was renowned for that rare combination of courage and modesty.

The second battle of El Teb, fought on 29 February, was a very
different affair from the first. Some 6,000 Mahdists entrenched in a
zariba near the site of the first battle were engaged by Graham's force,
which included 3,000 infantry, artillery, machine guns, 10th Hussars,
19th Hussars and mounted infantry. Having successfully silenced the
enemy's artillery with his own, Graham advanced towards the zariba,
only to find the enemy horsemen dashing forward at them in small
parties. Despite their reckless courage they were shot down by the
steady fire of British infantry and, continuing the advance, Graham
captured the enemy position and guns. The British cavalry under
Herbert Stewart then pursued those of the enemy who were retiring,
only to encounter numerous enemy horsemen on the flanks as they did
so. As a result the 10th and 19th Hussars suffered proportionately far
greater casualties (about seventy) than did the British infantry and
artillery (just over one hundred). But it had been a clear victory, with
well over 2,000 Sudanese dead. Graham returned to Trinkitat, and
then two weeks later fought another battle at Tamai, where Osman
Digna commanded in person. It was a bloody and indecisive affair, for
although Graham could claim a victory in driving the Sudanese from
the field, he had suffered well over 200 casualties, about half killed,
half wounded, and at one point a British square, or rectangle to be
precise, had been penetrated. Tamai, it will be remembered, was
another of the places referred to by Charles Carrington where
'savages' successfully argued the toss with 'civilized men' at close
quarters on rough ground. They would do so again at Abu Klea, where
we will shortly be witnesses to another battle. Graham's campaign

was over and although he had done what was demanded of him in relieving garrisons, although also the Suakin base remained in British hands, to the Mahdists it seemed that they had expelled their infidel enemies from eastern Sudan, over which Osman Digna still held sway.

In the same month that Graham and his force returned to Cairo, March 1884, Wolseley was warning the cabinet that Gordon was in serious danger in Khartoum. He could not evacuate it as the Mahdist forces were closing in all round him. Baring strongly supported Wolseley. Even Queen Victoria wrote to Gladstone, saying she trembled for General Gordon's safety, adding how awful it would be if anything befell him. Both Baring and Wolseley pressed the Government for an expedition to relieve him, and as early as 8 April Wolseley had produced an actual plan to do so at the request of the Secretary of State for War, Lord Hartington. In April too, communications between Khartoum and Sennaar province, the main source of grain, were cut. Finally in May Berber itself was captured by the Mahdists, which meant not only that Khartoum was cut off by the Nile route, but that the desert route from Suakin by way of Berber would now be much more hazardous. At this point we may perhaps see what sort of plan Wolseley had in mind, what those on the spot thought about it, and what the three other principal players in the drama – Gordon, Gladstone and the Mahdi himself – were up to.

It was clear that Wolseley saw the Khartoum Relief Expedition as one which would finally clinch his longing to be thought of as one of the great captains of history. It was to be 'the biggest operation the English Army has *ever* undertaken', and even when it came to what was perhaps the most crucial question of all – which route should be taken – he was in no doubt.

> I would propose to send all the dismounted portion of the force up the Nile to Khartoum in boats, as we sent the little expeditionary force from Lake Superior to Fort Garry on the Red River in 1870. That force had to traverse a desert region, destitute of supplies, for a distance of 600 miles, taking provisions with it for three months in boats ... Remembering the great superiority of river over land transport, the ease with which stores of all sorts are carried in boats, the great distance, comparatively speaking, that can be traversed daily in boats, and the vast saving that there would be in expense, I have no hesitation whatever in saying that the river route from Wady Halfa to Khartoum is infinitely preferable to any other.

Yet, as Adrian Preston has pointed out in his admirably edited version of Wolseley's campaign journal,* there was powerful dissent from this view, particularly by the soldiers on the spot, Graham, Evelyn Wood and Stephenson, and by Baring, all of whom regarded the Nile route as

* *In Relief of Gordon*, Hutchinson, 1967.

impracticable, favouring instead the Suakin–Berber desert route. Quite apart from the difficulties of sheer distance and of the cataracts presented by the Nile, there was, as officers of the Royal Engineers emphasized, another strategic reason of great significance for choosing the Suakin–Berber route and for joining the two by railway, if there were any intention of maintaining some long-term influence in the Sudan in the future. It was with considerable strategic insight that one of these Royal Engineers, Major Clarke, predicted that Wolseley's proposal would do nothing to solve the Sudan's future problems. It might relieve Khartoum and allow garrisons to be withdrawn, but this would simply encourage the extension of Mahdism, with its inevitable threat to Egypt, so that sooner or later yet another military expedition to Khartoum would have to be mounted.* But a Suakin–Berber railway would put Berber within twelve hours of Royal Navy ships, and so give the British easy access to and control of both Khartoum and the Sudan.

At the time Wolseley put forward his plan, however, there was still no decision to relieve Gordon at all, although in that same month, April 1884, Gordon's own behaviour was giving rise to much concern. In the middle of the month he had cabled to Baring in terms that set alarm bells ringing in both Cairo and London:

> Of course my duty is evacuation and the best I can hope for is establishing a quiet government. The first I hope to accomplish. The second is a difficult task and concerns Egypt more than me. If Egypt is to be quiet, Mahdi must be smashed up. Mahdi is most unpopular, and with care and time could be smashed. Remember that, once Khartoum belongs to Mahdi, the task will be far more difficult . . . evacuation is possible, but you will feel effect in Egypt and will be forced into a far more serious affair in order to guard Egypt. At present it would be comparatively easy to destroy Mahdi.

So much for Gordon's original instructions from the cabinet! What he was now suggesting was that the Sudan should be reconquered, the Mahdi smashed and Egypt's security thereby guaranteed. But the truth was that there were no means of doing so, and as for evacuation being possible, two things were fast becoming clear – first, that Gordon had no intention of withdrawing, that it was contrary to his whole nature to embark on retreat, that he was determined to remain in Khartoum and by doing so force the British Government's hand to mount an expedition to relieve him, destroy the Mahdi and re-occupy Sudan; second, that even if Gordon were set on evacuation, it would no longer be possible as the tribes north of Khartoum were rising in support of the Mahdi and, as we have seen, had taken Berber itself in May.

Meanwhile, at home, support for an expedition to be mounted was

* As indeed it was – by Kitchener 1896–8 with its climax at Omdurman when he destroyed the Dervish army, commanded by the Mahdi's successor, the Khalifa.

gaining ground. As early as March Lord Randolph Churchill had asked in the House of Commons what the British Government was intending to do. 'Are they going to remain indifferent to the fate of the one man on whom they have counted to extricate them from their dilemmas, to leave him to shift for himself, and not to make a single effort on his behalf?' Gladstone, however, refused to face facts. At this juncture of affairs his single-mindedness did him a disservice. He was too immersed in his plans for introducing a Reform Bill. Even the relatively trivial matter of the atheist, Charles Bradlaugh, who although elected to Parliament had refused to take his seat, seemed to take precedence over impending tragedy in the Sudan. Again in May Lord Randolph Churchill attacked the Prime Minister: 'I have compared his efforts in the cause of General Gordon with his efforts in the cause of Mr Bradlaugh. If a hundredth part of those invaluable moral qualities bestowed upon the cause of a seditious blasphemer had been given to the support of a Christian hero the success of Gordon's mission would have been assured.' It took a great deal of pressure to move Gladstone, but at length public opinion, Selbourne, the Lord Chancellor, the Secretary of State for War, Hartington, Queen Victoria herself did move him, and in the autumn of 1884 he asked the House of Commons for £300,000 so that operations for the relief of General Gordon could if necessary be undertaken. 'It was,' writes James Morris, 'like a parable: Gordon the half-mad hero in Khartoum, Gladstone the embattled man of conscience at Westminster, Victoria the Queen-Empress furiously underlining her diary entries at Windsor. Of course the only man to lead the rescuing armies up the Nile was Lord Wolseley. Among all the figures of the fable, it seems, he alone knew his purpose throughout.' On 9 September 1884 Wolseley arrived in Cairo.

By this time Gordon was almost the sole remaining European in Khartoum. Ever since March when he had sent the Mahdi a gift and offered him the governorship of Kordofan and a parley – an offer that was instantly and contemptuously rejected – the Mahdi's forces had been drawing closer to Khartoum. Later that month Gordon sent Stewart with about 1,000 bashi-bazouks (Arab and Egyptian irregulars) and two Egyptian officers to attack and disperse Dervishes at Halfiyeh, eight miles north of Khartoum. It was a complete fiasco, the bashi-bazouks simply taking to their heels the moment about sixty Dervish cavalry rode towards them, and rushing back to the boats on the Nile. About one-third of Stewart's force were killed or wounded and his poor opinion of them wholly vindicated. Gordon was so furious that he ordered the execution of the two Egyptian officers. After the fall of Berber and as the Mahdi's forces advanced ever nearer to Khartoum by the Blue Nile, Gordon made one last attempt to re-establish an escape route. He sent 1,000 men under Mohammed Pasha in late August with the aim of reaching Sennaar. If this were done, he

would then dispatch Stewart to re-take Berber. But after some initial
success Mohammed Pasha's column was ambushed and he and half
his men killed. The last throw had failed.

Yet Gordon held on. In September he sent Stewart, Power (*The
Times* correspondent and British consul), Herbin, the French consul
and a dozen others downstream in the steamer *Abbas* in the hope that
they would get through in order to tell Baring and the whole world
what was happening, so that reinforcements might be sent. They got as
far as Abu Hamed, about a hundred miles north of Berber, but went
aground there. All were killed except a stoker. Gordon himself did not
hear of this until November, by when Wolseley was well on his way –
and we will join him shortly – but in Khartoum it was Gordon himself
who was at once the inspiration and organizer of defence. 'He used
every ruse and device to keep the enemy at bay,' says James Morris,
'and his people's spirits up.' Fortifications, mines, river patrols,
ammunition factories, medals for The Siege of Khartoum, morale-
raising band concerts, messages smuggled out in the hope they would
be intercepted, giving assurances that he could hold out indefinitely,
even bogus messages from Wolseley's relief force. His defiance was
absolute. He would tell a Khartoum merchant that when God was
handing out fear to everyone in the world, his own turn was last and
then there was no fear left. A call from the Mahdi for surrender was
dismissed with the retort that he was in Khartoum like iron, awaiting
the imminent arrival of the English. James Morris, perhaps more than
anyone else, has given us a sense of what this martyr of Empire's
feelings and thoughts were during those last weeks of the siege.

> He admired his Mahdist enemies, he enjoyed war and responsi-
> bility, and if he despised his Egyptian soldiers, he was indubitably
> attracted by the stalwart Sudanese . . . He was terribly alone. He
> had no intimate friend in the city – he spoke little Arabic, nobody
> else spoke English. Yet he never sounds unhappy. He had, like so
> many of the Victorian imperial heroes, like Napier, like Hodson,
> like Colley, a vivid sense of theatre: and there in the throttling heat
> of his palace roof he was playing the most splendid of all tragic
> roles, to the best of all audiences. He made sure it was all recorded
> for posterity, and he did not fail to stage manage the last curtain to
> legendary effect.

But before we see the curtain come down, we will take a look at what
the British Army was doing to try and change the ending from one of
heroic tragedy to one of last-minute rescue.

It will be recalled that Wolseley favoured the Nile route, and on
arrival in Cairo he proceeded with his plans accordingly. He intended
to concentrate his army of some 95,000 men at Korti, about 200 miles
from Khartoum across the desert, but much further, of course, by
river. His aim was to achieve this concentration by mid-December, but

delay after delay put his programme back by more than a month. One special feature of his plan was the creation of a 2,500-strong Camel Corps as a striking force which could make a dash across the desert if necessary. Wolseley had with him all the members of the 'Ring' that he could muster, including William Butler, Redvers Buller, Brackenbury and Charles Wilson. Buller was Chief of Staff and not a very good one, adding to the army's delay in reaching Korti by failing to make proper arrangements either for buying enough camels or the forage for them. He also fell down on the provision of coal by Thomas Cook and Sons which stopped for a whole fortnight all steamers moving from Assuan to Wady Halfa. Other delays were caused by the sheer nature of the country through which the army had to move, whether overland or by river. The *Official History* called the Nile expedition a campaign waged more against nature and time than against man. 'Had British soldiers and Egyptian camels been able to subsist on sand and occasional water, or had the desert produced beef and biscuit, the army might, in spite of its late start, have reached Khartoum in November. But as things were, the rate of progress of the army was dependent on the rate of progress of its supplies.'

All these delays obliged Wolseley to modify his plans and at the end of December, while still at Korti, he decided to send the Desert Column under Herbert Stewart across the Bayuda Desert to Metemmah, and from there make a dash over the last hundred miles to Khartoum. Meanwhile the River Column under Major-General William Earle would move up the Nile to Abu Hamed, Berber and Shendi, which was opposite Metemmah. From there they would be able to supply the Desert Column. The plan was all very well, but again was dogged by the need to establish a supply base at Jakdul for the Desert Column. All this coming and going quickly alerted the Mahdi's forces to what Stewart was going to do, so that when he finally set off from Jakdul in mid-January, the Mahdi had concentrated 10,000 of his finest troops at the Abu Klea wells, and this was something that one of the stars of Charles Wilson's intelligence staff, Captain Herbert Kitchener, despite all his excellent work elsewhere, had failed to discover. Let us now accompany Stewart and his Desert Column as they encounter those Fuzzy-Wuzzys who were 'the finest o' the lot'.

Stewart's square, as it advanced on the morning of 17 January 1885, to seize the Abu Klea wells – for his column was in urgent need of water – and to deal with the Dervishes opposing them, must have made a magnificent spectacle. In front were 160 Mounted Infantry and 180 Guards' Camel Regiment with three guns in between them; on the left flank a similar Mounted Infantry force with a company of Heavy Camel Regiment (5th and 16th Lancers); in rear some 350 of another Heavy Camel Regiment, manned by Household Cavalry and Dragoons; on the right flank more of the Guards' Camel Regiment, some Royal Marines and 125 Royal Sussex. In the centre of the square were camels loaded with water, supplies, ammunition, medical stores. Men of the Camel Corps made a fine showing. Count Gleichen, Adjutant of the Guards' Regiment, judged their uniform to resemble that worn in the English Civil War with its 'bandoliers, breeches and stocking-like puttees'. Lord Anglesey describes it in detail:

> The brown leather bandoliers, worn over the left shoulder, held fifty rounds of rifle ammunition. The breeches were made of yellow-ochre Bedford cord; the puttees were dark blue. On the head was worn a khaki-coloured pith helmet ... grey serge jumpers were worn, though the men also had with them red serge ones. A brown waistbelt, with a pouch attached, holding twenty rounds, a haversack and brown ankle boots completed the uniform ... the arms carried were a rifle in a Namaqua rifle-bucket.

The camel itself was not, according to Robert Baden-Powell, a lovable beast, but a great philosopher – 'apparently entirely indifferent as to what is going on round him so long as he can chew the cud and curl his lips in contempt at men. Wounds he will accept with philosophic calm, merely giving expression to a grunt or an annoyed gurgle when he finds that his inside has been perforated by a bullet ...' These then were the men and animals who were attacked by the Dervishes as they moved from their zariba towards the Abu Klea wells. Colonel Talbot, commanding the Heavy Camel Regiment, tells us what happened:

> After marching for about two miles at a very slow rate, the enemy's flags, which had been visible since leaving the zariba, suddenly became animate, and a large force of Arabs, distant some 500 to 700 yards, sprang up, and advanced as if to attack the left leading corner of the square. The square was at once halted, but immediately afterwards was moved to the right on to a slightly elevated knoll – a simple movement for men, but difficult for camels, many of which remained outside the square when it halted.

There was some confusion caused by British skirmishers being *outside* the square and preventing those inside it from engaging the advancing enemy, and it was at this point that two dramatic events occurred. First, Burnaby, attempting to help returning skirmishers with covering fire, found himself also outside the square and under attack from a number of tribesmen. Coolly parrying the long spear of one Fuzzy-Wuzzy, he was distracted by that of another striking his shoulder and, turning to fend off this new opponent, allowed the first one to drive his heavy spearpoint into his throat. He fell from his pony, and although he struggled to his feet, laying about him with his sabre, half a dozen Dervishes were upon him to finish it. The second thing was that the Fuzzy-Wuzzys actually got inside the square. Here we must let Etherington of the Royal Sussex Regiment tell us how it looked to him:

We were only two deep in square still within fifty yards of the enemy, when our skirmishers retired, and we opened square to let them in. At that moment the Mahdists charged, but were repulsed. A second charge failed, but at the third they succeeded in breaking one corner of the square, and then the position became very serious indeed. Probably their success was due to the fact that our men at that corner were not used to the bayonet but to the sword. Anyhow, the Soudanese broke a British square, and that is something to their credit . . .

It was at this point that Gunner Smith won the only Victoria Cross of the campaign. When the square was broken, Major Guthrie stuck to the guns (seven-pounders), and fought till he fell wounded. Then Gunner Smith rushed to the rescue. He had lost his rifle, but he caught up a gun spike, beat off the Soudanese, and dragged the Major back into the square.

When the square was re-formed a lot of the Mahdists were inside, but you may be sure that none of them lived to get out again . . . At last the Gatling guns were got into action, and that practically ended the battle. The Soudanese were simply mown down. Their bodies flew up into the air like grass from a lawn-mower. But their pluck was astonishing. I saw some of the natives dash up to the Gatling guns, and thrust their arms down the muzzles, trying to extract the bullets which were destroying their comrades! Of course, they were simply blown to atoms.

The battle lasted off and on from eight in the morning to five in the afternoon, when the Soudanese finally fled. We did not pursue them, but with a ringing cheer we dashed to the wells, for we had drunk nothing all day, and were nearly maddened with thirst. Altogether sixty-five of our men were killed, and a hundred and eighty wounded, while about two thousand natives lay dead upon the sand.

We may perhaps understand now what Kipling meant when he wrote that this particular enemy of the beggars in red was the only thing that did not give a damn for a Regiment of British Infantry. We may well say with him:

> So 'ere's *to* you, Fuzzy-Wuzzy, at your 'ome
>   in the Soudan;
> You're a pore benighted 'eathen, but a first-
>   class fightin' man;
> An' 'ere's *to* you, Fuzzy-Wuzzy, with your
>   'ayrick 'ead of 'air –
> You big black boundin' beggar – for you broke
>   a British square!

For all that, however, and even though Abu Klea was the principal battle of the campaign, Stewart and his Desert Column were still a

long way from Khartoum. Stewart never did get there. On the
following day, during a further engagement with the Mahdists as the
Desert Column made its way towards the Nile, Stewart was mortally
wounded, and Sir Charles Wilson assumed the command. On 19
January he and his men repulsed another Dervish attack and occupied
Gubat. Meanwhile Wolseley at Korti (Hartington, War Secretary, had
forbidden him to go forward with the Desert Column, as he had
wished) was waiting for news. He received it on 21 January, as his
campaign journal records:

> Messengers arrived from Stewart. They left him at Abu Klea wells
> on the morning of 18th instant, so they have come in well, 150 miles
> in three days on the same camels all the way. Stewart had a real big
> fight on the 17th inst. A regular El Teb or Tamai over again: our loss
> has been heavy arising from the unsteadiness of the heavy Camel
> Regt. which allowed the enemy to break into the square. Poor devils
> they have suffered for it, as out of 64 killed, 35 belonged to that
> Regt. There were 9 officers killed and 9 wounded; amongst the
> former poor Burnaby who was stabbed by a lance through the
> jugular. All the correspondents speak most highly of the manner in
> which our soldiers fought and also of the way in which Stewart
> handled his troops. He and his staff were for some minutes in great
> danger: I believe they were knocked down in melee and Stewart had
> his horse killed. His loss would have been irreparable, and I dread to
> think of his being killed in some of these early affairs.

A week later, on 28 January, Wolseley heard of Stewart's wound,
although not yet of his death. Wolseley at once dispatched Buller to
Metemmah to take command as he did not trust Wilson, who was not
one of the 'Ring'. He noted too in his journal of the 28th that four days
earlier on the 24th 'Wilson with two steamers and 20 men of Sussex
started for Khartoum'. What they found there meant that there was no
longer any purpose in trying to relieve the city, for when the leading
steamer, under fire from shells and bullets, came within sight of the
palace, its crew saw, not the Union Jack flying from the roof, but
hundreds of Dervishes crowded by the river among the Mahdi's
banners. 'It was,' writes James Morris, 'one of the great moments of
the imperial story, and to dramatize it further still twenty men on
board the ship were dressed in scarlet – the last British soldiers ever to
wear the red coat of Empire into battle'. They were, of course, too late,
for two days earlier, as they later learned, Gordon had bravely met his
martyr's death, pierced by a Dervish spear as he stood at the top of the
stairs by a balcony, then cut to pieces when he fell.

> Too late! Too late to save him,
> In vain, in vain they tried.
> His life was England's glory,
> His death was England's pride.

Would they have been too late if Gladstone had listened to Wolseley and Baring in March 1884, when they both urged him to send an expedition? It was not until September of that year that Wolseley reached Cairo and began to organize the relief operation. Wolseley himself was in no doubt where the blame lay, and when he heard on 4 February of Khartoum's fall (he did not yet know that Gordon was dead), he could not help reflecting that the prize had been so near and yet had been snatched from his grasp. If Gordon were killed, it would be better than captivity and 'the beginning of a glorious new life'. And what a fuss there would be in England! 'If anything can kill old Gladstone this news ought to, for he cannot, self-illusionist though he is, disguise from himself the fact that he is directly responsible for the fall of Khartoum . . . that it was owing to his influence, active measures for the relief of Gordon were not undertaken in time . . . What an ending to all our labour, and all our bright hopes is this!!.'

Certainly nothing made Gladstone more unpopular at home than Khartoum's fall and Gordon's death. The Queen made no secret of her distress and anger. The initials of the Prime Minister's soubriquet, G.O.M. (Grand Old Man) were reversed to become Murderer of Gordon.And even though his Government survived a vote of censure in the House of Commons, when in June 1885 seventy-six liberals abstained from voting on an amendment to the budget, Gladstone resigned and was succeeded by Salisbury. In that same month died too the Mahdi, whether of typhus or poison administered by an embittered, ravished woman of Khartoum remains a mystery. He was succeeded by the Khalifa Abdullahi, who was to cause the British a good deal of trouble until finally brought to account, fittingly enough, by Herbert Kitchener in 1898, thirteen years after he had recorded in his report: 'Never was a garrison so nearly rescued, never was a commander so sincerely lamented'. The effect of it all on Wolseley was, according to Adrian Preston, that it broke him 'physically, morally and professionally'. We may perhaps think of this as something of an over-statement, when we recall that he became a Field-Marshal, a Viscount, Commander-in-Chief of the British Army from 1895 to 1900, and lived until 1913. Yet it is true that in the Sudan he met with a check to his hitherto unbroken run of success, from which he was never quite to recover. After the fall of Khartoum, the British Government wisely decided to withdraw its troops behind the Wady Halfa frontier, while hanging on to Suakin, so that Wolseley's final months in command of a British army in the field were spent in extracting his columns to Korti. His appreciation of what would be needed to conduct a counter-offensive against the Mahdi – reinforcements of twelve infantry battalions, four cavalry squadrons and two horse artillery batteries – coming at a time, March 1885, when further trouble was brewing in Afghanistan where Russia was once more playing the Great Game, was quite enough to convince Gladstone's cabinet that they could not afford the risk of two simultaneous Imperial campaigns. In July 1885 Wolseley was back in London and honest enough to record in his journal 'so ends my unsuccessful expedition for the relief of Khartoum'.

We may perhaps take note of one more British expedition 'acrost the seas' before witnessing a unique military spectacle at home, for it was the road to Mandalay that the British soldier would be taking towards the end of 1885, and his presence there and subsequent stories of it gave rise to one of Kipling's best known and loved ballads. Although the British had long been in Lower Burma as a result of the wars in 1824 and 1852 which we have already looked at, Upper Burma was a native kingdom, which since 1878 had been misruled by King Thibaw. When in 1886 Thibaw sought to confiscate the property of the Bombay-Burma Company in order to hand its valuable assets over to the French, Lord Randolph Churchill, Secretary for India in Lord Salisbury's first administration, was not slow to send an ultimatum, and rapidly follow it, when ignored, by dispatching 10,000 troops from India to occupy Mandalay, deport Thibaw and annex his kingdom to the British Crown. And so Kipling's Tommy found 'a neater, sweeter maiden in a cleaner, greener land' and as the Upper Burmese did not exactly lie down under British rule, there would be opportunities for him to answer the call: 'Come you back, you British soldier, come you back to Mandalay!' We shall find ourselves in London shortly, where we can understand Tommy's cry:

> An' I'm learnin' 'ere in London what the ten-year
>   soldier tells;
> 'If you've 'eard the East a'callin', you won't never 'eed
>   naught else'.

With Salisbury as Prime Minister again from 1886 to 1892, there would be in the seat of power another great Imperialist to keep the Army busy. But let us now during the early part of his second Premiership, take a last look at our beggars in red as they come on parade for a very special ceremonial occasion in London.

CHAPTER FIFTEEN

Soldiers of the Queen

Queen Victoria really was the first arbiter of the world, and had imposed a British peace upon it. It could scarcely be described, however, as a peaceful century for the British themselves. 'If we are to *maintain* our position as a *first-rate* Power', wrote the Queen herself, with sundry underlinings and sudden capitals, 'we must, with our Indian Empire and large Colonies, be *Prepared* for *attacks* and *wars, somewhere* or *other*, CONTINUALLY'. She was right. The cost of Empire was an almost ceaseless running battle against reluctant subject peoples, so that a professional soldier in the 1890s could have spent almost all of his working life on active service.

JAMES MORRIS

On 21 June 1887, however, quite a lot of them were engaged in a different activity. They were the supporting players for one of those splendid Imperial productions which only the British could stage. It was the celebration of Queen Victoria's first jubilee, and in *The Times* of the previous day there appeared some appropriately glowing tributes that the Queen was completing 'the fiftieth year of a reign prosperous and glorious beyond any recorded in the annals of England'. It went on to suggest that Her Majesty would derive profound satisfaction, as would all those of her subjects who were 'right-minded', from the reflection that her Jubilee was not disturbed by strife. 'The vast empire over which she reigns is at peace with the rest of the world'. This was something of an exaggeration, as *The Times* itself conceded by referring to what we have just recorded at the end of the last chapter – a considerable force of British soldiers engaged in bringing the people of Upper Burma to their senses. But this, it seems, was regarded as a mere matter of internal security, and not to be thought of as a real intrusion on the British enjoyment of what was clearly going to be a party of great rejoicing, a party for which one cartoon in *Punch* displayed the British Lion dressed in garish tights fashioned from the national flag. All sorts of promises were made in newspapers about the decorative and processional treats being prepared for public view, with Indian princes, tribal chieftains, the crowned heads of Europe, every sort of colourful uniform to be imagined.

The public was not to be disappointed. In reporting Jubilee Day, *The Times* managed to fill twelve columns of its leader pages. Let us join its reporter as he witnesses the scene outside Buckingham Palace at ten o'clock on the morning of Tuesday 21 June 1887. The Yeomen of the Tower are already inside the gates, together with 500 bluejackets, while 1st Battalion, Scots Guards have taken post outside the Palace marking off a huge square. The Life Guards, the Royal Horse Guards and 10th Hussars, all with their bands, are opposite the Palace, and with the arrival of the Duke of Cambridge, Lord Wolseley and glittering staff officers, troops are called to attention and the crowds cheer. The real business of the day got going an hour later when with fanfares of trumpets and the National Anthem the foreign Sovereigns left the Palace in their carriages, surprisingly enough closed, and then at half past eleven with more fanfares, bands playing, kettledrums rolling, the Queen herself, preceded by the Royal ladies, was greeted with boundlessly enthusiastic cheers, and was followed by a brilliant cavalcade of horsemen, her sons, grandsons, the Indian cavalry and escort of 1st Life Guards. The only hitch in the affair was caused by the Marquis of Lorne's horse which, taking exception to the tumultuous cheering, succeeded in getting rid of its illustrious rider along Constitution Hill. Lorne was unhurt and returned to the Palace on foot, where he found another horse. The procession made its way up Constitution Hill, through the Arch (Hyde Park Corner), down Piccadilly, past Trafalgar Square, along the new Northumberland Avenue, the Embankment and then turning right through Parliament Square to Westminster Abbey. Everywhere troops were lining the streets. Among those to be seen were the Royal Fusiliers, the Rifle Brigade, Scots Greys, Horse Artillery, Royal Marines, the London Scottish, Grenadier Guards, Royal Dragoons, even the Volunteer Medical Corps and the Chelsea Pensioners. Every sort of dignitary was in the Abbey for the Thanksgiving Service and the Queen noted later in her Journal:

> *God Save the Queen* was played, and then changed to Handel's *Occasional Overture*, as I walked slowly up the Nave and Choir, which looked beautiful, all filled with people. The Royalties of highest rank were seated within the altar rails. The House of Commons was below us to the left, and I recognized several persons amongst them, but did not see Mr. Gladstone, though he was there . . . I sat *alone* (oh! without my beloved husband, for whom this would have been such a proud day!) where I sat forty-nine years ago and received the homage of the Princes and Peers . . . The service was very well done and arranged. The *Te Deum*, by my darling Albert, sounded beautiful . . . Came back another way until we got into Piccadilly . . . We only got back at a quarter to three. Went at once to my room to take off my bonnet and put on my cap.

> Gave Jubilee brooches to all my daughters, daughters-in-law, granddaughters, granddaughters-in-law, and pins to all my sons, sons-in-law, grandsons, and grandsons-in-law and George Cambridge.

George, Duke of Cambridge, was still Commander-in-Chief of the British Army* whose regiments and battalions had figured so splendidly in the Jubilee celebrations. Only relatively few were on parade, but then it is perhaps worth recalling that the whole Army, compared with the huge, conscripted armies of the Continental powers, was small and composed entirely of volunteers. There were some 200,000 men in the Army altogether, with about 700 artillery pieces and 25,000 horses. Roughly half the Army was at home or in Ireland, one-third stationed in India, 30,000 or so in the Colonies. The infantry of the line usually had fifty battalions serving in India; more than twenty in Ireland; nearly thirty spread about the world on garrison duties in Malta, Gibraltar, Egypt, Ceylon, Singapore, Hong Kong, South Africa, Bermuda, West Indies and Canada; the rest were at home. Cavalry regiments, apart from those in Britain, were deployed in Ireland, South Africa, Egypt and India. The Royal Artillery were always about – as their proud motto, *Ubique*, testified – whenever there was some serious campaigning to do, and the equally omnipresent Royal Engineers were all over the Empire building roads, railways, bridges, barracks, schools, cathedrals, even towns.

Yet to most European Emperors and their general staffs, the British Army – its social standing, glittering uniforms, splendid traditions and unrivalled battle experience notwithstanding – was negligible. It had not been involved in a European campaign since the Crimean blundering thirty years earlier; it had no General Staff; did no proper strategic planning; was largely officered in a casual way by members of the landed gentry; and recruited its ordinary soldiers from Ireland or down-and-outs – indeed to go for a soldier was still thought of as a last resort, choosing a trade which was far from reputable, even shameful. And for all its paradoxical splendour, it was, writes James Morris, 'small, scattered and cumbersome'. Viscount Wolseley was clearly conscious of certain shortcomings in the nation's defences, when in Jubilee Year he effected a number of reorganizations in the Army. In language as relevant now as it was then he put the case like this:

> It seems to me that as we all insure our houses, I hope most seriously that the nation will insure its house by having *at all times* a sufficiently strong Army and Navy, so that when any fire does occur in this great national house our fire engines may be in proper order; that there may be plenty of water; that the engines may work easily

* He was not finally got rid of until 1895, having held the position for nearly forty years. His successor was Wolseley.

and well; that everything may be thought out beforehand;* and then you may rest assured that it will not be the fault of the soldiers and sailors of the Army and Navy if success is not achieved. Depend upon it, when the fire-bell rings and the fire-engines are required, the soldiers and sailors – the firemen of the country – will be in their places, and will endeavour, to the best of their ability, to do the duty for which they have been organized.

He went on to say that what they were trying to do – and here again today's generals would do well to pay attention – was to get rid of 'what I may call the theatrical side of the British Army, and to introduce business-like habits, and to reduce our curiously constituted Army into a real fighting organization'. The whole idea was to be able to put into the field – 'if untoward events should happen' – two strong Army Corps and a division of Cavalry, some 60,000 men. Wolseley did not trouble himself with speculating as to exactly when and where trouble might arise that would demand the dispatch of what was in modern parlance a strategic reserve. He knew it *would* arise and therefore wanted to be ready for it. He was wholly right, and the pity of it was that he did not cap it all by pressing there and then for the creation of a General Staff (not finally done until after Haldane became Secretary of State for War in 1905) which could have busied itself examining strategic problems and making contingency plans. Wolseley, however, still had faith in his 'Ring'. Yet the *United Services Gazette* (30 April 1887) noted with approval what he was trying to do, observing with satisfaction that a force of 60,000 would be something 'larger than England had ever had in the field since the days of Marlborough, a larger British force than Wellington ever commanded, and twice the strength of the little Army we sent in 1854 to the Crimea'. The article ended with a hope, often since then reiterated and as apt as ever today that 'the ardour displayed in Pall Mall will not be quenched by financial cold water from the Treasury'.

At this time the Chancellor of the Exchequer was no less a figure than Lord Randolph Churchill, whose ideas about the economical administration of Army and Navy came in for sharp censure from another contemporary publication (*The Broad Arrow and Naval & Military Gazette*, 18 June 1887). The writer complained not only that Lord Randolph attached excessive importance to his own opinions – which of us does not? – but also that these opinions were not based on mastery of his subject. It was all very well to draw attention to the high cost of the British Army, and indeed to the instances of waste or extravagance, but it was absurd to compare its cost with that of Continental armies. These latter armies were raised by universal, compulsory service; their soldiers received by way of remuneration a

---

* It can hardly be said, however, that Wolseley lived up to this ideal, when the Boer War of 1899 came along, and *he* was Commander-in-Chief.

mere pittance; there was no need to spend money on securing a plentiful reserve; it was unnecessary for the Continental Powers to keep regiments on the move to stimulate interest and efficiency; nor did the Continental Powers have to transport men and *matériel* all over the world or engage, as England did, because of its great Empire, in continuous, expensive and demanding colonial wars. Moreover, there was gross misapprehension of what the Army Estimates for 1887–8 were actually for. The unenlightened seemed to thing that the £18 million voted for the Army was to pay simply for Wolseley's two Army Corps of 60,000 men. This indeed would have been excessive. But it was far from the fact of the case. The £18 million was to pay for both the Regular Army at home and in the colonies – over 150,000 all ranks (the cost of the British Army in India, some 60–70,000 men, was met from the finances of India, which also, of course, paid for the Indian Army) *and* for auxiliary services, pensions, ordnance. Even so, compared with the millions of men under arms for the European Emperors, it was a small army considering its cost.

Considering too all that we have been seeing it do – in Egypt, in Afghanistan, in Zululand, the Sudan and a score of other places – and when we remember that it was deployed in the greatest Empire the world had ever seen, comprising a quarter of the globe's land surface, with Dominions, colonies or protectorates in every continent and every ocean, an Empire on which the sun really never did set, containing over 370 million people of different races, religions, customs, laws – when all this depended for its security on so ridiculously small an Army, with a few regiments and battalions spread about here and there, we may suppose also that the whole thing was a colossal bluff. So it was to some extent. But there was, of course, always the Royal Navy. And there was the Indian Army. Like the British Army itself, the Indian Army was composed entirely of volunteers, and there was never a shortage of them. As we have noted before, recruits came from the martial peoples, Mahrattas and Sikhs, Dogras, Rajputs, Muslims and Gurkhas, to whom soldiering was an honourable profession, and these Indian soldiers fitted readily into the tight loyalties and proud traditions of the British regimental system. As we saw earlier, a remarkable degree of trust and liking grew up between British officers and their Indian soldiers, which surmounted all the obstacles and differences of race, religion, personal habits and beliefs that existed between them. This mutual confidence was such that it was enhanced by danger and hardship. But it depended essentially on the soldiers being under command of the officers they knew and trusted. After all, the system had survived and triumphed over the terrible bloodshed and emotional shocks of the Mutiny itself. The Indian Army owed its loyalty to Victoria, the Queen Empress. About the same size as the British Army, some 200,000, it meant that in time of peace, apart from the huge reserves in India which could be called upon if necessary, Queen Victoria had at her command more than 400,000 soldiers. Moreover, the Indian Army did not confine its activities to India. James Morris has pointed out that 'You could do things with Indian troops that you could not do with British . . . the Indian Army was like a Praetorian Guard of Empire, set apart from the public control, and available always for the protection of the Inner State.'

We have followed the fortunes of these fellows in both of Victoria's armies for a hundred years. What have we seen? We have seen endurance and eventual victory against Revolutionary and Napoleonic France; disaster and perseverance in Afghanistan; hopeless blundering redeemed by matchless courage in the Crimea; tragedy and triumph in India; a host of wars in Africa, fighting Ashantis, Arabs, Zulus, Boers, Fuzzy-Wuzzys. But we have seen much more than this. We have been privileged to observe at close quarters the men who did it all. Led more often than not by brave, fine, dedicated commanders, we have seen numerous models of what Wellington called 'the article', and later christened Thomas Atkins, the profane, drunken, philosophic, staunch soldier of the Queen, the beggar in red himself, who had to endure so much and yet invariably did his duty, stuck to his post, outfaced and outfought his enemies:

> If your officer's dead and the sergeants look white,
> Remember it's ruin to run from a fight:
> So take open order, lie down and sit tight,
> And wait for supports like a soldier.

There were all sorts of endearing absurdities and eccentricities thrown in, a host of 'characters' to enliven life on active service, an assortment of rules and regulations that gave rise to both wonder and mirth, a collection of anecdotes of which those of us who love the Army never tire. There was, for example, what must in general have seemed a sublimely superfluous regulation forbidding officers of field rank to wear spurs when climbing into balloons. What bizarre incident, we may ask ourselves, inspired military officialdom to publish so esoteric an instruction in the first place? There was that remarkable soldier 'Wully' Robertson, who rose from being a cavalry trooper to become a field-marshal and Chief of the General Staff. When first offered a commission, he refused it because the regiment concerned, 16th Lancers, expected an officer to have £300 a year of his own, while a lieutenant's pay was only £120. Later he did accept a commission, noting that it was not altogether agreeable to be seen drinking water in the mess, while others drank champagne. There were many entertaining stories about his dropping of aspirates, such as opposing all civilian criticism of his conduct of war by bluntly replying: 'I've 'eard different' or in a crisis of command: 'Get 'aig' (Haig was Commander-in-Chief in France 1915–18), but his strategic grip was sound enough.

There were jokes about Aldershot and its innumerable public houses, many of which were named after the Army's Commander-in-Chief, so that when asked the whereabouts of The Duke of Cambridge, supposedly visiting Aldershot for some review, the irrepressible soldier humorist replies that he doesn't know because he's teetotal. There were those soldiers who were not teetotal and as a result found themselves rewarded with pack-drill and a fortnight's CB for 'drunk and resisting the Guard':

> I've a head like a concertina: I've a tongue like a button-stick:
> I've a mouth like an old potato, and I'm more than a little sick,
> But I've had my fun o' the Corp'ral's Guard: I've made the cinders
>   fly,
> And I'm here in the Clink for a thundering drink and blacking the
>   Corporal's eye.

There was always India and the North-West Frontier, not only for the famous Indian regiments belonging to the Punjab Irregular Frontier Force ('Piffers'), but for the British infantry too where active service, even campaigning on a small scale, was the order of the day. 'The routine of the Frontier', wrote Philip Mason, 'accustomed men to bullets and to taking cover, to guards and sentry duty which had real purpose, to night marches and sniping . . . it was infinitely superior to a field-day at Aldershot.' It was here that the British Tommy discovered that Gunga Din* was the better man, that if he looked after his rifle properly, it would shoot straight for him, that it was no good ducking when first under fire; it was here too that the gentlemen-rankers found that life was not a spree all the time, that they could take a step or two *up* the rungs of the ladder, that hope and honour had not been altogether abandoned, that they might after all not be 'Damned from here to Eternity'. James Morris has reminded us that for the late-Victorian British, the adventure of the North-West Frontier – with its harsh terrain, its fierce tribesmen, its unrelenting yet honourable enemies, both the idea and the reality of it all – had a very special appeal. The British Army had frequently had cause to advance to and beyond the Khyber Pass, to fight and refight its wars against the Afghans, to respond to various hands being played in the Great Game, and now at the time of Victoria's first jubilee they were on guard beyond the double-decker bridge over the Indus at Attock.

> Across it their armies moved, year after year, on their way to the forts, cantonments and entrenchments of the tribal country and the Afghan frontier. On the lower deck the infantry swung by, the commissariat carts, the cavalry with their lances and fluttering pennants: on the upper deck the troop trains clanked their way

---

* Gunga Din was the name Kipling gave to Juma, the heroic regimental *bhisti* – water carrier – of the Guides at the siege of Delhi.

towards Peshawar, bareheaded soldiers lolling at their windows, or singing bawdy songs inside. . . Trumpets blew at Attock, officers trotted up the hill to the artillery mess in the fort, the flag flew above the ramparts, and all the way along the Peshawar road were carved regimental crests, the dates of old campaigns, or simply the initials of British soldiers, scratched on a stone as the battalion rested on the march.

Those regiments whose crests were carved there had, of course, seen active service in campaigns far from India itself, as well as on the Frontier. We have seen in this story how expeditions were mounted from India to take part in wars as far removed as Abyssinia, China, Egypt, the Sudan, Burma and Afghanistan. In following these regiments, whether from the British or Indian Armies, we have observed one unchanging feature quintessential to both – the unchanging loyalty, dedication to duty, comradeship and sacrifice which spring from the idea of Regimental tradition, pride and service. Not all the neglect and parsimony of successive governments could deny it. We must hope that this lesson of history, as I have urged in the Preface, will not be ignored by those planning the Army's future. How telling is it that today's Indian Army guards its regimental system as fiercely and proudly as ever it did in the days of the Raj. But then, as Philip Mason wrote: 'The Indian Army was, after all, the child of the British and the British had been called by a continental observer – a loose federation of regiments.'

There have been many who have recalled with artistry and eloquence the soldiers of the Queen and their deeds, among them Lady Butler, battle artist *sans pareil*, some of whose pictures are reproduced in this book; Rudyard Kipling, 'the discoverer of Tommy Atkins as a hero of realistic romance', whose *Barrack Room Ballads* are so frequently quoted here, including one from which this book's title is taken – see the verse on page v, one in which another verse tells us exactly what the beggars in red had achieved as we come to the end of the story:

> We 'ave 'eard o' the Widow at Windsor.*
> It's safest to let 'er alone:
> For 'er sentries we stand by the sea an' the land
> Wherever the bugles are blown.

With pictures, verse and fiction these two artists did much for the British soldier. Sir John Fortescue put down the hard facts in his incomparably authoritative and distinguished *History*. Who has done more than these three? One perhaps, one who, like his hero, Nelson, both made history and wrote about it, who might be thought of as the greatest Briton of his day, who had also been a soldier, and who

---

* It was said that Queen Victoria did not greatly care for this poem.

recorded his own military deeds and daring together with those of a million others. In 1889 Winston Churchill joined the Army Class at Harrow. He himself tells us how it came about:

> This orientation was entirely due to my collection of soldiers. I had ultimately nearly fifteen hundred. They were all of one size, all British and organized as an infantry division with a cavalry brigade. . . The day came when my father himself paid a formal visit of inspection. All the troops were arranged in the correct formation of attack. He spent twenty minutes studying the scene – which was really impressive – with a keen eye and captivating smile. At the end he asked me if I would like to go into the Army. I thought it would be splendid to command an Army, so I said 'Yes' at once: and immediately I was taken at my word.

It was an important day for the British Army and for the British people. One of Winston Churchill's subsequent colleagues in war and peace was that 'superior person', George Curzon, who in the same year, 1889, published a book called *Russia in Central Asia*, in which he expressed among other opinions this one:

> Whatever be Russia's designs upon India, whether they be serious and inimical, or imaginary and fantastic, I hold that the first duty of English statesmen is to render any hostile intentions futile, and our frontier impregnable, and so to guard what is without doubt the noblest trophy of British genius and the most splendid appanage of the Imperial Crown.

He need not have worried. Even though as Viceroy, he allowed himself to indulge in imagining some fantastic Russian designs upon India, and taking such extreme measures as dispatching British bayonets to Lhasa, the Great Game went on being played successfully. British soldiers went on guarding the North West Frontier and earning their pay by keeping the peace and waging war. But by then they would have ceased to be beggars in red and become instead gentlemen in khaki.

A Note on Changes in Organization and Uniforms

(Extracted from an article by Sir Charles Oman, 'The British Army and Royal Jubilees', *Journal of the Society for Army Historical Research*, Volume XIV.)

The first real and officially celebrated Royal Jubilee was that of George III in 1809, but long ere that date the whole organization, no less than the appearance, of the army had been repeatedly changed. The war with France, which commenced with the fighting in America in 1755, and which developed into the continental struggle of the Seven Years' War, had led to wholesale additions to the armed forces of the Crown, as well as to some fresh developments in the way of new corps. The first British Light Cavalry were the 15th, 16th, 17th and 18th Light Dragoons raised in 1759. A more abnormal creation was the first corps originally intended to be colonial, the Royal Americans raised in New York and Philadelphia in 1755 and given the regimental number 60th in 1757. It had a considerable German element along with the colonial. This abnormal regiment of no less than four battalions continued to serve in America throughout the 18th century. It saw no European service until 1798 when its fifth battalion – a recent addition – was used in the suppression of the Irish rebellion, and later sent to Portugal with Wellington in 1808, where it had a most distinguished career. This was the first green-coated rifle battalion in the British Army – the famous Rifle Brigade, originally the 95th, was raised in 1800, two years later than the 5th/60th, and trained by Sir John Moore.

In the period of the Seven Years' War an immense number of new infantry corps were embodied. Their numeration ran up from the 51st to the 124th Foot, and in addition many provincial and local corps were raised, and some of the old regiments were authorized to form second battalions. There was, of course, an immense disbandment of newly-formed corps at the peace of 1763, and the only permanent additions to the army were the infantry regiments finally numbered from 50 to 70. Many of them had borne higher numbers at the time of their original levy, but got nearer to the top of the list owing to the disappearance of corps that had originally stood senior to them. In the cavalry line there only survived the new 15th, 16th, 17th and 18th Light Dragoons. The 19th, 20th and 21st Light Dragoons were disbanded.

It was after the peace of 1763 that considerable varieties of uniform spread throughout the army. As was to be the case again during two other great wars, the changes were made in conscious imitation of foreign armies of great repute. In 1763 it was the victorious host of Frederick the Great which served as the example, not only in the matter of drill but in that of clothing. In imitation of the Prussian uniform the old rather loose and amply-skirted coats disappeared, and were replaced by tighter and narrower ones, exposing more of the chest, stomach and thighs, and making the waistcoat more conspicuous. This was by no means an improvement for practical purposes. Perhaps the most conspicuous mark of the period in uniform was the substitution of the double cross-belt at the breast, which superseded the single broader buff belt of 1750 and earlier days. The three-cornered hat for battalion companies, and the mitre-shaped cap for Grenadiers, still continued – the latter in many regiments now being made of fur instead of cloth.

The American War of Independence, starting in 1775 and developing into the world-wide war with France, Spain and Holland which only ended in 1783, caught the British Army in one of its normal stages of low cadres and slack administration, which always intervened between war and war in the 18th century. The army which fought out this desperate struggle had to be improvised just as the army of the Seven Years' War had been. Once more new corps were raised – the numbers of the foot regiments went up to 105, in addition to many 'second battalions' for old corps. More than 20,000 'Provisionals' (Loyalist militia) served in America against their rebellious compatriots, and Hessians and Hanoverians were hired as in the old wars of 1742–8 and 1756–63. Irregular corps like Tarleton's 'Legion' and Simcoe's 'Rangers' made themselves no small reputation. The direction from London was abominable – mainly owing to that wretched minister, Lord George Germaine, who always left his generals in the lurch. But the actual commanders in the field, even Burgoyne and Cornwallis, who had such bad luck, were nearly all competent officers set an impossible task by misdirection from home.

There was, of course, the usual general disbandment of superfluous corps on the peace of 1783, ending by 1785 in the disappearance of all infantry regiments with a higher figure than 73 and cavalry regiments numbered above 19. The period of the American War saw the transformation of many of the old heavy cavalry corps of the Line into light cavalry: all the units between the 8th and the 13th became no longer red-coated Dragoons furnished with the musketoon, but adopted a blue uniform with a round, black leather helmet, and were served out carbines instead of the heavier weapon. This uniform for light cavalry lasted down to 1812, save in the case of four or five regiments who were turned into Hussars in 1806–8.

The extreme length of the next great struggle with France, which lasted practically without a break from 1793 to 1815, was the cause of the complete transformation of the appearance and organization of the British Army in the next generation. In its earliest years all the evils of the old wars reappeared. Hastily raised and ephemeral new regiments – the highest number of the Foot was the 135th and the Light Dragoons the 33rd, of which thirty or so never filled their ranks and were drafted into older corps – were authorized. Horse artillery was first embodied in 1793, and had its own soldier-drivers: for the field batteries (or companies as they were still called) the Corps of Royal Artillery Drivers was raised in 1794, and the civilian hireling disappeared. Rifle corps with special weapons and training start with the green-coated 5th/60th in 1798, and were developed by Coote Manningham's famous 95th (later the Rifle Brigade) in 1800. The Royal Military Artificers were turned into Royal Sappers and Miners in 1812, under special pressure from Wellington. Mounted military police (the Staff Corps Cavalry) appear in 1812. Proper transport was at last provided by the Royal Corps of Waggoners in 1794, who became the Royal Waggon Train in 1803. [There were many] expensive mistakes and abortive experiments before Wellington could count on an efficient force of all arms in the Peninsula. Even when it had been created, he found plenty to criticize in its organization and its personnel. But, as he remarked in a moment of confidence, 'If I ever got into a scrape – they fought me out of it'.

In Wellington's army of the Jubilee year, 1809, the most archaic-looking regiments were the Heavy Dragoons, who still wore the broad-cocked hat and jack-boots which went back to the old wars. The more numerous Light Dragoons had the blue jacket, much belaced in front, and the black leather helmet with bear-skin crest, and plume at the side. The Horse Artillery – a most distinguished if small fraction of the Peninsular Army – had a uniform precisely similar to that of the Light Dragoons. The companies of Field Artillery, on the other hand, had assimilated their uniforms to that of the infantry of the Line in cut, but not in colour; they wore blue coats while the ordinary Foot regiments had red. Both, by the third year of the Peninsular War, had grey trousers in substitution for the gaiters, whose buttons had worried the soldier for so many generations; and felt shakos, with a brass plate with the regimental number or badge in front and a plume at the side. Highland regiments, of which there were now ten in existence, were of course wearing the kilt, and a plumed bonnet much smaller than that which was prescribed in later years. There were four battalions of Rifles in dark green. In addition Wellington had, of the faithful Hanoverian 'King's German Legion', four (afterwards three) Line battalions and two light battalions, who were dressed respectively in red and dark green.

All the follies of powdered hair and 'clubbed' pigtails had vanished by the time the Peninsular War began, and both officers and men wore their own hair, cut rather short. An equally great boon was the serving out of long grey overcoats for winter wear. The one evil invention of the period was the 'stock', the stiff leather contrivance which supported the high collar of the regimental coat. It constricted the neck. On hard service men often unbuttoned their collars and turned their stocks aside. Shortly before the Peninsular War ended there were several conspicuous changes in uniform in the cavalry. The Heavy Dragoons and the Household Cavalry gave up their cocked hats in favour of a brass helmet of rather too lofty a build, and replaced their jack-boots and leather breeches by overalls of grey webbing with a broad red stripe. The Light Dragoons at the same time lost their black helmet with the bearskin crest in favour of bell-topped shakos.

But the most sweeping changes in uniform only came after Waterloo, when the general reduction of the army which always followed a peace was accompanied by lavish alterations in the direction of decorative splendour in accordance with the acute sartorial megalomania of King George IV – then Prince Regent. The second battalions were all disbanded and the Line regiments with numbers from 94 to 104 disappeared, except the old 95th Rifles, who were taken out of numeration and saved as the Rifle Brigade. Similarly in the mounted arm all the Light Dragoon regiments from the 18th to the 25th were disbanded. But the regiments which survived suffered from the Prince Regent's hobbies. It was he who put the 1st Guards into bearskins – the 2nd and 3rd Guards only got fur headgear some time later. He made the Life Guards and Blues into cuirassiers, with helmets of preposterous height. He adorned Hussars with long aigrettes and profusely furred pelisses. He made several Light Dragoon regiments into Lancers, with the peculiar Polish square headdress and baggy Cossack trousers. The infantry of the Line went into the bell-topped shakos and had their sensible grey trousers turned into white ones – impossible to keep clean save by lavish pipe-claying. The Highland regiments got much larger feathered bonnets and furred sporrans, and an additional amount of gold lace on their coats. All these alterations were in the line of display, not of practical utility, and the rude shock of the Crimean winter of 1854–5 was required to show the pernicious consequences of most of them in field service.

Two curious foreign influences may be traced in the British

uniforms of the later Victorian era – the first was 'gallicism', when the high shako gave way to a low headdress like the French képi, accompanied by a sensible rejection of the narrow 'coatee' in favour of the tunic, which had sensible skirts of medium length meeting in front. The other curious transformation of head-gear was the substitution in the early seventies of a felt helmet for the képi. This change came in at the same time as Lord Cardwell's great scheme for the creation of 'linked battalions', by which all corps which had not a second battalion were amalgamated into two-battalion regiments, of which (in theory) one was to be abroad and one at home in normal times. Any illustration of Queen Victoria's army at the time of the Jubilee of 1887 shows the helmet in use for all Line regiments (except Fusiliers, Rifles and Scottish corps) to be very similar to that for the Field Artillery, Royal Engineers, and the departmental corps (ASC, etc). The Household Cavalry and the Heavy Dragoons (except the Scots Greys) show metal helmets. The six Lancer regiments wore the square-topped old Polish headgear, and the Hussars and Horse Artillery the fur busby. Most of this array lasted down to the epoch-making date of 1914.

Bibliography

Anglesey, Marquess of, *A History of the British Cavalry*, Leo Cooper, 1973, 1975.
Army Quarterly and Defence Journal, Ed. T.D. Bridge.
Blackwood's Magazine, June 1979, William Blackwood & Sons.
Blake, Robert, *Disraeli*, Eyre & Spottiswoode, 1966.
Broad Arrow and Naval & Military Gazette, The, 1887.
Bryant, Arthur, *The Years of Endurance, Years of Victory, The Age of Elegance*, Collins, 1942, 1944, 1950.
Cronin, Vincent, *Napoleon*, Collins, 1971.
Cecil, David, *Lord M.*, Constable, 1954.
Churchill, Randolph S., *Winston S. Churchill*, Heinemann, 1966.
Churchill, Winston S., *A History of the English-Speaking Peoples*, Cassell, Vol. 3, 1957; Vol. 4, 1958.
— *My Early Life*, Collins, 1930.
Ensor, Sir Robert, *History of England 1870–1914*, Oxford University Press, 1936.
Fortescue, Sir John, *A History of the British Army*, Macmillan, 13 Vols, 1899–1930.
Fulford, Roger, *Hanover to Windsor*, Batsford, 1960.
Garrett, Richard, *General Gordon*, Arthur Barker, 1974.
Griffith, Samuel B. II, *In Defense of the Public Liberty*, Jonathan Cape, 1977.
Haswell, Jock, *The British Army: A Concise History*, Thames & Hudson, 1975.
Hazlitt, William, *Selected Essays*, The Nonesuch Press, 1934.
Herbert, A.P., *Why Waterloo?*, Methuen, 1952.
Hibbert, Christopher, *The Dragon Wakes*, Longman, 1970.
Hopkirk, Peter, *The Great Game*, John Murray, 1990.
Holmes, Richard, *Coleridge: Early Visions*, Hodder & Stoughton, 1989.
Howard, Michael, Ed., *Wellingtonian Studies*, Gale & Polden, 1958.
Hugo, Victor, 'The Battle of Waterloo', Haldeman-Julius Company.
Irish Hussar: A Short History, QRIH Regimental Association, 1986.

Journal of the Society for Army Historical Research, National Army Museum.

Keegan, John, *The Face of Battle*, Jonathan Cape, 1976.

Longford, Elizabeth, *Wellington: The Years of the Sword* and *Pillar of State*, Weidenfeld & Nicolson, 1969, 1972.

Macaulay, Thomas Babington, *Critical and Historical Essays*, Dent, 1907.

Macdonnell, A.G., *Napoleon and his Marshals*, Macmillan, 1950.

Macrory, Patrick, *Signal Catastrophe*, Hodder & Stoughton, 1966.

McGuffie, T.H., *Rank and File*, Hutchinson, 1964.

Mason, Philip (Philip Woodruff), *The Men Who Ruled India*, Jonathan Cape, 1953.

— *A Matter of Honour*, Jonathan Cape, 1974.

Maurois, André, *Disraeli*, John Lane The Bodley Head, 1927.

Morris, James/Jan, *The Pax Britannica Trilogy*, Faber & Faber, 1968.

Napier, Sir William, *History of the War in the Peninsula*, 1834–40.

Oman, Sir Charles, *A History of the Peninsular War*, Oxford University Press, 7 Vols, 1902–31.

— *The British Army and Royal Jubilees*, Vol. XIV, *Journal of the Society for Army Historical Research*, National Army Museum.

Pocock, Tom, *Horatio Nelson*, The Bodley Head, 1987.

Preston, Adrian, Ed., *In Relief of Gordon*, Hutchinson, 1967.

Queen Victoria, ed. G. E. Buckle, *Journals 1887*, 1926–32.

Read, Jan, *War in the Peninsula*, Faber & Faber, 1977.

Ridley, Jasper, *Lord Palmerston*, Constable, 1970.

Stanhope, Earl, *Conversations with Wellington*, The World's Classics, Oxford, 1938.

The Times.

Trevelyan, G.M., *English Social History*, Longmans, Green & Co., 1942.

Usherwood, Paul & Spencer-Smith, Jenny, *Lady Butler: Battle Artist*, Alan Sutton/National Army Museum, 1987.

United Services Gazette, 1887.

Watson, J. Steven, *The Reign of George III, 1760–1815*, Oxford University Press, 1960.

Watson, S.J., *Carnot*, The Bodley Head, 1954.

Woodham-Smith, Cecil, *The Reason Why*, Constable, 1953.

Woodward, Sir Llewellyn, *The Age of Reform, 1815–1870*, Oxford University Press, 1962.

Index